D1570104

PANEL TO THE SCREEN

PANEL TO

STYLE, AMERICAN FILM, AND COMIC BOOKS DURING THE BLOCKBUSTER ERA

THE SCREEN

DREW MORTON

UNIVERSITY PRESS OF MISSISSIPPI / JACKSON

www.upress.state.ms.us

The University Press of Mississippi is a member
of the Association of American University Presses.

First printing 2016

Library of Congress Cataloging-in-Publication Data

Names: Morton, Drew, 1983– author.
Title: Panel to the screen : style, American film, and comic books during the
blockbuster era / Drew Morton.
Description: Jackson : University Press of Mississippi, 2016. | Includes
bibliographical references and index.
Identifiers: LCCN 2016020358 (print) | LCCN 2016031386 (ebook) | ISBN
9781496809780 (hardback) | ISBN 9781496809797 (epub single) | ISBN
9781496809803 (epub institutional) | ISBN 9781496809810 (pdf single) |
ISBN 9781496809827 (pdf institutional)
Subjects: LCSH: Film adaptations—History and criticism. | Motion pictures
and comic books. | Superhero films. | Comic strip characters in motion
pictures. | Motion picture production and direction—United States. |
Motion picture industry—United States. | BISAC: LITERARY CRITICISM /
Comics & Graphic Novels. | SOCIAL SCIENCE / Media Studies. | SOCIAL
SCIENCE / Popular Culture.
Classification: LCC PN1997.85 M685 2016 (print) | LCC PN1997.85 (ebook) | DDC
791.43/6—dc23
LC record available at https://lccn.loc.gov/2016020358

British Library Cataloging-in-Publication Data available

For Nicole, my Peach

CONTENTS

ix   Acknowledgements

3   Introduction: Comics Are in Right Now

PART ONE
Definitions and Historical Context

---

21   **CHAPTER 1**
"It's Perfect. It Looks Just like the Book!": Scott Pilgrim, Stylistic Remediation, and Transmedia Style

40   **CHAPTER 2**
Camp, Verisimilitude, Noir, and Neon: The Historical Evolution towards Stylistic Remediation

---

PART TWO
Remediation in Comic Adaptations

---

65   **CHAPTER 3**
The Dread of Sitting through Dailies that Look like Comic Strips: Graphical Remediation in *Dick Tracy* (1990) and the Remediation of the Multiframe in *Hulk* (2003)

87   **CHAPTER 4**
"He Cared More about the Appeasement of Fanboys . . . ": Spatiotemporal Remediation in *300* (2006) and *Watchmen* (2009) and Textual Remediation in *American Splendor* (2003)

PART THREE
Remediation beyond Comic Adaptations

115 **CHAPTER 5**
Derived from Comic Strip Graphics: Remediation beyond Comic Book Adaptations in *The Matrix* (1999), *The Good, the Bad, and the Ugly* (1966), and *The Dark Tower: The Gunslinger Born* (2007)

138 **CHAPTER 6**
"There, That Looks Much Better": The Joker, *Sin City*, *The Spirit*, and the Dialogical Process of Remediation

175 **CONCLUSION**
Comics Are in Right Now?

185 Notes

205 Bibliography

221 Index

ACKNOWLEDGMENTS

This book—like most academic monographs—is the product of almost a decade worth of thinking, research, and writing. The kernel of what would evolve into two videographic works and a book began in Benjamin Schneider's class on Film Adaptation at the University of Wisconsin-Milwaukee on the eve of the release of *Sin City*. I was fascinated with the film and how the filmmakers were extensively utilizing green screen technology (still a rather novel idea at the time!) to visually remediate the original text. However, I was unable to do much with the idea because the film was still very much an outlier, and as a young undergraduate, I had yet to develop my analytical toolbox. Those shortcomings dissipated as I revisited the idea as a master's student at the University of California, Los Angeles. While enrolled in Janet Bergstrom's classroom, I made an early video essay on the topic that she was especially complementary of. Thus, my first set of thanks goes to Ben and Janet for helping me develop as a Cinema and Media Studies scholar and for nurturing my intellectual curiosity.

I owe a round of thanks to the colleagues who helped guide the evolution of my video essay to a monograph. Specifically, my dearest thanks to Cliff Hilo, David O'Grady, Jennifer Porst, Maya Smukler, Julia Mitsuko Wright—and to Steve Mamber, whose initial skepticism of my project pushed me to more clearly articulate my methodology and focus when it came to my prose. I also owe a great deal of thanks to the following practitioners and scholars who aided me in this endeavor. Specifically, Glenda Ballard, Christine Becker, Will Brooker, Nick Browne, Scott Bukatman, Amy Carwile, Ron Clohessy, Corey Creekmur, Blair Davis, Doris Davis, Kevin Ells, Ally Field, Philippe Gauthier, Harrison Gish, Catherine Grant, Richard Grusin, Christian Keathley, Derek Kompare, Rob King, Jonathan Kuntz, Geoff Long, Andrew Martin, Scott McCloud, Ross Melnick, Celia Mercer, Misha Mihailova, Jason Mittell, Andrei Molotiu, Bryan Lee O'Malley, Denny O'Neil, Tasha Oren, Patrice Petro, Avi Santo, Suzanne Scott, Matt Zoller Seitz, Jeff Shuter, Vivian Sobchack, Chuck

Tryon, Phil Wagner, Mark Waid, Tami Williams, Edgar Wright, Matt Yockey, and my students.

I would like to extend a big thanks to the friends and colleagues who read the manuscript and provided valuable feedback. One of the most difficult aspects of writing your first book is finding an accessible tone without sacrificing intellectual depth. In order to do that, I needed some fresh perspectives. Michelle Bumatay, Michael Clarke, Doug Julien, Bob Rehak, and Ben Sampson all read drafts and their comprehensive feedback ensured that the official revision process was defined by a series of mole hills rather than mountains, and for that I thank them deeply.

Obviously, this project would not have been possible without the Fantastic Four. John Caldwell was immensely kind and constructive in his feedback. Writing a book can be a frustrating process and John was always available with a supportive and uplifting email. Similarly, Denise Mann consistently pushed me to further explore the industrial aspects of stylistic remediation, a challenge I attempted to address with the support of her large network of industrial practitioners. As already noted, Janet Bergstrom was supportive of my project from its infancy to the present. An interdisciplinary project always flirts with the disaster of alienating the audience and Janet's notes for clarification were incredibly fruitful in sculpting an accessible and rigorous manuscript. Finally, I owe Henry Jenkins a tremendous thanks for his perspective on this project. In addition to being the primary model for my academic voice, Henry provided suggestions to flesh out the historical context of this project. Despite being a rival USC Trojan, Henry was incredibly generous with his time and words of encouragement.

Furthermore, I owe my appreciations to the University Press of Mississippi team (Valerie Jones, Lisa McMurtray, Vijay Shah, Robert Norrell), their anonymous readers whose feedback helped bring the manuscript to the finish line, my editor Leila Salisbury, my family, and friends. Dad, Mom, Amy, Larry (RIP), Tyler, and Heidi, thank you for decades of support—even when some of you thought my pursuit of a career as a Cinema and Media Studies scholar was a bit reckless. Neal Long, thank you for taking me into a comic book store in 2006 and getting me back into the habit of reading comics. Our friendly arguments about different titles provided a very different and potent fuel to this project!

Finally, I reserve my most emotional and loving thanks for my wife Nicole Alvarado, to whom I dedicate this book. Academia can be both an exhilarating and, at those bleakest early morning hours (many of which involved the inevitable and necessary task of revision), a lonely and depressing career. Through every step in the evolution of this project, I had the support of Nicole. She accompanied me to San Diego Comic-Con for a decade, aided me in tracking down participants for interviews, gave me swift kicks to the backside when it came to oversimplifying aspects of her favorite medium (animation), read numerous drafts, and provided an abundance of love when I found myself beating my head against a mentally constructed wall. This book is a representation of my evolution as a scholar. Nicole has been with me every step of the way and I dedicate this to my beautiful and thoughtful wife.

PANEL TO THE SCREEN

INTRODUCTION

Comics Are in Right Now

Film scholar Dudley Andrew offers a useful insight when considering the practice of cinematic adaptation. Andrew writes, "The making of a film out of an earlier text is virtually as old as the machinery of cinema itself. Well over half of all commercial films have come from literary originals."[1] Filmmakers rely on previous texts such as theatrical plays and the novel for content, but also to capitalize upon a pre-established audience base as well. Yet despite Andrew's observation and Columbia Studios Director of Publicity Whitney Bolton's allegedly quantifiable claim from a 1940s production memo that "If you want to sell a story to a Hollywood studio, write a comic strip. That, according to statistics, should increase your chances by about thirty per cent," Hollywood studios have only recently turned to the comic book for source material.[2] Take, for instance, this telling rift in chronology: the debut of Jerry Siegel and Joe Shuster's Superman occurred in *Action Comics* #1 in June 1938. However, the character did not appear in a feature until *Superman and the Mole Men* in 1951. A similar cinematic fate befell Bob Kane and Bill Finger's Batman, who first appeared in *Detective Comics* #27 in May 1939 and did not appear in a feature until the self-titled film in 1966.[3]

As scholar David Bordwell has observed, "Comic-book movies were scarcely a genre in the studio era, but they became a central one with the arrival of the blockbuster."[4] Indeed, shortly after the release of Steven Spielberg's *Jaws* (1975), arguably the origin of the contemporary blockbuster, Richard Donner directed *Superman: The Movie* (1978) for Warner Bros. Yet as M. Keith Booker describes, despite the positive reviews and box office success of the film and some of its sequels, "The Superman franchise was still regarded in Hollywood as a one-of-a-kind special case, so that Superman films remained the only major example of graphic cinema for a decade."[5] The industry-wide

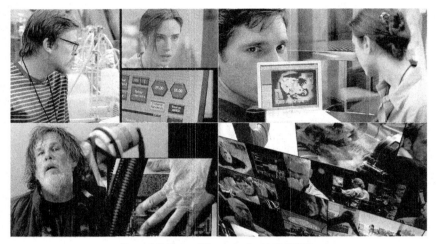

Figure I.1. The multiframe in the *Hulk* (2003).

Figure I.2. High contrast, low key lighting in *Sin City* (1991).

trend of adapting comic books to the screen would not reach critical mass until the success of another Warner Bros. film in 1989, Tim Burton's *Batman*.

Soon after the success of *Batman*, slews of adaptations ranging from children oriented superheroes like the *Teenage Mutant Ninja Turtles* (1990, 1991, 1993), the maturely realized *The Crow* (1994, 1996, 2000, 2005), and the hardboiled strip *Dick Tracy* (1990) began to hit multiplexes. The box office and critical response to the top two films of 2012, Joss Whedon's *The Avengers* and Christopher Nolan's *The Dark Knight Rises*, are indicative of the widespread success comic book films are currently enjoying. Nearly each month of the summer blockbuster season brings at least one superhero film and this looks to be the pace for the next few years (over twenty-five superhero films are slated for release between 2016 and 2020). As Matthew P. McAllister, Ian Gordon, and Mark Jancovich write, "Modern comic book-based films have helped establish the industrial formula of the Hollywood popcorn blockbuster: fantastic action movie as cultural event."[6] Yet this proliferation has had a particular effect on the stylistic devices of both media forms. Specifically, films (both adaptations of comics and original properties) have increasingly relied on the formal characteristics of the comic book (such as panels, speed lines, the dissection of motion, flat compositions) and comics have found themselves drawing upon formal devices derived from film (such as the film noir compositional technique of high-contrast lighting and Photoshop assisted motion blurring to produce a more cinematic look).

The objective of this book is to account for and investigate the intricacies of this stylistic practice, defined here as stylistic remediation. The stylistic characteristics of comics and film are in a dialogue with one another. For instance, comic book attributes such as the multiframe have appeared in film adaptations like Ang Lee's *Hulk* (2003, Figure I.1) while film noir stylistics such as high contrast, low-key lighting provided the formal foundation of Frank Miller's *Sin City* comics (1991–2000, Figure I.2). Yet while comic books and film are often viewed as being formally analogous (partially due to the comic's similarity with the filmic storyboard and the reliance of both media on visual storytelling, which has led some to equate the comic panel to the cinematic frame), there are in fact great differences between the two media.

A brief overview of a handful of these formal attributes would be useful at this stage (this overview should not be viewed as being comprehensive and will be elaborated upon throughout the book). First, comic books are typically illustrated while film is a photographic art form, meaning that the former has its roots in the graphic arts while the latter has an ontological relationship to reality. Hence, it is easier for the former to be fantastic (stories and images are limited only by the mind of the artist) while the latter is confined by such real world factors as a production budget and technology. Secondly, comic art relies on sequential snapshots of time—mobilized across the space of the page—to represent a narrative. Film, on the other hand, typically presents multiple shots of space individually, across time. In film, montage and classical film editing perform the work of spatiotemporal closure that is required of the reader of comics. For instance, while a split-screen in *Hulk* may "look" like a page of comic book panels, it functions differently. The sequential images of comics that provide its formal foundation are "read" in dialogue with one another. The panel in the upper left corner of a page takes place before the panel at the bottom of the page. In the case of filmic split-screens (including those in *Hulk*), there is a temporal synchronicity between the individual frames. In other words, the viewer is getting multiple spatial perspectives on the same moment in time. This spatial presentation of the narrative, in this instance, is bound together with temporal glue. Thus, while these two media are in a stylistic dialogue with one another, this dialogue involves aesthetic compromise—a formal translation rather than a transposition.

Four interrelated questions guide this inquiry. First, how does stylistic remediation complicate the idea of media specificity? Second, what role have horizontal integration and conglomeration had in the process of stylistic remediation? Third, what is the industrial motivation behind remediation, both in films and comics? Finally, is the remediation of comic book stylistics into films fundamentally a by-product of technologies and an indication of a larger ontological shift from cinema to digital cinema? Research and analysis would suggest that this trend cannot be fully comprehended without regard of these three factors: industrial practices, the evolution of special-effects technologies, and consumption. All three of these contexts must be given due attention and considered on a case-by-case basis in order to avoid broad generalization.

Adaptation vs. Remediation

As Andrew notes, adaptation is the modification of a prior text from one medium into another. Remediation, as outlined by theorists Jay David Bolter and Richard Grusin, is the representation of one medium in and by another. Remediations are not necessarily adaptations. Take, more broadly, the example of the ebook. This medium retains the content, the form of the book (printed pages bound together), and the practice of reading (linearly, left to right and top to bottom) exhibited in its analog predecessor. The ebook's remediation of literature does not modify a prior text as it transitions from one medium to another; it simply re-represents it.

Conversely, adaptations are not necessarily remediations. For instance, many film adaptations borrow content without representing the source medium in the process. Nolan's Batman series, in contrast to Ang Lee's *Hulk*, avoids representing the defining formal characteristics of the comic book medium. He does not depict the Dark Knight's actions by fracturing the film frame into smaller panels. Moreover, Nolan does not define his approach to mise-en-scène in relation to the comic book by engaging in caricature or the saturated four-color palate that defined the first fifty years of the American comic book and films like Warren Beatty's adaptation of *Dick Tracy* (1990). Putting aside comic book adaptations for a moment, a notable and accessible example of remediation in an adaptation is John Lounsbery and Wolfgang Reitherman's *The Many Adventures of Winnie the Pooh* (1977). The film features the written page and illustrations that come to life before our eyes as a device used to smooth the transition between scenes.

Moreover, adaptation is often a one-way process insofar as the source is only translated once. For instance, the film adaptation of *The Many Adventures of Winnie the Pooh* was not itself adapted back into a book. A reader may find a novelization of an original film property, but will rarely find an adaptation based on an adaptation. Remediation, on the other hand, is often reciprocal and dialogical. As I will describe in an analysis of the Scott Pilgrim transmedia franchise, 8-bit video games informed the style of the comics, flavored the adaptation of the film, were re-remediated into their own low-resolution video game, and ultimately came back around to the comics in an elaborate box-set slipcase showcasing 8-bit art renderings of the characters. In cases of dialogical remediation, it becomes increasingly difficult to determine where one medium ends and another begins. The relationship between the modern webpage and television newscast is a perfect example of this slippery (and historically contingent!) slope of media specificity. The website's evolving remediation of formal principles from newspapers, magazines, and television news has produced a formal hybrid that bears the markers of all three media forms. At the same time, television news has been stylistically reinvented to incorporate multiple windows and text panels, making it look more and more like its world wide web offspring. Moreover, this dialogical process can be—and often is—ongoing.

It is important to note that remediation, as Bolter and Grusin define it, is not strictly limited to discussions of form, as interactivity and other factors can also be tied to the concept. This study, however, focuses primarily on the stylistic aspects of the process. Hence my desire to differentiate this study with the term "stylistic remediation." While it will be defined in greater depth in the following chapters, stylistic remediation can be generally defined as the representation of formal or stylistic characteristics commonly attributed to one medium within another. Like remediation, stylistic remediation differs from adaptation as a critical concept in two ways: it is not tied to a specific text, and it can be linear or dialogical. Also, while the term and concept of adaptation are used by practitioners within these two intertwined industries, the term or concept of remediation has not appeared within trade papers or interviews. Essentially, the term is being applied onto this stylistic practice retroactively.

The Contemporary Industrial, Cultural, and Technological Contexts of Stylistic Remediation

To describe this formal practice and to make stylistic remediation a relevant critical and theoretical term, attention must be given to industrial practices, advances in technology, and the role of an increasingly visible and vocal fan community. While these contexts will be analyzed in depth within the individual case studies that follow, a brief overview will be helpful. First, with regard to industrial practice, Eileen Meehan suggests in her essay on the success of Tim Burton's *Batman* that "economics must be considered" as a motivating factor in the rise of superhero films.[7] Throughout her essay, Meehan suggests that the conglomeration and horizontal integration of the Hollywood studio system gave studios the ability to progress towards an increasingly coordinated form of industrial practice. Thus, in the case of *Batman*, Warner Bros. was not only able to buy the rights to the property in a package deal (Warner Communications Inc., then a part of Kinney National Company, purchased DC Comics in 1967), but to market one product through several media forms (soundtrack albums, trading cards, toys). In this sense, Meehan concludes, the social, economic, and cultural success of the film "is best understood as multimedia, multimarket sales campaign [sic]."[8] Undoubtedly, the success of a property can be linked to horizontal integration and savvy marketing. Yet this link can serve as only a partial justification of the cause. After all, just because a conglomerate spends millions of dollars and pushes a lot of cross-promotional merchandise at the public does not necessarily mean that a franchise will become a box office success. For instance, the pre-established property of a Japanese anime series, the talents of the Lilly and Lana Wachowski (both of whom co-directed *The Matrix* series), and a rumored $80 million in marketing support were ultimately unable to lift the box office grosses for *Speed Racer* (2008) above its $120 million production budget. The industrial-economic aspect with regard to the comic book films is undeniable, but it also requires, amongst many factors, an audience already knowledgeable and passionate about a pre-established property.

The industrial gauge of a comic's success with the public was, until recently, based around a quantified ranking produced by Diamond Comic Distributors (DCD).[9] Essentially, DCD calculates the ranking by tracking sales from their distribution company to individual comic book retailers. While this ranking is problematic insofar as a retailer could order five hundred copies of the latest Superman title and only sell ten, the DCD numbers are the determining factor in what titles remain in publication. According to Valeria D'Orazio, a comic book writer who was formerly an assistant editor at DC Comics, "We lived or died by those Diamond numbers. They were The Numbers."[10] Thus, it is normally the bestselling and consequently longer running books like *Superman*, *Batman*, *Spider-Man*, and *Watchmen* that are adapted into films. However, these numbers only tell part of the story. After all, if studios were optioning properties based on sales numbers alone, our contemporary moment would be an odd time to start because comic book sales peaked in the decade leading up to the self-regulatory enforcement of the Comics Code in 1954.[11] Essentially, there is a second factor being considered by studios in this contemporary moment and that is the relationship between the comic book reader and the filmgoer. This relationship has chiefly manifested itself through two avenues worthy of brief discussion: comic book cultural prestige and the visibility of fan communities.

The reshaping of the cultural worth of comics changed the industry. For instance, in the 1970s Warner Communications Incorporated (WCI) owned DC Comics and the rights to Superman. At the time however, the conglomerate had no interest in adapting the property into a film, viewing the superhero primarily as a licensing cash cow.[12] Moreover, there was the concern that comic book films were inherently campy and would not prove to be a fruitful investment.[13] When approached by a trio of European film producers (Ilya and Alexander Salkind and Pierre Spengler), WCI sold the rights and agreed to distribute the film via a negative pickup deal. Significantly, the producers were only able to secure financing for a budget of an extraordinary $30 million after addressing the camp fears by hiring famed screenwriter Mario Puzo (*The Godfather* films) and casting acclaimed actors like Marlon Brando and Gene Hackman. Tellingly, Warner Bros. only agreed to provide financial aid towards budget overruns (which allegedly soared to a cost of $80 million faster than a speeding bullet) after they had seen footage, already sunk money into marketing the film, and the film's release date was jeopardized by the disgruntled producers . . . who allegedly held the negative for ransom.[14]

Yet despite the monumental success of *Superman*, studios still looked at comic book films with uncertainty for multiple reasons. First, budget over-runs occurred on many of the films, as many special-effects technologies needed to be invented from scratch (this was the case for *Superman* and for George Lucas's production of *Howard the Duck*). Secondly, box office success was difficult to grasp, as the 1980s witnessed huge financial failures in *Supergirl* (1984, estimated budget of $35 million, domestic box office gross of $14 million), *Red Sonja* (1985, estimated budget of $35 million, domestic box office gross of $7 million), and *Howard the Duck* (1986, estimated budget of $52 million, domestic box office gross of $16 million). Significantly, by the tail end of the decade, even Superman lost money (*Superman IV: The Quest for Peace*, 1987, estimated budget of $30 million, domestic box office gross of $15 million). Overall, the failure of these films can also be attributed to a range of factors, including their inability to capture the tone of the source material. Notably, while the *Superman* cycle began with the producers attempting to address concerns of camp, the pendulum quickly swung the other way. The producers fired director Richard Donner, who spoke the virtues of cinematic realism, and hired comedy director Richard Lester.

After the slew of comic book film failures in the mid-1980s, Hollywood began a drive to account for tonal direction by going back to the source mate-rial. However, a larger, related, question lingered: who was the audience for these films? For decades, comic books had traditionally been read by youth (due in part to the dominance of the Comics Code), but the audience had shifted during the 1970s and 1980s. Beginning in the 1970s, independent underground comix (a genre of comics that was published outside of the reg-ulation of the Comics Code) attempted to cater to the adult reader by embrac-ing controversial topics such as the counter-culture, drugs, and sexuality. The comic book's shift from a lowly children's form to a high art medium capable of capturing an adult audience is temporally marked by what might be con-sidered "the medium's greatest year: 1986."[15]

1986 marks a significant year for the comic book due to the release of three seminal texts: Alan Moore and Dave Gibbons's *Watchmen*, Art Spiegelman's *Maus: A Survivor's Tale*, and Frank Miller, Klaus Janson, and Lynn Varley's *Batman: The Dark Knight Returns*. For the release of the third title, comic book publisher DC began utilizing a new square-bound binding for the lim-ited series which they called the "Prestige Format" in order to differentiate the dark and gritty project from other comics produced for youth. As comic book historians Randy Duncan and Matthew J. Smith note, "Miller's take on the Dark Knight drew more attention than the character had received since the campy TV show of the 1960s. Miller had brought Batman back to his violent roots and provided a grittier, less sanitized vision of vigilantism."[16] The financial success of Miller's comic allegedly jumpstarted production on the film, which had spent nearly a decade in pre-production. Like the producers of *Superman* before them, the producers of *Batman* vowed to avoid the campy qualities of the TV series by injecting prestige into the title—specifically through the casting of Jack Nicholson as the Joker.

The *Batman* example provides a perfect bridge from discussing the recently acquired prestige of comics to the second industrial factor that has been known to make or break a comic book adaptation: fan communities. When the casting of comedian Michael Keaton as Batman was announced, long time readers were incredibly disappointed. They feared that the property had shifted from the dark, adult, vision of Frank Miller's work to the camp qualities of the TV series. In November 1988, the *Wall Street Journal* reported that fan publications were receiving hundreds of protest letters.[17] When Warner Bros. got wind of the reaction, they responded by cutting a trailer that inspired an enthusiastic response. According to *Newsweek*, "When the trailer went into general release at Christmas, word of mouth spread among the fans and beyond. . . . 'By the start of the year,' says Rob Friedman, Warner Bros. president of worldwide advertising and publicity, 'there was a feeding frenzy that we took advantage of, and to a certain extent fueled.'"[18] As Friedman's quote helps illustrate, marketing can fuel and capitalize upon a fan base, but it does not necessarily produce one.

Over the past twenty years, comic book conventions, especially San Diego Comic-Con International (SDCC), have proven an invaluable resource for industrial personnel in both developing content for comics and film and—one might argue more so—for marketing such properties. While SDCC has been the Mecca for comic book fans since 1970, it has experienced a monumental growth in attendance from 1989, the year *Batman* was released, to 2009. Specifically, from 1970 to 1989 the attendance of SDCC grew from approximately three hundred to eleven thousand people (an average yearly growth of approximately 563 visitors). In contrast, from the 1989 to 2008 SDCC attendance jumped from eleven thousand to one hundred and twenty-six thousand attendees (an average yearly growth of approximately six thousand visitors).[19] As SDCC became larger and larger, studios increasingly relied on the convention both as a means of legitimating product with fans and as an instrumental mechanism in driving cultural awareness. After all, who "sells" a product better than satisfied fans, the core audience of a film? In the words of Fox Chief Marketing Officer John Hegeman (who produced Guillermo del Toro's *Hellboy*), studios need to hold onto this core fan audience because a film cannot be financially successful without their support. At the same time however, studios have gradually shifted towards a two-tiered marketing approach, utilizing more interactive forms of marketing (alternate-reality games, presentation panels at SDCC) to engage with fan communities while also drawing on more traditional and accessible forms (television spots, merchandising) aimed at the casual consumer.

However, conglomeration, horizontal integration, comic book cultural capital, and the rise of fan cultures do not complete the picture on the recent rise of the comic book films. After all, SDCC was formed in 1970, providing a face to the comic book fan community eight years before the release of *Superman* and nearly two decades before the onslaught of post-*Batman* adaptations. The final contextual puzzle piece that needs to be briefly considered is the influence of technological developments in filmmaking (specifically special effects and computer-generated imagery) during the past twenty-five years. As Booker notes, before the early 2000s:

> the technology available for filmmakers simply did not allow them the range and scope that have always been available to comic artists, whose creativity was limited only by their own imaginations. After all, it costs very little to draw an action scene (relying on readers to fill in much of the detail) that might cost millions of dollars to produce for the screen—-if it can be produced at all.[20]

Yet when placed alongside the other factors so far examined, Booker's judgment, while no doubt being true to a point, is also problematic. Of course, CGI gives director Bryan Singer the ability to stage an extraordinary action sequence featuring Superman rescuing Lois Lane from a malfunctioning space shuttle in *Superman Returns* (2006) with great ease. However, CGI is also an incredibly expensive tool. For instance, James Cameron's *Terminator 2: Judgment Day* (1991) featured a groundbreaking 300 visual effects (VFX) shots and cost roughly $102 million to produce while *Superman Returns* contained 1,400 VFX shots, pushing its budget to $261 million.[21] Without the financial backing of a horizontally integrated corporation and a pre-established fan base ensuring an economic return on the massive financial investment on films whose budgets surpass the $100 million mark, Booker's analysis verges on the terrain of technological determinism.

While technological innovations are part of equation, it is significant that many of these films utilize technology to remediate comic book stylistics. Take, for instance, this excerpt from critic Richard George's review of Zack Snyder's *300* (2007):

> Synder's use of blood and slow motion gives the movie a flair of its own that also seems to channel panels in a comic book. The blood takes on a very flat, 2-D

effect that keeps the violence within limits while also making it unique in cinema. We've all seen blood fly in horror movies, but things are done a bit differently here. Miller and colorist Lynn Varley used a similar technique, resorting to paint blotches splattered throughout the battles rather than going for something pains-takingly realistic. The result is something both artistic and viscerally exciting . . . Last but not least in Snyder's arsenal of techniques is slow motion combined with freezing frames . . . Snyder will rush along in a battle only to suddenly drop the frame rate down drastically. The effect is something almost akin to a panel.[22]

In the case of *300*, as was the case with Robert Rodriguez and Frank Miller's *Sin City* (2005), CGI is used by the director as a means of reaching beyond narrative source material towards stylistic fidelity. Yet this analysis of stylistic remediation is not merely the product of over-zealous formal analysis, as Sny-der (specifically in the case of *300*) often used Frank Miller and Lynn Varley's original panels as storyboards, going so far as to instruct his VFX team to "build this."[23] As I have argued here, the slew of comic book films to grace the screen and the evolving stylistic characteristics that have marked them can-not be simplified to a focus solely on the realm of industry, the consumer, the US cultural context, or technology. All of these contexts exhibit significant influence upon one another.

Due to the complex interrelationships that define this context, the scope of this book is limited with regard to temporality, geography, and textual exam-ples. Temporally, the most justifiable boundaries for this study are the years between 1978 and 2013. 1978 brought not only the first release of a comic book film in the blockbuster era, *Superman: The Movie*, but also the release of Will Eisner's *A Contract with God, and Other Stories*, a long form comic that is often considered (erroneously) to be the marker for the birth of the American graphic novel.[24] 2013 provides a poetic end point, as it marked the release of Zack Snyder's cinematic reboot of the Superman mythos, *Man of Steel*.

With regard to geography, this investigation is limited—for the most part—to comics and films produced in the United States. Admittedly, this process can undoubtedly be viewed as international, as Franco-Belgian and Japanese films based on sequential art are incredibly common. Moreover, as will be discussed in the *Scott Pilgrim* case study, some formal explorations analyzed here have been gleaned from international texts (specifically, Jap-anese manga). However, a geographical limitation must be set in order to investigate the intricacies of this phenomenon in depth. This geographical boundary can be justified from two fronts. First, comics and graphic novels from other countries often follow different representational paths. To be more specific, in his discussion of representations of time in international comics, scholar Scott McCloud notes different temporal segmentations from country to country, particularly noting an "east/west split." As McCloud writes:

> Traditional western art and literature don't wander much. On the whole, we're a pretty goal-oriented culture. But, in the east, there's a rich tradition of cyclical and labyrinthine works of art. Japanese comics may be heirs to this tradition, in the way they so often emphasize being there over getting there. Through these and other storytelling techniques, the Japanese offer a vision of comics very different from our own.[25]

McCloud's assertion is echoed in scholar Roger Sabin's history of comics. Sabin argues that beginning with comic strips (the predecessor to the comic book and graphic novel), American comics followed "a quite different evolutionary path" than their international counterparts.[26]

Secondly, the cultural history of comics in Japan and the Franco-Belgian region is markedly different from here in the United States. With regard to Japanese readership, 40 percent of the publishing industry is made up of "manga" (the Japanese term for comics) while comics make up only 3 percent of the industry in the US. Moreover, the property rights for Japanese comics are held by individual creators, not publishing companies. The publishing format is also significantly different, as manga are published in black and white and have a relatively low production value. Moreover, the cultural history of Franco-Belgian comics differs from our own insofar as, in the words of scholars Randy Duncan and Matthew J. Smith, "The French and Belgians have always embraced the comics medium as an art."[27] Most notably, the French cultural ministry partially funded a comic book museum and research center, the Cité Internationale de la Bande Dessinée (CIIBDI) since 1974. The only nation with a comic book industry analogous to our own is the United Kingdom. However, much like the relationship between the US and UK film industries, American publishers have hampered the growth of the UK industry by launching competition in the form of international subsidiaries (such as Marvel UK) or by luring creative talent (such as Alan Moore, Dave Gibbons, Neil Gaiman, and Grant Morrison) to American productions.

Finally, with regard to the selection of film texts, this investigation is focused primarily on feature films. The torrent of animated and live-action television shows based on comics produced during the past thirty years featuring such characters as Spider-Man, the X-Men, Batman, Superman, and the Justice League would complicate industrial, stylistic, and consumption contexts beyond what can be successfully addressed by this volume. However, the role of television and some of the texts produced for it, most notably some of the Batman television series produced throughout the years, will not be completely ignored. The medium has played an undeniable and evolving role in the relationship between comics and film. Furthermore, live-action and animated television shows rarely engage in stylistic remediation (with one notable exception being MTV's *The Maxx*).[28] In fact, the most common point of formal convergence is both media's emphasis on seriality. This may be because stylistic remediation is often tied to the extensive use of CGI, which inherently raises production costs.

Finally, the industrial rationale behind many comic book films from this period has been to move as far away from television product as possible, as the "campy" stigma of earlier, televisual, incarnations proved to be a major concern. As *Batman* producer Jon Peters noted when faced with a lawsuit by TV's Batman, Adam West, after he was rejected as a candidate for the film: "I never saw the TV show but this has nothing to do with the television show."[29] During the bulk of the timeframe analyzed in this study, studios producing comic book films have sought to differentiate their product from television in their continual quest for cultural prestige, be it through the casting of Marlon Brando or Jack Nicholson, the hiring of critically lauded directors (Christopher Nolan, Bryan Singer, Ang Lee) and comic book personnel (Frank Miller, Dave Gibbons), and the embrace of a comic book stylistic devices. Essentially, a film's embrace of comic book form holds a lot of water with its main fan demographic. Adapting comic books to film without considering style is akin to making a musical without dance sequences; it misses something fundamental about the original text.

The Layout of the Book

The first chapter, "Scott Pilgrim, Stylistic Remediation, and Transmedia Style," covers Edgar Wright's adaptation of Bryan Lee O'Malley's comic series. Despite being one of the last case studies in this book temporally, I begin with it because it is one of the richest texts in existence for outlining the concept of stylistic remediation as almost all forms that will be outlined in this volume's formal taxonomy are present within it. Specifically, Wright fractures his film frame into a series of panels, visually represents sounds, and utilizes O'Malley's drawn assets as a replacement for the photographic frame, making it the closest the cinema has ever come to remediating the form of the comic. Moreover, the stylistic remediation present across the Scott Pilgrim texts became the basis of a transmedia campaign. However, the film was also a financial disaster that prompted Hollywood studios to reevaluate stylistic remediation and the influence of fan communities. Essentially, the box office demise of *Scott Pilgrim vs. the World* (2010) also diminished a rich trajectory of stylistic remediation in comic book adaptations. Thus, it serves as the perfect primer for introducing the theoretical concepts at work here and how they are informed by the aforementioned contexts.

While the first chapter focuses on the contemporary period, the second chapter, "The History of Remediation Between Comics and Film," takes a broader approach to the cultural, industrial, and technological history that has defined the relationships between film and comic book media since 1936. While the chapter does not fully define or engage with the theory of stylistic remediation, it does consider how the cartoonish nature of the *Batman* television series (1966–1968) and Comics Code titles pushed the team behind *Superman: The Movie* to work against that stylistic path by embracing cinematic realism. As the medium of comics became culturally reevaluated however, certain approaches to stylization—specifically the noir infused mise-en-scène of Tim Burton's Batman films (1989, 1992)—were embraced and accepted by fans. However, as the commercial and critical reception of Joel Schumacher's Batman films (1995, 1997) illustrates, stylistic remediation that veers on camp is often met with fan hostility. In addition to fan reception and the cultural reevaluation of comics, these stylistic approaches have also been reenforced by such industrial trends as the increased integration and oversight of media conglomerate holdings and the visual norms of special-effects technology.

Thus, chapters I and II establish the basics of the multifaceted theoretical toolbox mobilized here, a general taxonomy of stylistic remediation, and the historical context for the practice. Chapters III and IV, by contrast, focus on a set of case studies in which those remediations occur. By analyzing comic book adaptations ranging from Warren Beatty's *Dick Tracy* (1990) to Zack Snyder's *Watchmen* (2009), the basic taxonomy of stylistic remediation formulated in the first chapter will be elaborated upon. Specifically, by drawing upon theories of film and comic book form, these case studies outline the methods filmmakers use to seek formal equivalency and how radically different these superficially similar media forms actually are. Moreover, these chapters also continue to deepen the historical trajectories outlined in the second chapter by outlining the contexts for these titles by engaging with discussions of pre-production and post-production difficulties, filmmaking technology, and reception. Even when it is discussed and analyzed as being a formal creative choice, a fully elaborated theory of stylistic remediation cannot be divorced from the real world factors that shape it.

The fifth and sixth chapters are similar in structure to the two chapters preceding them in their theory, methodology, and concern for context. However, the main objective of the two chapters—"Remediation Beyond Comic Book Adaptations" and "The Dialogical Process of Remediation"—is to move beyond the proving ground of comic book adaptations in order to define and elaborate upon how stylistic remediation is a phenomenon that differs from adaptation. Essentially, stylistic remediation can be present in films (*The Matrix, The Good, the Bad, and the Ugly*) and comics (Marvel Comics' *The Dark Tower*) that are not adaptations produced from visual content born from another medium. Specifically, *The Matrix* (1999) stylistically remediates the motion lines of comics within its bullet time sequences while Sergio Leone's construction of space eschews the conventions of the continuity system in favor of the spatial discontinuity present across comic book panels. *The Dark Tower* series (2007-Present), on the other hand, draws upon Leone's morally defined caricatures and the pacing leading up to short explosions of violence. Moreover, stylistic remediation can be a dialogic process in which ongoing remediations bear traces of their previous incarnations, which can be utilized as a marketing tool. The case studies illustrating re-remediation (for lack of a better term) include two analyses. First, an analysis of how film informed the design of the Joker in the comics and looped back around to his depiction in television and comics will be put forth. The second analysis centers on how film noir style influenced Frank Miller's comics, his co-directed adaptation of *Sin City*, and ultimately overwhelmed his adaptation of Will Eisner's *The Spirit* (1940-Present).

What emerges from this layout is the formulation of a new meta-theory of style—stylistic remediation—and how a style can migrate across different media forms. As this study will prove, style can be as much a commodity as the superheroes Iron Man, Batman, and The Avengers are. When the flattened, artificial, impressionistic mise-en-scène of Frank Miller's *300* graphic novel is remediated both by film (Zack Snyder's film adaptation) and television (*Spartacus*), it has separated itself from an adaptation and has become, like the birth of bullet time from *The Matrix*, a formal trademark of its own. However, the migration of a style is also informed by real world limits, and like kryptonite to Superman, nothing kills it faster than economic failure. When the fictional publisher George Christopher noted in HBO's *Bored to Death* that "comics are in right now," he was only partially correct. In the fall of 2009 (when he uttered that phrase), films based on comics and comic book style were "in," not comics themselves. One year later, after the box office implosion of *Scott Pilgrim* and *Kick-Ass*, the "right now" of Christopher's phrase had begun to diminish with regard to stylistic remediation.

Nothing symbolizes the trailing off of this trajectory as much as Zack Snyder's most recent film, *Man of Steel* (2013). Snyder's *300*, *Watchmen*, and *Sucker Punch* (2011) are all stylistically informed by the formal vocabulary of comic books. For instance, throughout all three films, Snyder manipulates the temporal status of his images via speed ramping. By transitioning individual shots from slow motion to fast motion to the "normal" speed of 24 frames per second, the filmmaker captures the fluid relationship between space and time both within and between comic book panels. Perhaps due to the embarrassing economic and critical reception of *Sucker Punch*, Snyder's *Man of Steel*, an adaptation of Superman, shows few signs of its director's previously established style. In fact, the film's strong adherence to cinematic realism conceals the identity of Snyder behind the "serious" tone of his producer, Batman auteur Christopher Nolan. Contemporarily, the stylistic remediation of comics by film has temporarily lost out to formalism that adheres to the norms of realism. However, stylistic remediation is not a movement. It is, like the theory that defines it, dialogical.

PART

DEFINITIONS AND HISTORICAL CONTEXT

ONE

CHAPTER 1

"It's Perfect. It Looks Just Like the Book!": Scott Pilgrim, Stylistic Remediation, and Transmedia Style

Introduction

On the opening night—August 13, 2010—of Edgar Wright's film *Scott Pilgrim vs. the World*, a full crowd attended a screening in one of Los Angeles's many neighboring cities, Century City. Century City is similar to Culver City or Burbank. It is a city founded on the movies. While Culver City serves as the geographic home base to Sony Pictures Studios (which is located on the former Culver Studios lot), Century City gets its "Century" from studio mogul William Fox. The AMC multiplex located in the Westfield Century City mall is across the street from Fox's headquarters, and on that Friday night, the theater was packed. The audience roared with laughter at comic writer/artist Bryan Lee O'Malley's cultural references. They clapped after Wright's creative staging of the film's numerous action set pieces. When the lights came up, a female patron seated near me turned to her friend and said "It's perfect. It looks just like the book."

While *Scott Pilgrim* may have been successful earlier that summer at San Diego Comic-Con and the multiplexes located in the posh shopping malls just a few minutes from the beaches of Santa Monica and Malibu, it failed miserably at the box office. Despite garnering complementary reviews from critics and an "A-" CinemaScore from average viewers (CinemaScores are based on a sample of audience members after a screening of a film), the $60 million ($85–90 million before tax breaks) film came in fifth place during its opening weekend. That weekend, *Scott Pilgrim* earned what industrial analyst Nikki Finke described as being "a pittance": $10.5 million.[1] Eventually, the film

21

grossed $47 million globally, $13 million less than its hefty production budget (ignoring any additional marketing costs).

Like *Kick-Ass* (2010), another adaptation released that year based on a niche comic book property, the film's studio—Universal—seemed to have huge expectations for *Scott Pilgrim*. During that summer's San Diego Comic-Con, the film was positioned as one of the Con's main attractions. The outdoor "Scott Pilgrim Experience" took up the courtyard of a neighboring hotel complex and drew massive crowds waiting to get autographs and to collect free merchandise. Moreover, the Con produced lines that sprawled city blocks for "secret" advance screenings. Prior to the film's release, four of the five top selling titles on Amazon.com were *Scott Pilgrim* titles and the property was one of the leading "trending" topics on the social networking site Twitter. Despite the Comic-Con hype, social network visibility, and being a movie that looks just like the book, *Scott Pilgrim* also led to a decline in the formalist trend of stylistic remediation under analysis here.

Yet despite being an economic disaster, *Scott Pilgrim* is also one of the richest case studies illustrating the process of stylistic remediation at work in the adaptation of a comic book to a film. As the excited theater patron noted, it looks just like the book. But what does this exactly mean? In the following section, I will elaborate on this proclamation by briefly outlining what makes both film and comic books distinct media forms by dissecting their ontological differences. Then, we can begin to look at how Edgar Wright and Universal attempted to compromise those differences via stylistic remediation, a process which eventually—through comics, a film, a soundtrack, and a video game—became a means for a media conglomerate to attempt to unite its transmedia properties. In short, like bullet time in *The Matrix* before it, the stylistic remediation of *Scott Pilgrim* became a type of transmedia style.

Adaptation vs. Stylistic Remediation Redux

Filmic adaptation involves the transformation of both the form and content of a previous text from another art form onto film. For decades, these adaptations, when subjected to scholarly textual analysis, were often defined by and against their source texts. As film adaptation scholar Robert Stam has outlined, this theoretical framework of "fidelity criticism" perpetuated a prejudice against adaptations that often resulted in self-defeating paradox. He writes, "A 'faithful' film is seen as uncreative, but an 'unfaithful' film is a shameful betrayal of the original. . . . The adapter, it seems, can never win."[2]

Yet thanks to the efforts of scholars like Stam, adaptation theory has finally broken free of the intellectual shackles of fidelity criticism. Specifically, Stam—guided by the work of post-structuralists—has encouraged alternative methodologies such as "intertextual dialogism" that "refers to the infinite and open-ended possibilities generated by all the discursive practices of a culture, the entire matrix of communicative utterances within which the artistic text is situated, which reach the text not only through recognizable influences, but also through a subtle process of dissemination."[3] Thus, for Stam, adaptation theory should situate its texts within a cultural context and view them as being engaged in an intertextual dialogue defined by co-presence rather than a hierarchy defined by an original and its copy. As his theory has evolved (Stam originally proposed "intertextual dialogism" in 2000) into the twenty-first century, he has encouraged scholars to view adaptation within the realm of the "post-celluloid world" in which new media theories can play a valuable role in expanding the field and its metaphors.[4]

Hence my desire to mobilize one of the foundational texts of new media theory—Jay David Bolter and Richard Grusin's *Remediation: Understanding New Media*—to continue Stam's move beyond fidelity criticism. Remediation, as examined by Bolter and Grusin, is the representation of one medium in another.[5] While adaptations can engage in the process of remediation if, in the words of Bolter and Grusin, the original medium is "appropriated or quoted" in the adaptation, remediations do not rely on a previous text from another art form for material to translate.[6] Rather, remediations translate the art form itself. While remediation undoubtedly occurs in adaptations of previous texts (be it *Sin City* the film or the graphic novelization of *Batman*), an analysis defined by a focus on adaptations only gives us a piece of the puzzle. This is because remediation is often a broader, dialogical, artistic, socioeconomic process.

As Bolter and Grusin eloquently describe, "Established media, such as film and television, respond by trying to incorporate digital media within their traditional formal and social structures. . . . What is new about new media comes from the particular ways in which they refashion older media and the ways in which older media refashion themselves to answer the challenges of new media."[7] In this specific case, remediation analyzes the translation of aspects of one medium (film noir lighting) into another medium (film noir lighting as remediated by Frank Miller's drawings in the *Sin City* comic), which can ultimately be reacted to by the original form (Frank Miller's remediations by film noir lighting in the comic as re-remediated by Frank Miller and Robert Rodriguez's adaptation). My own critical term, stylistic remediation is an elaboration upon Bolter and Grusin's theory in order to place emphasis on the remediation of formal and stylistic attributes that are specific to one medium or the other.

Definitions aside, now we can turn to defining the formal properties that are being remediated in the film *Scott Pilgrim vs. the World*. Comics Studies scholar Pascal Lefèvre's analysis serves as an excellent starting point.[8] For Lefèvre, the relationship between the forms of the comic and film can be broadly defined across three formal attributes: sound, iconography, and space. Elaborating upon Lefèvre's schema, we can also consider the remediation of text (as separate from sound) and temporality. With regard to sound, comics have a textual soundtrack with diegetic sound expressed through word balloons (dialogue) and graphically embellished onomatopoeia (noises).

O'Malley's *Scott Pilgrim* comics engage in both of the formal norms of representing sound. Word balloons run in abundance (while "silent" comics exist, they are largely a formal outlier) and large, block letter outlined, words like "Kroww" and "Krak" stand in for the sounds of a fist fight. Furthermore, O'Malley's comic exemplifies a unique formal means of representing the sound of music. Specifically, the title's hero is the bass player in a band called Sex Bob-omb and the first graphic novel, *Scott Pilgrim's Precious Little Life* (2004), showcases the band practicing the song tentatively titled "Launchpad McQuack." The artist utilizes a remediation of sheet music and textual captions that stand outside the panel to represent the song. Thanks to the inclusion of a chart featuring guitar chords and lyrics, O'Malley informs the reader that "you can play along with Sex Bob-omb at home! It's easy, because they're kind of crappy!" Essentially, and this will be elaborated upon shortly, O'Malley's comic also remediates other media.

While Wright does not go as far to re-remediate O'Malley's remediation of music, the director continuously underlines diegetic sounds with visual onomatopoeia via the process of aural remediation. For instance, when Wright depicts the band opening "Launchpad McQuack" (before segueing into the credits), he visually represents the drummer's count into the song and the "Yeah" of the band's vocalist with words serving as icons. Essentially, despite the change in medium from "silent" comics to "sound" cinema, the adaptation—like the *Batman* live-action television series that inspired it—stylistically remediates the comic's representation of sound. As the filmmaker noted in a personal interview, "I really like the style of the artwork and the film is a comedy, not gritty or realistic. I just really wanted to embrace the pop art nature of comics. Maybe because of the *Batman* television series, which I always liked as a kid but became a dirty word in the 1980s when *The Dark Knight Returns* came out. But there are things about the '60s and '70s books—the colors—that really embraced the pop art and fun that I appreciated."[9] Essentially, this double-layered representational mode encourages the viewer to approach the adaptation as a text that can also be read and watched.

The second formal discrepancy between comics and film in our broad taxonomy is their differing modes of representation. Film is a medium that was—until recently—powered by the motor of photography. Photography, on the other hand, remains a little explored route in American comic art. Drawing—be it through inks, pencils, paint, commercial off-set lithography, or even digital methods—is the primary tool of visual expression. Comic scholar Scott McCloud's map of the pictorial language of the comic proves useful here. McCloud, who utilizes the form of the pyramid, constructs his map on a two-axis system.[10] The horizontal axis, which he dubs "The Representational Edge," is marked by a spectrum of comic representational methods. For the author, "Reality" (at the far left) and "Meaning" or "Language" (at the far right) defines the spectrum of representation utilized by comics practitioners.[11] For instance, photography and photorealist cinema are placed upon the left side of the pyramid while minimalist illustration styles stand at the far right. McCloud complicates his horizontal axis with the vertical axis "The Retinal Edge," which is crowned by "The Picture Plane."[12] Essentially, as images ascend the pyramid, they become more abstract, which renders them neutral on the "Representational Edge."

With regard to the pictorial pyramid, O'Malley's compositions would veer towards the minimalist side of the representational edge and be slightly elevated upon the retinal axis, far from the domain of photorealism. This is because the series—including publication format, narrative arc, and representational mode—owes much to Japanese manga. First, the title was not sold in single, monthly issues that define the majority of American comics. Rather, *Scott Pilgrim* was packaged in a small digest form by Oni Press and published on a release pattern of roughly one volume a year. The digest form (approximately 7.5 by 5 inches) is strikingly smaller than the usual comic book format (approximately 10.25 by 6.5 inches) and is more familiar to American comic book readers as the typical format that manga is published in. Moreover, the intertwining arcs of Scott's quests for identity and true love are narrative characteristics of modern *shōjo/shoujo* (the first is the female variation, the second is the male) manga.

Finally, O'Malley's character designs (specifically the large, round, eyes of the characters and the minimal use of lines to define emotion) are also in dialogue with the manga aesthetic. For the sake of illustration, here is a page of O'Malley's *Scott Pilgrim* placed next to a page of Koge Donbo's *Kamichama Karin* (2003–2005, 2007–2008), a popular Japanese manga that also became

Figure 1.1. O'Malley's *Scott Pilgrim*.

a television anime (cartoon). In both figures, we notice that both artists have abstracted their characters from the photorealistic by providing few details beyond the mouth and eyes (although Kim Pine, in panel one of *Scott Pilgrim*, has freckles and Steven Stills, featured prominently in the final panel, has what looks to be the beginnings of a beard). Moreover, the eyes of the characters in both titles are often either large circles (panels 1, 2, and 4 of *Scott Pilgrim* and the final panel of *Kamichama Karin*) or "closed" by the use of the line (the final panel of *Scott Pilgrim*, the first three panels of *Kamichama*).

Perhaps more obvious is that the settings in both titles are minimally established, with the exception of the middle panel of *Scott*. Moreover, both

Figure 1.2. Donbo's *Kamichama Karin*.

artists place their characters against white, black, or "subjective" backgrounds that symbolize the emotion of the character (an adrenaline rush in the final panel of *Scott*, the love and excitement in the first panel of *Kamichama*). This mode intersects with a difference in the representation of motion between American and Japanese comics that Scott McCloud outlines. Specifically, Japanese comics often engage in a representation of motion not typically seen in their American cousin: "subjective motion."[13] Essentially, McCloud writes that Japanese artists began to provide subjective point-of-view panels (his example is a motorcycle chase) to engage the reader beginning in the late 1960s. American comic artists, on the other hand, rarely rely on subjective points-of-view. Instead, American artists rely on dialogue and facial expression to capture psychology. In Japanese comics, such as *Kamichama*, emotion defines the literal space of the setting.[14]

For the most part, Wright's adaptation allows the photographic apparatus to define his representation. Admittedly, he occasionally embeds characters in the subjective spaces that O'Malley borrows from manga, abstracting his characters from their surroundings via green screen technology. However, there is one prolonged sequence that stands in complete opposition to the photographic mode. During Scott's (Michael Cera) fight with Ramona (Mary Elizabeth Winstead)'s first evil ex (Satya Bhabha), Wright—like O'Malley before him—intercuts a flashback. In this flashback (which depicts Ramona's relationship with the antagonist), Wright shifts away from photographic realism to literally—using the actual panels of O'Malley's comic—represent the flashback with an animated comic strip. Aside from the addition of color (O'Malley's original books were published in black and white, but were later reprinted in color), the graphic representation has not been altered from its original medium. Essentially, this is not an adaptation of the comic. By utilizing the original art work and panel transitions, Wright's representation of the flashback is a graphical remediation of O'Malley's art in motion.

The third characteristic that defines the formal relationship between these two media is that of temporality. For the most part, film is a medium in which time and movement are in sync, correlated by the relatively stable temporal definition of the individual film frame as being 1/24th of a second (the exception would be slow or fast motion or, as I will discuss, speed ramping). This correlation between time and space does not exist in comics. Not only can the duration between sequential panels vary in a multitude of ways, but the temporal definition of an individual panel is not equated with the instant, as a photograph might be.[15] As McCloud has argued, an individual panel can include a multitude of temporal durations with actions ranging from a split second to half a minute (or longer), partially defined by the artist's use of sound and dialogue.[16]

Moreover, the comic's establishment of time is further complicated by the figure of the reader. The reader of a comic book can ponder over individual panels for as long as he or she pleases. Hence, there is a tension in the reader's experience of the text, which is amplified by the multiplicity of images presented to him or her. Essentially, the path of comprehension in the comic is not defined by the medium or the filmmaker. As Will Eisner describes in his study of theory and method and the comic, the attention of the reader cannot be controlled via time. Instead, the "sequential artist" must utilize composition and the conventions of reading to control the reader.[17]

On the other hand—and depending upon the exhibition venue—the viewer of a film remains relatively passive in their temporal reading of a cinematic sequence. In a theatrical setting, the viewer is incapable of controlling the constant and absolute march of cinematic time. However, thanks to home video formats such as DVD, Blu-Ray, and digital streaming, the home viewer is capable of temporal manipulation (pausing, replaying, and skipping thanks to the remote control). This, of course, depends upon the viewer. While new technologies have allowed viewers to "read" films like comics, there are plenty of cinephiles who look upon such manipulation as an act of spectatorial blasphemy that ruptures both the spatiotemporal and narrative flows of the text.[18]

The fluid temporality of comics is apparent in O'Malley's representation of Scott's fight with the first "evil ex." The majority of the sequence is represented by a blending what McCloud describes as moment-to-moment panels (panels that represent a fraction of a second, much like the individual frame of a reel of film) and action-to-action panels (panels that, when placed in dialogue with one another, represent a longer duration of time). The fight sequence begins with two moment-to-moment panels: one temporally encapsulating Scott blocking a punch and the other Scott throwing a punch. However, following these moment-to-moment transitions, the temporality of both the panels and the sequence begins to get hazy. For instance, one panel features a landed punch and an exchange of dialogue, which—if we consider the panel akin to the film frame—lacks stable temporal definition. After all, the time it takes to punch someone is shorter than the time it takes to ask "What?" As McCloud describes, our cognitive predisposition towards art (painting, photography) as the representation of a single instant in time does not apply to comics. Time dictates the representation of space in film while the opposite holds true of comics.

Wright captures the fluid definition of time in the first shots of the fight sequence. The confrontation begins with shots filmed at 24 frames per second (the audience is able to gauge the frame rate thanks to dialogue). However, after the initial introduction, the evil ex jumps into the air and hovers in slow motion. Wright juxtaposes this with a shot of Scott asking "What do I do?!" that is filmed, once again, at regular speed. The filmmaker then cuts back to the evil ex jumping in the air, underlining the elongated duration with the use of sound. Finally, Wright returns to Scott, who is now part of the same elongated temporal continuum (he removes his guitar in slow motion). Essentially, the director utilizes shots composed at different frame rates to stylistically remediate the fluid temporality of O'Malley's comics. The temporal definition of the individual film frame no longer remains static at 1/24th of a second; it has become malleable and ambiguous.

Finally, the remediation of space, characterized by the metamorphosis from the comic book panel to the cinematic frame, is often simplified by theoreticians who simply equate a comic book with a storyboard, or treat them as two forms of media that produce narratives through sequential images. Yet the difference between the two media with regard to their methods of producing space is vast. Analyzing the difference between comics and cinematic storyboards, the panels of the comic are often interdependent images of space and time, featuring narrative text, and presented in unison. Storyboards (the composition of which can vary drastically based upon the artist and the preproduction staff) often lack narrative text and the legibility of comics. They are blueprints for shots; the frame may feature movement vectors (arrows or boxes to indicate a zoom, pan, tilt, or dolly shot) and other variables that comics do not include. Essentially, storyboards are not legible in the same way comics are because they are not the ultimate, presented, result. The former are often paired with a screenplay—linked with scene and shot numbers—making them incapable of telling a story in isolation.

With regard to their construction of space, comics produce a tension best illustrated by the phenomenological response the reader experiences. While McCloud is correct when he describes comics formally as being "Juxtaposed pictorial and other images in deliberate sequence," there is a tension in how the reader actually engages with the images.[19] Often, the reader grapples with a comic one image at a time because the frames of each panel are closed compositions. Moreover, the closed compositions of the comic panel are often reinforced by the spatial characteristics of the comic book page. Specifically, the gutter (the white border around the images) segregates the individual frames from the overall page. The gutter directs space inwards (both in terms of the frame and the overall page) and fractures time and space into an overall sequence which provides the reader with a preferred route towards narrative comprehension.

Yet regardless of the closed nature of the comic panel, readers are often faced with a series of complex compositions that threaten the narrative flow of the page. As theorist Thierry Groensteen observes:

> A page of comics is offered at first to a synthetic global vision, but that cannot be satisfactory. It demands to be traversed, crossed, glanced at, and analytically deciphered. This moment-to-moment reading does not take a lesser account of the totality of the panoptic field that constitutes the page (or double page), since the focal vision never ceases to be enriched by the peripheral vision.[20]

Many of these techniques are drawn from a process of visual differentiation. For instance, the eye is naturally drawn to compositions that are unlike others around it. Visual differentiation, in terms of the comic, can be exemplified through a number of techniques, including color, symmetry, and the shape of the panel.

O'Malley represents the fight scene between Scott and the first evil ex through alternations of pages defined by the multiframe (pages which feature a grid like structure of panels) and panel-less splash pages. The sequence begins with a series of multiframed pages that structure the panels around the exchange of physical violence: Scott is punched in one panel, he deals a blow in the second panel. Then, O'Malley shifts into splash pages that depict temporally discrete actions (Scott punching the evil ex, the evil ex falling after the barrage of punches) within the same space. Essentially, O'Malley's construction of space—like his representation of temporality—is fluid. One moment, he asks his reader to put individual panels in dialogue with one another, and with the flip of a page, he asks the reader to provide intra-panel closure.

Wright spatially remediates the shifting dimensions of O'Malley's comic book panel through a variable aspect ratio. Returning to Scott's fight with the first evil ex, Wright begins the sequence with a widescreen ratio of 1.85:1 (the bulk of the film was shot this way). However, the director quickly narrows and widens the frame in conjunction with the fight. For instance, when Scott is attacked, the frame narrows. When he counter-punches, the frame opens back up to its initial aspect ratio. Moreover, the flashback sequence is depicted in what would be considered a full screen aspect ratio (1.33:1). This cinematic multiframe of moving panels prompts the viewer to provide spatiotemporal closure in the same way that he or she would approach a comic book page with. Essentially, the sequence implicitly and explicitly remediates the space of O'Malley's comic by alternating between the filmic equivalent of a splash page and that of a paneled multiframe.

Stylistic Remediation as Transmedia Style

Furthermore, O'Malley's work in the Scott Pilgrim series lets us see how stylistic remediation can become a form of transmedia style, as the author/artist self-consciously utilizes the title as a sandbox for remediation. While manga and music are a part of O'Malley's style, it is also defined by the narrative and stylistic attributes of the video game. For instance, his protagonist is tasked with facing off against his lover's seven evil exes, which provides each volume in the six book series with a climactic boss battle (one of the duels involves twins, hence the seven exes and the six books). Moreover, once Scott defeats an ex, he is showered with coins (a device borrowed from the *Super Mario*

Figure 1.3. *Sonic the Hedgehog 2* intro (1992).

Figure 1.4. *Scott Pilgrim* intro (2007).

games) and power-ups (including an extra life). Furthermore, volumes two (*Scott Pilgrim vs. the World*), four (*Scott Pilgrim Gets it Together*), and five (*Scott Pilgrim vs. the Universe*) begin with "title sequences" that pay homage to popular video games.[21]

O'Malley's stylistic remediation is not merely a means of dressing up his young adult tale of budding romance. In fact, the style paves the way for metaphors and narrative devices that do not have any resonance in day to day reality. For instance, Scott's "boss battles" with the seven exes are a metaphor for his conflict with Ramona's romantic baggage. Moreover, O'Malley builds in the device of the "continue" into the narrative. In video games, if a player's actions lead to the death of a character or a less-than-desirable outcome, the player is sometimes offered the ability to "continue," which takes the player back a few sequences into the gameplay and allows him or her to try again. In the comic, when Scott is faced with losing Ramona forever, he decides to continue (after a "game over" page) his quest for her love. Finally, the extra life Scott earns comes into use when he is killed by Ramona's final evil ex, Gideon.

Focusing on the device of the extra life, O'Malley both remediates its narrative use and three stylistic attributes of the video game in his representation of the reward (Figure 1.5). A floating copy of Scott's head, the extra life is differentiated from the natural world of the comic. First, it is a one-dimensional representation. Within the three-dimensional space of the comic, the extra life is flat, giving it the appearance of the paper cutouts of early Nintendo scrolling adventures such as *Super Mario Bros.* (1985). Secondly, the device is later re-introduced with the text "Scott had an extra life!" The content of the text is not as noteworthy as O'Malley's choice of font: an 8-bit typeface modeled off of early computing software (he uses this font in many of the battle scenes). Finally, O'Malley applies a half-tone effect to the extra life (specifically visible in the representation of Scott's hair), further differentiating it from the "reality" of the comic through the stylized appearance of early low resolution video games.

Like the many other attributes of the comic already described, Wright re-remediated O'Malley's initial remediations of video game style. We are given a barrage of visual information within the film frame—including a heads up display that features health and level up data. Included in Wright's re-remediation is the device of the 8-bit extra life icon (Figure 1.6). Like O'Malley's version, Wright's 8-bit icon is abstracted from the naturalistic diegetic world. When it rotates over Scott's head, we notice it is flat. Pixelated, it also mirrors the low resolution aesthetic that O'Malley attempted to capture with his use of half-tone dots. More significantly, the representation of Scott looks nothing

Figure 1.5. The 1-Up icon in O'Malley's *Scott Pilgrim*.

Figure 1.6. The 1-Up icon in Wright's *Scott Pilgrim*.

like its lead actor. It is not a CGI embellished representation of Michael Cera; it is a blocky remediation of the comic book's representation.

Significantly, Wright's remediation is not only a graphical re-remediation of O'Malley's art; it is also an example of how stylistic remediation can become transmedia style. Henry Jenkins defines transmedia storytelling as a story that is strategically parsed out across a series of texts in different media forms. For instance, the video game *Star Wars: Shadows of the Empire* takes place during the temporal gap that exists between two films—*The Empire Strikes Back* and *Return of the Jedi*—and centers on a subplot involving a rescue attempt of Han Solo. Transmedia style, on the other hand, can be defined as a unified series of texts in different media that are unified by a unique stylistic approach. In the case of the "Scott Pilgrim Experience," Wright asked Paul Robertson, the art director and lead designer behind *Scott Pilgrim vs. the World: The Game* (2010), to design the icon used in the film.[22] Moreover, the assets Robertson designed for the video game also appear within the last shot of the film. After the final credits roll, a end tag featuring the words "The End" appears. From off-screen left, 8-bit Scott Pilgrim jumps out and pummels the words to bits—just like Mario breaking a concrete block with his fists. Like any video gamer's favorite Italian plumber, Scott is showered with coins as a reward before he points at the viewer and vanishes.

While the game is stylistically linked to the film via the inclusion of its visual assets, the video game also stylistically remediates O'Malley's compositional style. During the age of graphical photorealism in video games, *Scott Pilgrim vs. the World: The Game* embodies a retro aesthetic defined by low-resolution graphics that perfectly fit O'Malley's minimalist character designs. The game's representation of Scott is simply an 8-bit colorized version of O'Malley's rendering. This was an intentional artistic decision. As O'Malley noted in a personal interview:

> We wanted to give people three separate experiences (the comic, the movie, and the game) . . . The thing about the game is, when they make a movie tie-in game it's usually something that feels shoddy, they do it quickly and it feels like a cash in. So the first thing we said when we sat down was that we didn't want to see the cheap polygon version of Michael Cera fighting bad guys. That's no knock on Michael Cera; I just don't want to play him in a video game right now. I was really adamant on doing a cartoon style and when Ubisoft hired Robertson, I knew we were on the right track.[23]

Yet the relationship between stylistic remediation and transmedia style deepens when we return to Paul Robertson's artistic role in the "Experience."

Significantly, the 1-up icon, 8-bit Scott Pilgrim, and the video game were not his sole contributions. The artist also designed a slipcase for the entire comic series that takes the form of an 8-bit remediation of O'Malley's artwork. Essentially, Robertson's work stylistically unites the comics, film, and video game from a visual standpoint, which makes the ancillary properties seem less—to borrow from O'Malley's turn of phrase—like "cash in[s]." After all, if both the book and the film embrace the stylistic devices of the video game, it is only natural that a video game exists. In short, O'Malley's initial stylistic remediation of the video game within the comic book medium organically motivates its transmedia sister properties.

Like transmedia storytelling, transmedia style rewards involvement in a property as it moves across multiple platforms. Unlike transmedia storytelling however, the success of individual texts is not compromised by consumer ignorance: it is merely a form of intertexual reference, not a form of narrative embellishment. Essentially, transmedia style is a form of textually motivated synergy that does not have the narrative payoffs of transmedia storytelling. At the same time however, it does not incur the potential financial risk of alienating the viewer/consumer with an elaborately designed, multi-platform, narrative. In other words, transmedia style provides visceral pleasure that can either be mentally registered or ignored and yet can still remain a potent marketing hook. For instance, filmgoers unfamiliar with both the comic and the fundamentals of the comic medium may still have been awed by Zack Snyder's formal explorations in *300* (2007).

Significantly, the production teams behind the various Scott Pilgrim texts had the opportunity to construct a transmedia narrative and chose not to. Shortly after their release, the comics occupied a unique position with regard to the film's production. The series was optioned by Universal Studios, who hired screenwriter Michael Bacall to draft the screenplay with Wright one month before the release of the second title in the series in the summer of 2005. The team quickly wrote a first draft of the screenplay, which only focused on the first two books, before putting the project aside. Wright then went on to focus on the follow up to his acclaimed breakthrough *Shaun of the Dead* (2004), *Hot Fuzz* (2007). Over the course of those two years, O'Malley's comic book series headed towards its eventual conclusion. Meanwhile Wright and Universal decided to adapt all six books into one film.

When production began on the film in March of 2009, O'Malley had yet to write the ending to the books. This left the screenwriters rudderless with regard to how to end the film. Thus, Wright shot an original ending in which Scott ends up with Knives Chau (Ellen Wong), rather than his dream girl Ramona Flowers. However, after negative test screenings, the director decided to reshoot the ending. Now in sync with regard to their production schedules, Wright and O'Malley revised the conclusion of the film. Thus, despite the fact that both texts were being developed simultaneously—a creative decision that can enable transmedia storytelling—the artists and studio did not want each medium to provide unique narrative information. The comic, the film (with slight alterations of course), and video game all construct the same story around the arc of Scott and Ramona's relationship.

Conclusion: The End of Stylistic Remediation?

It would be short-sighted to consider the progression from stylistic remediation to transmedia style that O'Malley, Wright, Robertson, and Universal practiced without considering its economic results. Recent box office reports have not produced confidence in the longevity of stylistic remediation. Out of the film adaptations analyzed in this volume, roughly half made their studios money (*American Splendor*, *Hulk*, and *300*). Contemporarily, two of the most hyped comic book films of 2010—*Kick-Ass* and *Scott Pilgrim vs. the World*—were considered box office failures. Matthew Vaughan's *Kick-Ass*, which features a prolonged sequence that stylistically remediates comic book graphics, was budgeted at $30 million. Like *Pilgrim*, the film benefitted from a great deal of hype (the product of a panel at 2009's San Diego Comic-Con and a secret screening at the 2010 South by Southwest Film Festival). Despite the hype however, the graphically violent film—which infamously features a thirteen year old girl blowing the brains out of the bad guys—finished with a global "limp return" of $96 million.[24] In the opinion of many entertainment journalists, the film failed for two reasons. First, its graphic violence led to an R-rating that prohibited anyone under the age of 18 from viewing the film theatrically. Secondly, according to Bill Gibron, writer Mark Millar and artist John Romita Jr. "are less than household names . . . [the film had] a lack of recognizability."[25]

The economic failure of *Scott Pilgrim* has been attributed to multiple factors. One of the most cited reasons is what is best described as Michael Cera saturation. The lead actor, who had become a cult hero after appearing on the television series *Arrested Development* (2003–2006), the Judd Apatow comedy *Superbad* (2007), and *Juno*, was beginning to be lampooned for being typecast as a sarcastic yet lovable loser. Both this perception of typecasting and Cera saturation rose after the massive success of *Juno*. The actor quickly experienced a critical and box office free fall from 2008 to 2010. For instance, *Nick and Norah's Infinite Playlist* (2008) grossed $33 million in comparison with a production budget of \$10 million, a far cry from the success of *Juno*. Then, the bottom began to fully drop out. Cera co-starred in *Year One* (also released in the summer of 2009) alongside Jack Black. The film carried a production budget of \$60 million and grossed a mere \$62 million. By the time *Scott Pilgrim vs. the World* hit the multiplex—at roughly the same time a scathing viral video entitled "The Michael Cera School of Acting" hit the web—Cera saturation had pushed potential moviegoers away from the film. As one commenter noted on Nikki Finke's article, "I don't care about watching Michael Cera doing his Michael Cera awkward love-struck schtick YET AGAIN. I like the guy, but god damn get a new schtick. . . . I AM TIRED OF WATCHING THE MICHAEL CERA STOCK CHARACTER. Good god, that's growing old."[26]

While Cera fatigue is a potential factor in *Scott Pilgrim*'s economic under-performance, Bill Gibron rightly attributes the film's implosion to an age-gap in Hollywood demographics and the studio's overestimation of a vocal, visible, and yet minuscule geek crowd. Gibron writes that "*Scott Pilgrim vs. the World* will end up being the last word on the season-long argument between 'gamers' and 'geezers'—and the old coots win a 'flawless victory' this time out. . . . It's easy to predict a real reevaluation of the whole subgenre—even with Hollywood grappling hand over hammer toe to grab the latest 'hot' comic release. . . . For now, the argument is over. In fact, it's gamer over."[27] Gibron's analysis is supported by an producer Neil Moritz, who spoke to me about the dangers of making an R-rated adaptation of Garth Ennis's *The Boys* in the wake of the reception of *Kick-Ass*. Moritz noted, "I really enjoyed *Kick-Ass* and I thought Matthew Vaughn did a great job, but I don't know if that was the most mainstream version of the movie. . . . The hard part is making these movies not to go to a very small, comic book fan base, but trying to broaden it out."[28] The failure of these films will not keep studios from green lighting comic book films, but it appears to have taught them some pivotal lessons. Stylistic remediation can be a costly means of appeasing the original fan base. Why aim for the minority when you need the majority to turn a profit?

Thanks to the high-profile failures of 2010, the future of stylistic remediation and transmedia style—with regard to comic book films at least—appears to be dim. The immense box office success of comic book films not practicing stylistic remediation like *The Dark Knight* (2008, production budget of \$185 million, grosses of more than \$1 billion dollars worldwide) and *The Avengers* (2012, production budget of \$220 million, grosses of more than \$1.5 billion worldwide) provides a strong incentive against the practice. While this is, in certain aspects, an apples to oranges comparison (*Kick-Ass* and *Scott Pilgrim vs. The World* are adaptations of independent comics rather than central titles in the DC and Marvel publishing lines), the budgetary gap between the two is beginning to narrow. *Scott Pilgrim vs. the World* carried a budget of $90 million that was shaved down to $60 million thanks to tax rebates. However, once print and advertising costs are factored in, the budget probably reached the $90–100 million mark (a significant leap, considering that *Sin City* was made for $40 million five years earlier).[29]

Yet there are two potential avenues for the future of the concepts of stylistic remediation and transmedia style. First, stylistic remediation is not limited to comic book films or transmedia properties. Stylistic remediation, like remediation, is an umbrella concept that can be embellished via medium specific theories that discuss style over narrative. Moreover, transmedia style as a theoretical concept—while limited to discussing transmedia properties—does not need to be limited to discussions of comic books or film. As this analysis briefly takes into account, we can consider such media as video games as mobilizing transmedia style. Furthermore, we do not need to limit such investigations to the realm of the visual, as the Scott Pilgrim soundtrack also remediates video game style through the use of vintage synthesizer soundboards. Secondly, while stylistic remediation and transmedia style have been currently encountering harsh economic realities at the box office, it remains a powerful means of marketing and appeasing a fan base. However, it is typically more successful when production costs are kept in the perspective of the small demographic that comic book fans are a part of. Just because *Scott Pilgrim*, like *Dick Tracy* before it, failed to recoup the production costs associated with such a flamboyant style, we cannot ignore the successes that have come out of this trend of stylistic remediation.

CHAPTER 2

Camp, Verisimilitude, Noir, and Neon: The Historical Evolution towards Stylistic Remediation

Introduction: Three Cycles

This chapter will sketch the historical, cultural, industrial, and technological contexts of stylistic remediation between comics and film. Given the interdisciplinary focus of this book, this chapter serves as a means of ensuring that every type of reader—the Cinema and Media Studies scholar, the Comics Studies scholar, and the uninitiated—is capable of starting off on the same page (or, to tip my hat towards the other side of the aisle, the same film reel). Despite the temporal breadth of this chapter (from roughly 1934 to 2013), it primarily focuses on three film cycles that span from the blockbuster period that began with *Jaws* in 1975 to the contemporary period. These cycles— exemplified by the *Superman* films of the 1970s and 1980s, the *Batman* films of the 1980s and 1990s, and what Bob Rehak has defined as the high fidelity adaptations of the late 1990s and early 2000s—provide illustrative case studies of the evolution of these various contexts in relation to remediation of style.[1] In the case of the Superman cycle, Warner Bros., a newly conglomerated Hollywood studio that had acquired DC Comics less than a decade earlier, was quick to overlook the value of the superhero. After it was licensed to a trio of independent producers, the production of the Superman films suffered technological challenges (which raised the budgets of the films) that needed to be surmounted in order to culturally distance the film from its source medium. At the time, comics, due to both the Comics Code and the *Batman* (1966–1968) television series, were viewed as being cartoonish and campy. Essentially, during the Superman cycle, realism was favored over the more formally flamboyant trajectory of stylistic remediation.

However, by the time of the Batman cycle, the stylistic pendulum had begun to swing the other way. Thanks to the cultural redefinition that reached a fever pitch in 1986, the comic book was once again viewed as a medium that could also appeal to adults. This redefinition finally persuaded Warner Bros. to greenlight a film adaptation of Batman. Tim Burton's overly gothic, German Expressionist treatment of the Dark Knight was a tremendous economic success that was lauded by fans for embracing the grim and gritty incarnations of the hero realized by such writer/artists as Frank Miller and Alan Moore. Moreover, thanks to lucrative licensing deals, the conglomerated studio system finally began to see the economic potential in comic book adaptations. Yet as Burton's work on the series continued, it became evident that the filmmaker's increasingly dark style had the potential to alienate families with children. In order to appease both parents and licensing partners, Warner Bros. hired Joel Schumacher to helm two films whose stylistic remediations owed more to the the *Batman* television series than *The Dark Knight Returns* (1986). Initially, the new stylistic direction offered by Schumacher paid off handsomely. However, it quickly angered adult fans of the series and became the target of intense mockery. Even the animated television ancillary text *The New Batman Adventures* (1997–1999) criticized Schumacher's films in an episode entitled "Legends of the Dark Knight."

The high fidelity cycle of the contemporary period has been defined by both filmmaking approaches. On one hand, Christopher Nolan's Batman films and the Marvel Universe films have taken the path towards cinematic realism. The high fidelity aspect of these films is illustrated by an increased attention to the narrative histories of their characters. Story arcs, rather than broad scenarios, are now providing filmmakers with material (Jeph Loeb and Tim Sale's *Batman: The Long Halloween* was a blueprint for Nolan). On the other hand, films like *Hulk* (2003), *Sin City* (2005), and *300* (2007) couple faithful adaptations of content with stylistic remediation. Moreover, in some cases, the filmmakers in the latter camp have openly collaborated with the original writers and artists, going so far as to construct elaborate reproductions of comic panels and to digitize textures from the comics and graphic novels for use in the film.

Comic Books, Film, and Television before the Blockbuster (1934–1968)

In order to more fully grasp the industrial and cultural affiliations between comics and film, a brief contextual history of the two industries during the three decades preceding the temporal window of this study is necessary.

According to comic book historian Bradford Wright, the birth of the comic book in the form of *Famous Funnies*, a bound collection of comic strip reprints, was far from an overnight success.[2] While the first issue, financed by Dell and printed by Eastern Color, sold out its initial run of 35,000 copies, newsstand distributors showed little interest in the product, prompting Dell to withdraw its financial support. The second series of 250,000 copies, released in July 1934, lost Eastman $4,000. After a lukewarm launch, Eastern began turning a profit with the sixth issue in the series, and according to Wright, by the time the twelfth issue hit newsstands "*Famous Funnies* was netting Eastern Color about $30,000 each month."[3]

The eventual success of *Famous Funnies* was not lost on other businessmen, most notably Major Malcolm Wheeler-Nicholson. In 1934, Nicholson founded National Allied Publications which, after he was forced out by his business partners in 1937, ultimately took its name from the title of its publication: *Detective Comics* (National Allied would become Detective Comics Inc., or DC Comics). In June 1938, DC published the debut of Superman in *Action Comics* #1. While the character was created by writer Jerry Siegel and artist Joe Shuster, it was owned by the publisher, which had purchased the intellectual property rights for a measly $130.[4] Superman, according to Wright, "won a large audience very quickly. At a time when most comic book titles sold between 200,000 and 400,000 copies per issue, each issue of *Action Comics* (featuring one Superman story each) regularly sold about 900,000 copies per month. Each bimonthly issue of the *Superman* title, devoted entirely to the character, sold an average of 1,300,000 copies."[5] Superman quickly became the first star established by both DC and the American comic book industry at large, successfully making comic books and superheroes synonymous for most Americans.

The success of Superman spawned a range of imitators from both inside and outside DC Comics. One of the most notable outside examples, Wonder Man, was developed by Victor Fox, a former accountant for DC who was privy to the rising sales figures of Superman. Fox's imitation, however, failed to appear in more than one issue because DC quickly sued their former accountant of copyright infringement. Attempting to catch lightning in a bottle twice, DC unleashed their newest hero, Batman, created by artist Bob Kane and writer Bill Finger. By 1941, Superman, Batman, and an assortment of other superhero titles (including Captain America, Captain Marvel, Green Lantern, and Flash) were vastly outselling comic strip reprints like *Famous Funnies*. Two years later, comic fever would be hard for publishers and vendors to ignore as the cheap illustrated books took over 33 percent of the newsstand market.[6]

The success of Superman and Batman encouraged DC to quickly license their properties for cross-media ventures. Less than three years after Superman's debut, DC National launched a radio series entitled *The Adventures of Superman* (1940–1951). Shortly thereafter, Paramount, which had acquired the screen rights, hired Fleischer Studios to produce a series of animated cartoons for theatrical release (1941–1943). The core audience for the comic, radio show, and animated shorts was obvious: children and young adults of both sexes. During World War II, the United States Army had been the largest purchaser of comic books.[7] However, as scholar Jean-Paul Gabilliet argues in his comprehensive study of the American comic book, "The most significant factor in comic book reading among adults was the presence of children and adolescents in the home.... Adults read comics in an opportunistic manner."[8] As the industry became aware of their main demographic, comic historian Roger Sabin notes, "comics were increasingly produced especially for them. The age range took a marked tumble."[9]

Due to this inherent appeal, sociologists began to express concerns over the effects of the comics on children. Did reading stories told through pictures infringe on a child's ability to read proper literature? As early as May 1940, *Chicago Daily News* literary critic Sterling North argued that the "violent stimulant" of comics would produce a generation "more ferocious than the present one" and that "America must band together to break the 'comic' magazine."[10] For the most part, these critiques, including Dr. Fredric Wertham's "The Psychopathology of Comic Books" published in July of 1948, were ignored throughout the 1940s. Comic books were a children's pastime which, according to Sabin, "were coopted into a vision of childhood that included climbing trees, flicking catapults, and playing tag."[11]

The booming comic book industry, however, was dealt a significant economic blow between 1946 and 1947 when publishers lost their largest consumer, the United States Army, and a glut of superhero comics over-saturated the market. In an effort to recapture adult readers, the industry began to explore other genres such as the Western, war, crime, and, most famously, horror. Horror comics, including *The Vault of Horror* (1950–1955) and *Tales from the Crypt* (1950–1955) published by William Gaines and his company Entertaining Comics (EC), became noteworthy for their lurid subject matter and abundance of gore. The turn towards other genres and adult readers was initially successful. By 1954, EC presses were printing 2.5 million books each month and fanzines focused on their contents began to circulate.[12]

However, EC's rise would be temporary. Its successful exploitation of the horror genre quickly raised the ire of parents and social reformers. By 1954, thanks to EC's graphic portrayals of violence and perversion and a thin linkage to a rise in juvenile delinquency, social critiques against comic books were no longer ignored. Wertham published his infamous study *Seduction of the Innocent: The Influence of Comic Books on Today's Youth* (1954), which claimed that horror and crime comics negatively affected youth. He quickly found an audience when his volume was excerpted in *Ladies' Home Journal*, rousing protests and inspiring several comic book burnings. On April 21, 1954, the Senate Subcommittee on Juvenile Delinquency called Wertham and Gaines to testify regarding the effects of comic books on America's youth.[13] While the subcommittee would announce its official conclusions in 1955 that "this country cannot afford the calculated risk involved in feeding its children, through comic books, a concentrated diet of crime, horror, and violence," the consequences of the public outcry and Senate hearings were quickly addressed by the comic book industry.[14] The industry proposed a solution—following in the footsteps of Hollywood and Major League Baseball—to hire a comics czar (Charles F. Murphy) to head the self-regulatory Comics Magazine Association of America (CMAA). The CMAA would establish an enforceable code forbidding "all scenes of horror, excessive bloodshed, gore and gruesome crimes, depravity, lust, sadism, [and] masochism."[15]

By 1955, poor public sentiment and the resulting enforcement of the Code produced both an industry and individual comics that "looked very different to" those that came before.[16] Essentially, the shockwaves killed off entire genres (horror and crime), publishers (EC), and due to the requirements of the code, any hope of capturing an adult audience. Notably, this "kid friendly" turn of events helped improve Dell Publishing's position in the industry. An established producer of the titles in the "funny animal genre," Dell had arranged licensing with Walt Disney (publishing *Walt Disney's Comics and Stories* from 1940 to 1962), Warner Bros. (publishing several titles including *Looney Tunes and Merry Melodies*, which later became just *Looney Tunes*, 1941–1962), and MGM.[17] By the 1950s, "Dell was the largest publisher of comic books in the world."[18] As Jean-Paul Gabillet writes, "The void created by the arrival of the Comics Code in 1955 was quickly filled by [publisher] Dell's morally irreproachable comics, which predominantly featured characters from animated cartoons.... The reality of the comic book industry during the second half of the 1950s: the disappearance of 'contestable' genres (romance, crime, horror) gave way, at least initially, to an increased value for 'acceptable' comics (whose contents targeted preadolescents)."[19]

Coincidentally, just as the comic book industry was finding its core audience of children entrenched, the Hollywood studio system was experiencing a similar identity crisis. Thanks to volatile mixture of factors, including the collapse of the vertically integrated studio system, the post-World War

II baby boom, and the correlation between the rise of television and decline
in film attendance, American film went from a mass medium to what film
historian Thomas Doherty has called "a less-than-mass medium" thanks to "a
shift in marketing strategy and production [that] initiated a progressive 'juvenilization.'"[20] Oddly, the shared audience demographic seemed to have been
lost on the studio system during this period. While Paramount had financed
the Superman animated shorts during the 40s and Columbia had produced
serials based on Batman (1943 and 1949) and Superman (1948, 1950), studios
largely avoided comic book properties during the 1950s.

Yet while the studios were apparently disinterested in comic books, television producers were not. As *The Adventures of Superman* radio drama reached
its end, DC commissioned a television unit to produce a feature film entitled
Superman and the Mole Men (1951) that the publisher could use as a "calling
card for a TV series."[21] Starring George Reeves and distributed by Lippert
Pictures, the film was a success and launched the successful syndicated TV
series *Adventures of Superman* (1952–1958).[22] While George Reeves's death in
1959 ended the production of *Adventures of Superman* and proposed spin-
offs failed to materialize, reruns still ran strong. The show's ongoing success
prompted DC to approach ABC to air a television series based on Batman
(which was subsequently produced by Twentieth Century Fox and Greenway
Productions). From the mid-1960s until 1978, television was the primary out-
let for the cross-media exploration of comics. Yet television's stance towards
stylistic remediation was fluid; the *Adventures of Superman* made little to no
attempt to remediate comic book style while *Batman* (1966–1968) wore it on
its sleeve to the point of backlash.

The *Batman* television program is significant for revealing the cultural
and industrial context behind the relationship between comics, television,
and film, particularly due to its approach towards stylistic remediation. As
media historians Lynn Spigel and Henry Jenkins argue, the *Batman* television series occupied a unique position between two distinct audience demographics. Thanks to a polysemic text that provided both a "fantasy portrayal
of real life" and a "camp sensibility," ABC was able to lure children and their
parents by positioning the series as the latest manifestation in pop art (Andy
Warhol was invited by ABC to attend a "cocktail and frug" party celebrating
its premiere).[23] By embracing pop art and camp (primarily through the utilization of a garish form of mise-en-scène, the flamboyant inserted titles that
captured the onomatopoeia of the comics, and wooden performance style),
the show perversely altered the perception of comics among adult viewers by
providing a "comfortable distance from the show's comic book materials."[24]
As Spigel and Jenkins describe, the sensibility held particularly high cultural

capital at the time (thanks no doubt to cultural critic Susan Sontag's 1964 essay "Notes on Camp"). The success of the show's first season pushed Fox to green light a feature film and DC to progressively lighten the tone of their comic book offerings.[25] Yet the camp craze and Batmania were temporary. By the time the second season aired, ratings were down and commentators noted that the show felt "too self-consciously campy."[26] The show would only last three seasons, ending in 1968.

The polysemic strategy utilized by producer William Dozier has cast a long shadow over the relationship between comics, film, and television. While Will Brooker notes in his cultural study of Batman that the show's camp qualities stem from many Batman comics of the 1960s and were further magnified within the comic after the success of the television program, the show would become the source of ire amongst many fans and even some comic book creators.[27] Perhaps in response to the rapid fall of *Batman*, the bulk of television programming based on comics produced in it its wake removed the polysemic element. Shows shifted formats from live-action to animated, and solely targeted the child audience. As Superman historian Jake Rossen notes, even the titles of properties were altered to mirror the "homogenized, dumbed-down approach" (the Justice League became the *Super Friends*).[28] Yet both the kid-friendly and the camp approaches were subsequently bound to stylistic remediation in the mind of the Hollywood studios and producers when it came to comic book adaptations. As Frank Miller would later note in the introduction to his *Batman: Year One* (1987), "If your only memory of Batman is that of Adam West and Burt Ward exchanging camped-out quips while clobbering slumming guest stars Vincent Price and Cesar Romero, I hope this book will come as a surprise. For me, Batman was never funny."[29] In film productions based off of comics, the industrial and cultural tide turned against stylistic remediation in favor of realism and verisimilitude, a sentiment best illustrated by a series of production cycles to which we will now turn.

The Superman Cycle (1978–1987)

Following the success of their films, *The Three Musketeers* (1973) and its sequel *The Four Musketeers* (1974), European producers Alexander Salkind, his son Ilya, and Pierre Spengler, contemplated where to turn their energies and recently acquired financial prosperity. Ilya proposed a film based on Superman, a risky proposition as the only historical precedents had been animated shorts, live-action serials, and low-budget films tied to television properties, none of which had sustained interest into the 1970s. The producers approached Warner Communications Incorporated (which had been formed in 1972 when Kinney National Company reorganized its entertainment assets, including DC Comics) to inquire about the rights to the property. According to Ilya, Warner Bros. head of production Dick Shepherd was more than willing to license the rights. "He said, 'Ah, sell it. It's not worth it. It's not a good property for a film.'"[30] While Warner Bros. was quick to endorse selling the rights, their comic book publisher was more ambivalent. DC had a "desire not to besmirch the image of their All-American Hero" and proposed contractual clauses which required their approval on aspects of the production.[31] When contractual talks stalled, Ilya contacted Warner Publishing (the parent company of DC), who signed the rights over to the Salkinds and Spengler for a period of twenty-five years in exchange for $3 million.[32] The negotiations also resulted in a negative pick up deal; the Salkinds and Spengler were left to fund the project while Warner Bros. would be given first look at the film for distribution. Finally, a clause required the Salkinds to accept input from a DC liaison.

For the producers, *Superman* had to be the complete opposite of every adjective that properties based on comics had become infamous for. The film had to be prestigious and realism became its dominant style. When interviewed by the *Los Angeles Times* in 1975, Salkind declared that the film would be "100% straight, no spoof, no satire. . . the opposite of a cartoon."[33] Essentially, the Salkinds did not want their project to show any signs of stylistic remediation. This move was not strictly cultural, as the producers also needed to secure financing for the film's massive budget. In order to do so, the producers hired screenwriter Mario Puzo (who had recently won Oscars for his collaborations with Francis Ford Coppola on the first two *Godfather* films) and cast both Marlon Brando and Gene Hackman (both recent Oscar winners as well) in the roles of Jor-El (Superman's father) and Lex Luthor (Superman's arch-nemesis).

The producers' quest for prestige and cinematic realism manifested itself both in front of and behind the camera. When the producers feared that Puzo's screenplay ventured towards camp, they hired Robert Benton, David Newman (both of whom co-wrote the New Hollywood touchstone *Bonnie and Clyde*) and David's wife, Leslie, to rewrite the screenplay. With the screenplay in an acceptable form—Puzo's original had been five hundred pages and was restructured to serve as the guide for not one, but two films that would be shot simultaneously—the Salkinds and Spengler began the quest for a director who could capture their desired style. After considering a range of candidates, including Steven Spielberg and Guy Hamilton, the producers settled on Richard Donner, whose belief in film's inherent verisimilitude led him to hang a sign with the noun painted on it in the film's production office.[34]

The one exception to Salkind's "100% straight" rule of style is the film's opening. The film begins with a black and white, Academy ratio shot of a fictional issue of *Action Comics* being opened before our eyes. The short sequence, clocking in at roughly a minute, stylistically remediates both the original comic (which is directly represented in front of the camera) and the George Reeves television program (paid homage by the choice of black and white film stock and the Academy ratio frame). Then, the film fades into cinematic realism defined by its primary style (color film stock, three-point lighting, and a widescreen aspect ratio). Significantly, this stylistic choice appears not to have been motivated by homage but by product differentiation. As Ilya Salkind notes, the sequence "was based on that idea of suddenly, bingo, we go from the small format to the big stuff."[35] The sequence announces that the filmmakers are following the philosophy "Out with the old, in with the new." This sentiment was also apparent in the film's advertising, which often contained the subheading "The Movie" following the title.

While the ties between comics, children, and derogatory tastes concerned the producers and pushed most film studios away from green lighting films based on such properties, there was a second concern. Could expensive and unreliable special-effects technology capture the amazing feats depicted in comics without killing any hope of a financial profit? While the Salkinds and Spengler pushed an advertising campaign exclaiming that "You'll believe a man can fly," the preliminary results were far from inspiring. A crew of experienced special-effects technicians—including production designer John Barry (*Star Wars*), Geoffrey Unsworth (*2001: A Space Odyssey*), and special-effects supervisor Colin Chilvers (*Battle of Britain*)—devised techniques that ranged from launching dummies in the air to a flying model airplane shaped like the hero in order to realistically bring the effect to life. Essentially, the crew needed to invent the technology as the shoot progressed, eventually settling on a set of catapults, wires, and cranes that were subsequently painted out and composited using blue-screen.[36] In contrast with the book, the animated shorts, and the television series, the flying sequences needed to be photorealistic; there needed to be a tactile quality visible in Superman's engagement with the world around him while he flies.

This desire for verisimilitude is particularly evident in the scene in which Superman (Christopher Reeve) saves Lois Lane's (Margot Kidder) life after her helicopter malfunctions. Donner sets the stage with a sequence that shows the helicopter spinning around on the roof top of the Daily Planet in establishing shots, only cutting in closer for a reaction shot of the fearful Lois. Similarly, when Superman inevitably appears, he is shot flying up the side of the building in a wide shot. Donner then goes on to shoot the sequence from above, below, and behind, only tightening the framing on Superman after he rescues Lois via a close embrace. Donner's audacity to shoot the sequence from a distance serves two purposes. First, we are close enough to notice that we're looking at an actual person, not a dummy. Secondly, we are given enough of the space around the superhero to realize that we cannot see any sort of wire rig. In short, we believe a man can fly.

As feared, the technological quest for such awe-inspiring results led to massive budget overages. Production on both *Superman* and *Superman II* (which were being shot simultaneously in an attempt to alleviate costs) went one year over schedule. Originally budgeted at $20–30 million, the budget for the two films soared to a reported $70–80 million. When an audit was later conducted, a significantly higher number was disclosed: $109 million, all of which was on the producers' shoulders due to the negative pickup deal they had with Warner Bros.[37] To put this in historical economic context, the production budgets for the blockbusters *Jaws* (1975) and *Star Wars* (1977) ranged from $7-$11 million. In 2006, Forbes produced a list of the most expensive films ever made (adjusted for inflation): *Superman* ranked nineteenth, the oldest film on the list aside from *Cleopatra* (1963).[38]

The budget overages pushed the Salkinds and Spengler to take corrective actions. First, they brought in *Musketeers* director Richard Lester to supervise Donner, who the producers blamed for the overages. Secondly, production on *Superman II* was halted in order to ensure that the first film could be completed without the budget going further off the rails. Relief finally came when Warner Bros. began infusing money into the project. The studio's injection of capital has been interpreted in several ways. According to Rossen, "Warner Bros. delighted in the overruns, figuring that eventually it could buy out the Salkinds and hoard the return for itself."[39] The *Los Angeles Times* tells a different story: the Salkinds allegedly held the film's negative hostage, ransoming it for a $15 million payment.[40]

When the film hit theaters in December of 1978, it became one of the most profitable in Warner Bros.' history, grossing $300 million worldwide. Moreover, critical reaction to the film was enthusiastic. In the context of the cultural prejudice against comic books and their adaptations, *Variety* critic James Harwood's review is illuminating. Harwood writes that the film overcomes "every challenge in presenting the man who leaps tall buildings in a single bound" and that the personnel involved will not "let the silliness get out of control. It's easy enough to just enter their world and adjust to the new realities."[41] While the film's success broke the gridlock on the sequel (which would ultimately be credited to Lester), it also inspired a flood of lawsuits. The night of the film's premiere, Mario Puzo sued for a greater share of the film's gross receipts. Two days after the release, Marlon Brando sued for $50 million, claiming that he was not paid his 11.3 percent share of the profits (he would later be paid approximately $15 million for roughly fifteen minutes of screen time).[42] Shortly after, stars Christopher Reeve and Margot Kidder literally followed suit.

Despite the judicial wrangling between the Salkinds, Warner Bros., and several members of the film's cast and crew, Lester's *Superman II* (1981) was also an economic success. Grossing $108 million domestically, the film was the third highest grossing film of the year (behind *On Golden Pond* and *Raiders of the Lost Ark*). For the most part, reviews were positive. However, some writers noted that the new director (who had previously directed the Beatles films *A Hard Day's Night* and *Help!* and the comedy *The Knack . . . and How to Get It*) had shifted away from Donner's embrace of realism. As Roger Ebert wrote in his review, "the whole film has more smiles and laughs than the first one. Maybe that's because of a change in directors."[43] The success of the film led the Salkinds to begin development on another follow up, advertising the film during the 1981 Cannes Film Festival. After negotiating a contract with Christopher Reeve and authoring a treatment that introduced new characters and subplots taken from the comic book series, Ilya Salkind approached Warner Bros., which now had exclusive distribution rights to the film.[44]

According to Rossen and his sources, Warner Bros. was ambivalent about the treatment and "dismissed the narrative as 'too sci-fi,' too embedded in Superman lore. . . was pandering to comics devotees and would require too much exposition for casual audience members."[45] The narrative and tone of the film took a turn for the worse when Richard Pryor expressed interest in the film and was ultimately cast for a fee of $4 million.[46] According to Superman aficionado, American film producer, and screenwriter Tom DeSanto (whose credits include the first two *X-Men* films), Pryor's performance brought the franchise to a halt for fans. DeSanto notes "Kryptonite never killed Superman but Richard Pryor sure did."[47] When Lester's $35 million film was released in summer of 1983, it was initially successful (grossing $13 million its opening weekend).[48] However, attendance steadily declined and the film ultimately grossed $60 million, a 50 percent drop from the previous film. While it is feasible that the Superman franchise experienced diminishing returns due to franchise exhaustion, reviewers took note of the franchise's continued trajectory towards humor. Giving the film a 2.5 star rating, Ebert wrote that the film is "the kind of movie I feared the original *Superman* would be. It's a cinematic comic book, shallow, silly, filled with stunts and action, without much human interest."[49]

The difficulties exhibited in the behind the scenes tensions of the first three *Superman* films are emblematic of many comic book films during the 1980s. For instance, the George Lucas produced adaptation of Marvel Comics' *Howard the Duck* (1986) experienced massive a budget overage due to special effect difficulties. Originally budgeted at $20 million, Lucas's effects firm Industrial Light and Magic was unable to complete a convincing look for the film's protagonist. By the time the techniques were refined and reshoots were performed by director Willard Huyck, the film reached a budget of $52 million.[50] The film would go on to gross just $37 million worldwide. Other comic book film properties that also had difficulties compromising budgetary costs with box office grosses included the Salkinds' Superman spin-off, *Supergirl* (1984, estimated budget of $35 million, domestic box office gross of $14 million) and the Brigitte Nielsen and Arnold Schwartzenegger film *Red Sonja* (1985, estimated budget of $35 million, domestic box office gross of $7 million).[51] A symbolic death to this cycle trend came when the Salkinds, faced with economic the disappointments of *Superman III* and *Supergirl*, sold the rights to Superman to the Cannon Group for $5 million. Eventually, even Superman went into the red when Cannon's *Superman IV: The Quest for Peace* (1987), budgeted at an estimated $17 million, grossed only $15 million domestically.

The Batman Cycle (1989–1997)

In October of 1979, less than one year after the success of *Superman*, producers Michael Uslan and Benjamin Melnicker formed Batfilm Productions and successfully secured an option for the feature film rights to DC's other signature property, Batman.[52] According to Uslan, the duo approached nearly every studio in town in an attempt to secure financing.[53] Finally finding a potential production company in Peter Guber and Neil Bogart's Casablanca Records and Filmworks, the four producers were unable to convince the production company's affiliated studio, Universal, to fund the project. While the film would eventually become a massive box office and critical success that would reignite America's Batmania for the first time since the ABC television series, it would take nearly ten years for the producers to get the film financed and produced. Despite the initial success of the *Superman* films, the Batman property still carried the cultural stigma of camp associated with the television series and studios were ambivalent to sign on. To put it simply, it would take a cultural shift in the public reception of both comic books and Batman to get the project off of the ground.

While the juvenilization of comics books following the enforcement of the Comics Code (1954) would face relatively little change for nearly a decade, two industrial shifts between 1954 and 1964 are worthy briefly noting. First, DC Comics found itself challenged as the top publisher in the industry as Marvel Comics (formerly Atlas Comics), under editor Stan Lee, began a "more human approach to its heroes." [54] Under Lee's editorial direction, Marvel launched a series of seminal superhero titles in the span of three years: *Fantastic Four* in 1961, *The Incredible Hulk* in 1962, and the *Amazing Spider-Man* in 1963. Secondly, in 1961, DC editor Julius Schwartz began to nurture comic book fandom by printing letters to the editor. According to comic historians Duncan and Smith, this provided fans with the ability to "build a community of their own." [55] Even if the publishers of the early 1960s lacked the ability to challenge the Code, the moves towards increasingly complex heroes and fan communities implies that they were beginning to move beyond children as their main demographic.

This public conception of comics and the Comics Code would be directly challenged in the late 1960s on two separate fronts. First, an influx of young talent began to break into both DC and Marvel. Many of whom, according to comic historian Bradford Wright, "entered the field as fans with career ambitions in the industry." [56] They did not view the comic book industry as a stepping stone or a last resort. Thus, comic titles began to deal with social issues such as the battle for racial equality and the Vietnam War in order to reach beyond the child audience and connecting "with the sensibilities of teens and young adults." [57] This trend manifested itself most significantly in 1970 when Stan Lee, upon the urging of the United States Department of Health, Education, and Welfare, penned a three issue arc for *Amazing Spider-Man* that depicted drug addiction. While the CMAA refused to give the arc its seal of approval, Lee was able to convince Marvel to publish it anyway. [58] The confining Code, like its cinematic equivalent, was beginning to be shed by the industry.

Secondly, the Code was also challenged by comic book writers and artists working outside of DC and Marvel. The emergence of underground comics, fueled by such talent as Robert Crumb, Gilbert Shelton, and S. Clay Wilson, brought forth a slew of comic books focusing on the counter-culture movement (most notably sex and drugs). However, the underground comics fad would be short-lived, ending in 1973 when the US Supreme Court declared that local communities could determine their own First Amendment standards with regard to obscenity. The underground's influence on the mainstream and American culture at large was relatively limited. For comic book historian Roger Sabin, the long-term achievement of the movement was setting the path for what would later become "alternative comics," "a new kind of avant-garde... typified by [Art Spiegelman's] *Raw*."[59]

Meanwhile, a new form of comic book distribution was embraced: direct marketing and the rise of the comic book specialty store. Comics had long been sold through newsstands and pharmacies, which carried limited titles and no back issues. This made some comic titles inaccessible, as readers had no way of catching up on them. A remedy to this unstable distribution practice came in 1973 when comic book fan Phil Seuling established the Sea Gate Distribution Company, planting the seeds for what would become the direct market system. Unlike the previous system (where news vendors would order books and then send overstock back to the publisher for credit), the direct market system stood as an intermediary between publishers and shops. By filling orders based on demand, publishers no longer suffered from miscalculating print runs. Meanwhile, vendors could order based on the tastes of their consumers. Thus, the direct market system both nurtured fans and encouraged publishers to take risks on titles, creating two modes of comic production: industrial and artisan. As scholar Mark Rogers describes, advance orders from retailers kept print quantities in check and facilitated the emergence of artisan publishers—who paid writers and artists with royalties and ownership rights—that "supported a wider variety of styles and genres ... more varied in score and more interesting aesthetically."[60]

This convergence of factors (including the challenging of the Comics Code, the shift in narrative content, the interlinked aim to capture older readers, and the rise of independent publishers, direct marketing, and the comic book specialty shop) can also be tied to the rise of the graphic novel. The graphic novel is a mode of comic production that entails a longer, sometimes self-contained narrative. In 1986, the mode—exemplified by Art Spigelman's *Maus: A Survivor's Tale*, Alan Moore and Dave Gibbons's *Watchmen*, and Frank Miller, Klaus Janson, and Lynn Varley's *Batman: The Dark Knight Returns*—would produce a significant shift in America's cultural value of comics. Spiegelman would go on to win a Pulizer Prize Special Award (1992) and Moore and Gibbons would go on to win a Hugo Award (1988). Shortly thereafter, comics were present in exhibitions at the Museum of Modern Art, taught in college courses across the United States (one of which was coincidentally taught by Batman producer Michael Uslan), and become the subject of popular journalism and academic articles. Thanks to the graphic novel and the factors that nurtured its existence, comics were able to shed the thirty year old stigma of being children's entertainment.

According to Warner Bros. animator, comic book writer, and *Batman: The Animated Series* producer Paul Dini, the cultural re-appraisal of comic books and the success of Frank Miller's *The Dark Knight Returns* gave Warner Bros. the courage to finally green light the film version.[61] With newfound zeal for the project, the studio and producers handed over the directorial reins to Tim Burton, whose unique visual style had made an impression on the studio when his modestly budgeted dark comedy *Beetlejuice* (1988, estimated budget of $14 million) grossed more than $70 million domestically.[62] Burton, who had worked with actor Michael Keaton on *Beetlejuice*, was quick to hire the actor as his hero. In the decades since *Batman* premiered, it seems odd to think of any other actor as an ideal fit for Burton's film. However, at the time, Keaton's screen credits (including *Night Shift*, *Mr. Mom*, and *Johnny Dangerously*) leading into the production of *Batman* caused many to write him off as a comedian. Amongst Batman fans, Keaton's persona was the exact opposite of the grim hero portrayed in Frank Miller's seminal interpretation. The initial response was famously pessimistic.

From July to November of 1988, press coverage of Keaton's involvement was overwhelmingly negative. On July 3, 1988, the *Los Angeles Times* ran a reader letter by Allan B. Rothstein entitled "Mr. Mom as Batman?" that is worth quoting at length:

> So Michael Keaton has been cast as Batman/Bruce Wayne ... ? He might have made a good Joker, but his comic style, which he seems unable to shake (but he can amplify) has doomed this promised "serious" treatment of Bob Kane's character to the same tired, boring level of artificial "camp" that made the TV series a hit yet simultaneously doomed it to an early cancellation. The painful lesson of "Superman III"—-when you don't treat venerable superheroes with respect the audience rejects the property—has been ignored in this cynical, opportunistic attempt to capitalize on the success of "Beetlejuice" ... Batman has been a popular character for almost five decades—not because he is a figure of comedy, but precisely because he is *not*, especially in the last couple of years. ... Better they should have filmed Frank Miller's "Batman: the Dark Knight Returns." But that would have required courage, taste, and imagination.[63]

Rothstein's letter perfectly illustrates a number of issues relevant to this chapter. First, his account eloquently offers up what doomed the *Batman* television show and the later *Superman* films to failure ("artificial camp") in the eyes of fans. Secondly, his letter acknowledges the cultural shift that comic books experienced during the 1980s (by referencing Miller and the renaissance of "the last couple of years"). Third, it depicts the reaction against camp ("precisely because he is *not*"). Finally, Rothstein merges all of these concerns by arguing that Keaton would put the final nail in the coffin, because casting a comedian as Batman would essentially hit the reset button on the cultural shift.

Significantly, this cynical account authored by a Batman fan living in North Hollywood was not an anomaly. On November 29, 1988, the *Wall Street Journal* ran a front-page article featuring a sketch of Keaton next to a sketch of Batman. The headline? "Batman Fans Fear the Joke's on Them in Hollywood Epic." The first line of Kathleen A. Hughes's article reads "Batman's sidekick, Robin, is officially dead, but for followers of the dynamic duo everywhere, the worst is yet to come: The caped crusader may turn out to be a wimp." While the bulk of the article is focused on the criticisms of fans regarding the film (many of which echo those of Rothstein), Hughes's article is notable for a number of reasons. First, given the article's placement, the film's core audience of fans appear to have gained a great deal of power by forcing Wall Street and Hollywood to reflect upon the project. Secondly, the article notes the length to which Warner Bros. was willing to go to address those criticisms "without changing the movie."[64] Specifically, Batman creator Bob Kane was hired as a creative consultant, the studio issued a public statement by Tim Burton to the *Comics Buyer's Guide*, and a marketing consultant asserted that "I've read all the drafts [of the script] and the only times I laughed were at some of the Joker's comments. . . . Nothing about Batman is a joke."[65] While this may all appear to be the done with the light touch of a seasoned public relations department, according to Nancy Griffin and Kim Masters's account of the careers of producers Jon Peters and Peter Guber, the Hughes article forced Peters to rush out an early trailer for the Christmas season with the hope of quelling the angry fan response.[66] By the time the film hit theaters in June of 1989, it was clear that the filmmakers and the marketing team at Warner Bros. had succeeded in ensuring that the core audience was appeased: the $35 million dollar film grossed over $400 million worldwide.

The visual design of Burton's film, credited to production designer Anton Furst (who won an Oscar for his contributions), is noteworthy for embracing the German Expressionist style. Apartment blocks are not so much refuges from work, but their own dark prisons (Figure 2.1). Skyscrapers, complete with towering spires, lick the moon while providing criminals with an abundance of shadowed cover on the serpentine streets below. This is not a cityscape founded on the modern principles of form following function; Gotham City's mangled metropolis is symbolic of the psychological torment of Bruce Wayne (and, by proxy, Jack Napier/Joker). Yet despite Burton and Furst's stylization, the film owes more to film noir than the design of the comics, even those of Frank Miller (most notably *Dark Knight Returns* and *Batman: Year One*).

Figure 2.1. Burton and Furst's Gotham City in *Batman* (1989).

It would be simplistic to describe this embrace of the baroque as only being present in films based upon comic books. Moreover, stylistic excess is not the product of the comic book's transformation into a culturally acceptable art form. As Justin Wyatt has traced from the late 1970s throughout the 1980s, the American film industry sought a way to redefine itself in what is commonly referred to as the "post-classical" period. "Post-classical" normally refers to the evolution in filmmaking norms that were initially established during the period covered in David Bordwell, Janet Staiger, and Kristin Thompson's *The Classical Hollywood Cinema: Film Style and the Mode of Production to 1960.* Essentially, scholars like Justin Wyatt, Thomas Schatz, and Geoff King have argued that industrial shifts in the mode of production (the shift from studio control to the rise of the producer and the production company, the end of vertical integration via the Paramount Decree, the rise of independent productions, and the influence of other media forms and international cinemas, etc.) have fundamentally altered film form. As Schatz writes, "Equally fragmented [he is referring first to the Hollywood film industry] perhaps, are the movies themselves, especially the high-cost, high-tech, high-stakes blockbusters, those multi-purpose entertainment machines that breed music videos and soundtrack albums, TV series and videocassettes, video games and theme park rides, novelizations and comic books."[67]

For Wyatt, the post-classical cinema is synonymous with what he terms "high concept." As Wyatt writes, "The term 'high concept' originated in the television and film industries, but it was soon adopted by the popular presses, who seized the term as an indictment of Hollywood's privileging those films which seemed more likely to reap huge dollars at the boxoffice [sic]." For Wyatt, "high concept can be considered as a form of differentiated product within the mainstream film industry. This differentiation occurs in two major ways: through an emphasis on style within the films, and through an integration with marketing and advertising."[68] Essentially, for Wyatt, Schatz, and to a lesser degree Geoff King, the post-classical style has produced a shift from narrative causality to spectacle and from spatial continuity rules to a more fractured representation of cinematic space. Yet as Bordwell later responded, high concept "remains a fairly isolated phenomenon. . . . [The Classical Hollywood System] is at once solid and flexible."[69] Moreover, as King acknowledges, "the classical style has not been abandoned. Far from it. The conventions of continuity editing and cause-effect narrative structure remain largely in place."[70] Essentially, and this will be elaborated upon later, stylistic remediation is a formal variable in what Bordwell refers to as the "bounds of difference" of the classical system: post-classical stylistic flourishes that essentially bend to the rules of the continuity system.[71]

While fans and audiences were onboard with Burton's surreal and foreboding stylistic interpretation of Batman, critical response was mixed. While many critics applauded the film's production design, some were perplexed by Burton's adult approach to the material. The opinions voiced in Roger Ebert and Gene Siskel's *At the Movies* foreshadow the problem the studio and the franchise would face over the coming years.

> SISKEL: As has been reported, this is a darker Batman, not at all like the campy '60s TV show. . . . Director Tim Burton obviously wants to . . . tell a more adult kind of story and that adult approach is what I found so refreshing about this Batman movie. We have so many films these days that are being made for the teenage audience. . . .
>
> EBERT: There's a great deal of hostility and anger in this film. . . . It's not a film for children. . . . It's not for kids, it's an extremely disturbing film.[72]

While Warner Bros. was quick to reassemble their winning formula of Keaton, Burton, and an adult approach for *Batman Returns* (1992), the studio was disappointed with the results. Budgeted at $80 million, the film grossed $266 million worldwide, producing a 40 percent slide in returns against a 225 percent increase in budget in comparison with the first film. While the film was not a box office failure by any stretch of the imagination, the studio felt that Burton had gone too far to the dark side, making the material questionable

Figure 2.2. The garish costumes of the Riddler and Two-Face in *Batman Forever* (1995).

for children. This was reflected not only by the box office receipts but in the studio's relationship with its licensing partners as well. Specifically, Burton's approach caused McDonalds to distance themselves from a Happy Meal tie-in.[73] According to a documentary covering the making of the film, the film's reception as not being kid friendly motivated the studio to push an already exhausted Burton out of the director's seat.[74]

With Burton relegated to an executive producer role on *Batman Forever* (1995), Joel Schumacher was brought in as his replacement. Hoping to make a film that would recapture a wide audience, the director saw the Batman comics of the 1940s and 1950s as an opportunity to move away from Burton's gritty portrayal of Batman in favor of a tone that would be bigger and lighter.[75] Replacing Keaton, the filmmaker cast Val Kilmer in the title role and, most notably, rising comedian Jim Carrey as one of the film's villains, the Riddler. Budgeted at $100 million, the kid friendly approach worked. The film grossed $336 million, an increase of 26 percent over the previous film. Notably, McDonalds pushed the film via their tie-in crystal drinking glasses.

Yet Schumacher and the studio went beyond abandoning the claustrophobia of Burton's noir style. The director's noteworthy alterations included adding nipples to the costumes of Batman and Robin, an animal print suit for Tommy Lee Jones's Two-Face (Figure 2.2), and a Batmobile that appears to have been draped in a zebra skin. Moreover, the director ditched Burton's preference for absolute blacks and overwhelming shadows in favor of electric neon colors (green in particular) and garish mise-en-scène.

Critics, including the *New York Times*' Janet Maslin, noted the stylistic shift and believed it to be an appeal to the youth audience. As Maslin writes, after noting the film is "so clearly a product that the question of its cinematic merit is strictly an afterthought," Schumacher's approach panders "more directly to a teen-age audience than either *Batman* or *Batman Returns* did."[76] Fans, despite the film's glowing box office returns, were livid with Schumacher's change in stylistic and tonal direction.

As documented by Will Brooker's *Batman Unmasked*, fans read the director's approach as a devolution towards the camp qualities of the *Batman* television series. As Brooker writes in his analysis of fan internet postings regarding Schumacher's *Batman Forever* and *Batman and Robin* (1997), "emerging from these posts is a dislike of the 'campiness' Schumacher brought to the movies, and in turn fear of any return to the 1960s television aesthetic."[77] As Brooker describes, the camp style has a basis in the Batman comics of the 1950s and 1960s. Fans have essentially engaged in a form of historical revisionism over the years, because the camp style became intertwined with a homophobic reaction against Fredric Wertham's infamous critique of Batman's less-than-traditional relationship with Robin.[78] Essentially, what differentiates the time periods of the Superman and Batman films is that the industry and fans appear to have accepted stylization (exemplified by the success of Burton's films) as an alternative to verisimilitude. However, the limit to that acceptance amongst fans ends where style takes on the negative connotations of camp.

These initial experiments in the stylistic remediation of comics into film died a relatively quick death. One of the film's predating Schumacher's flamboyant adaptation, Warren Beatty's *Dick Tracy* (1990, analyzed in more detail in the following chapter), left Walt Disney's Touchstone Pictures $57 million in the red. However, stylistic remediation may not have been the chief cause of the film's failure, as its style was applauded by most critics. Granted, it is problematic to equate critical response with a general audience. After all, it is common to see critically bashed blockbusters atop the box office almost weekly during the summer while some lauded films often go overlooked by the general public. However, one potent avenue for exploring the film's failure can be found in a general lack of cultural awareness amongst the public about the property. Essentially, Dick Tracy is not a hero on par with Batman or Superman. This may have resulted in lower attendance and ticket sales, which was unable to counter-balance Beatty's costly stylistic experiment (which carried a production budget of $101 million).[79] More red ink followed for stylistically experimental films. Rachel Talalay's *Tank Girl* (1995), based on the British comic by Alan Martin and Jamie Hewlett, grossed $4 million domestically against a production budget of $25 million. Essentially, stylistic remediation can be a means of roping in the main fan demographic for these films but—if poorly budgeted, far and beyond the niche audience—it can also be a costly gamble.

In 1997, like Superman before it, Batman experienced a tremendous shift in on-screen popularity. While it would make a profit once international sales were calculated, Schumacher's *Batman and Robin*, budgeted at $125 million, grossed $107 million domestically ($238 million worldwide). The film fell 62 percent from opening in first place during its first week of release to third place in its second, prompting top executives at Warner Bros. to publicly admit that the film "was a great disappointment. . . . It's just a crappy piece of product. Jesus Christ couldn't have saved this picture."[80] Warner Bros., under the impression that they had gone back to the well too quickly and too often with the property (the Schumacher films came out only two years apart), decided to cancel production of another sequel. As studio co-chairman Robert Daly was quoted after the failure of *Batman and Robin*, "It's not over. It could be three more years, or even four . . . There *will* be another *Batman*."[81]

The High Fidelity Cycle (2000–2013)

While this section jumps two years from the failure of Schumacher's film to the release of Bryan Singer's *X-Men* (2000), it would be incorrect to conclude that there was a drought of comic book films. 1998 to 2000 brought some successful theatrical films, such as *Blade* (1998). However, Singer's film exemplifies two significant industrial shifts that define the high fidelity cycle. First, after going though a cycle of economic highs and lows throughout the 1990s, Marvel Comics relied on licensing property rights for profit. According to Derek Johnson, 26 percent of Marvel's revenue came from licensing in 2002.[82] Yet by licensing away the rights, the publisher robbed itself of the ability to capitalize upon the success of its own properties in other media. For instance, the rights for *X-Men* were sold to Twentieth Century Fox for "a few hundred thousand dollars" while the four films (2000, 2003, 2006, 2009) went on to gross $1.4 billion dollars worldwide.[83] Essentially, thanks in part to the successes of the *X-Men* franchise at Fox, the *Spider-Man* (2002, 2004, 2007, 2012) franchise at Columbia Pictures, and their co-presentations with Paramount (*Iron Man*, *Thor*), the perceived value of the remainder of Marvel's holdings was enough to rebound the company from bankruptcy into a \$4 billion dollar deal with the Walt Disney Company.

Secondly, the film industry began culling talent for many of these films from a previously overlooked venue. The directors of three Marvel franchises, with the exception of *X-Men: The Last Stand* (2006) director Brett Ratner, all started their filmmaking careers in the independent sector. Bryan Singer, the director behind the first two *X-Men* films and later *Superman Returns* (2006), jumped to notoriety with his neo-noir *The Usual Suspects* (1996). Sam Raimi, the director of the *Spider-Man* trilogy, began his career in the Roger Corman tradition with *The Evil Dead* films (1981, 1987, 1993). Jon Favreau, director of the first two *Iron Man* films, began his career behind the camera as the writer of *Swingers* (1996) and the director of *Made* (2002). This trend is also exemplified in the Batman reboot franchise (2005, 2008, 2012, helmed by *Memento* director Christopher Nolan) and *Sin City* (2005, co-directed by *El Mariachi* director Robert Rodriguez).

Moreover, as comic book writer/artist Jim Steranko has noted, the writers, directors and producers now involved are "real comic fans. . . playing with material that they grew up with and they had a love for."[84] No doubt a by-product of these directors' own fandom, many of these projects involved comic book personnel creatively. While Bob Kane had been brought in as a creative consultant on Burton's *Batman*, it remains unclear whether or not he actually collaborated or just endorsed the film to appease fans. However, the practice became more commonplace and visible during the 2000s. Notable examples include Guillermo del Toro's collaborations with comic book writer and artist Mike Mignola (*Blade II* and the films based on his own series, *Hellboy*), Rodriguez's work with writer and artist Frank Miller (*Sin City*), and Zack Snyder's collaboration with illustrator Dave Gibbons (*Watchmen*). The result of this hiring practice is what scholar Bob Rehak has begun to describe as a "high-fidelity" trend that sometimes takes the form of stylistic remediation.[85] It is important to note, at this point, that high-fidelity adaptations or fan directors do not necessarily make for a more successful film, as the following case studies focused on such films as *Dick Tracy* (1990) and *The Hulk* (2003) will establish. To assume a fan-made product would automatically be successful with critics and the box office would merely embrace an intentional fallacy, glossing over the complex reception these films experience.

In the majority of cases, the high-fidelity trend manifests itself in the adaptation of tone and particular storylines (for instance *Batman: Year One* and *Batman: The Long Halloween* in *Batman Begins*), concerned with fidelity to the original content more often than with the form. However, at its most extreme, this high-fidelity approach (which is often a product of technology, respect for a given property, and fear of negative fan reaction), can also involve the remediation of style. While it is problematic to fully segregate form and content in specific cases, there does appear to be two separate trajectories in how filmmakers grapple with comic book form: ignorance or embrace. In the case of *Watchmen*, which Rehak specifically analyzes, Warner Bros. and director Zack Snyder attempted to situate the film within the fan community as a faithful adaptation by emphasizing the stylistic linkages between the film and its source. Specifically, Snyder repeatedly acknowledged using the comic as a storyboard for the film. Moreover, Gibbons was hired as a creative consultant, which was highlighted both at San Diego Comic-Con (he produced an exclusive teaser poster in 2007 and was a key participant at panels and the DC booth in 2008) and on the DVD's special features. A similar rhetoric surrounds the film *Sin City*. For instance, in the DVD documentary *How it Went Down*, Robert Rodriguez describes how he wanted to make "*Frank Miller's* [emphasis added] *Sin City*" by using green screen to "take cinema and try to make it into this book." Significantly, Rodriguez approached Miller with early footage not only to get his blessing, but to bring him onboard as a collaborator. The green screen allowed the filmmakers to move beyond the camera, to digitally draw on film.

This historical overview sets the scene for analyzing stylistic remediation within Warren Beatty's *Dick Tracy* (1990) and Ang Lee's *Hulk* (2003). Specifically, Beatty's blend of makeup effects, cinematography, and production design attempts to replicate the minimalist, caricature driven, drawing style of Chester Gould. Ang Lee's film, on the other hand, draws upon the comic book multiframe as one of its defining stylistic devices. Lee's fractured split-screens move the cinematic frame into the realm of becoming a formal hybrid where shots become panels to be arranged across the newly established grid of the screen. In so doing, both films attempt to realize adaptation beyond the notion of content and story, seeking to find a cinematic means of being faithful to the original text and medium via stylistic remediation.

PART
REMEDIATION IN COMIC ADAPTATIONS
TWO

CHAPTER 3

The Dread of Sitting through Dailies that Look like Comic Strips: Graphical Remediation in *Dick Tracy* (1990) and the Remediation of the Multiframe in *Hulk* (2003)

Introduction: Elaborating and Complicating the Taxonomy

With the formal taxonomy of stylistic remediation and the various evolving contexts grounding this stylistic practice broadly defined, we can begin to expand upon it (specifically within film adaptations of comic book properties). As mentioned before, the formal relationship between comics and film tends to be oversimplified due to the former's overstated and ultimately superficial similarities to the filmic storyboard. This chapter will explore how two unique aspects of form comics—graphical representation and the multiframe—were remediated by filmmakers Warren Beatty in *Dick Tracy* (1990) and Ang Lee in *Hulk* (2003). Essentially, the remediations exemplified by both films illustrate the disjunction between the formal vocabularies of the film and the comic.

Specifically, how can a filmmaker attempt to find a cinematic equivalent for the varied modes of graphical representation practiced by a cartoonist? In Chester Gould's *Dick Tracy* (1931–1977), the hero's smooth, modern, character design stands in stark contrast to the grotesque caricatures that antagonize him. Beatty, utilizing a hybrid of cinematography, production design, and makeup effects found a way to draw on film. He captured Gould's schizophrenic graphical style by moving beyond the photographic properties of the medium. Ang Lee, on the other hand, utilized CGI to find the point of contact between the multiframed grid of the comic book page and the cinematic frame. Yet as the case study of *Hulk* will illustrate, while Lee's experiments with split-screen look like multiframes, they do not function the same way. Essentially, his exercise in stylistic remediation is an act of formal compromise between the contradictory norms of two media. Finally, the contexts for stylistic remediation will continue to be fleshed out and nuanced by these case studies. Specifically, the high economic cost of such a process—and its questionable benefit—will begin to become a significant factor in its longevity.

Graphical Remediation in Dick Tracy (1990)

According to comic scholar Richard Marschall, adventure comic strips were a relatively new phenomenon in 1931 when Chester Gould submitted a detective strip titled "Plainclothes Tracy" to *New York Daily News* and *Chicago Tribune* publisher Joseph Patterson.[1] Marschall writes that Patterson may have been inspired by the rise of gangster activity in Chicago to revamp the strip with Gould into the hardened and gritty *Dick Tracy* we are familiar with today.[2] Despite making its debut in a smaller publication—the Detroit *Mirror*—"public interest and acceptance were swift. . . . *Dick Tracy* soon became a national phenomenon" spawning radio shows (1934–1948), serials (1937, 1939, 1941), and feature films from RKO Studios (1945–1947).[3] As of 2011, with writer Mike Curtis and artist Joe Staton at the desk, *Dick Tracy* was still running as a syndicated strip distributed by Tribune Media Services.

A film based on Gould's *Dick Tracy*, much like DC's *Batman*, gestated in Hollywood for a long period of time. Optioned by Paramount in 1977 while the Hollywood trades were buzzing about the upcoming *Superman* adaptation, the film started off in the hands of producer Art Linson and director Floyd Mutrux with a tentative start date of summer 1978 that was never met.[4] In 1983, John Landis was attached to direct, but he was removed after being indicted for involuntary manslaughter in the deaths of Vic Morrow and two children during production on *Twilight Zone: The Movie* (1983).[5] Three years later, in January of 1986, Paramount president Ned Tanen dropped the film because the budget was "way, way too high."[6] By the end of the year, producer Warren Beatty had moved the film to Disney.[7] The film was finally green lit by Walt Disney Pictures in 1988, eleven years after the rights had been purchased. The film carried a rumored budget of $30 million and Beatty was to serve as producer, director, and star.[8]

Information regarding Hollywood budgets is normally kept under firm lock and key, making it difficult to surmise what precise factors had driven the costs of Beatty's film up so dramatically. However, it seems reasonable, given the budgets on the *Superman* films and many other contemporary examples analyzed in the previous chapter, that special effects are a major factor in budget overruns. While Beatty's film did not draw upon CGI or teams of computer engineers, a large team of designers including prosthetic makeup technicians (John Caglione Jr., Doug Drexler), a cinematographer (Vittorio Storaro), a production designer (Richard Sylbert), and visual effects technicians (Michael Lloyd and Harrison Ellenshaw) was assembled to match the style of Gould's original strip. The team's task was to ensure that the film drew upon "Chester Gould's original strips as a 'bible,'... [giving everything] a generic look," a costly endeavor in itself.[9] This analysis, following the lead of Michael Cohen's thoughtful essay "*Dick Tracy*: In Pursuit of a Comic Book Aesthetic," will specifically analyze the mise-en-scène produced for the film by Beatty's design team and how they began to grapple with the ontological difference between the comic and the film image.

The differences between the comic and the film image began with the historical roots of their present day forms. Film, born out of advances in photography, has the unique ability—even when manipulated—to provide the viewer with an indexical tie to reality. As film theorist André Bazin notes in his seminal essay "The Ontology of the Photographic Image," photography and film both have an essential "objective character" due to the fact that "there intervenes only the instrumentality of a nonliving agent" between the originating object and its reproduction.[10] For Bazin, photography and film form an image of the world "automatically, without the creative intervention of man."[11] Even if we become aware of the manipulation of the image, that only lends itself to the acknowledgement of a reality beyond the diegetic world presented: the reality of the film production. Comics, on the other hand, are rooted in the parodic tradition. Their representational mode is founded upon deformation and caricature, providing the reader with a feeling of artifice. This drawn interpretation, like painting, is translated by the viewer as being the product of a living agent who forms an image that, to comic theorist Pascal Lefèvre, has "subjectivity . . . built into the work."[12] Essentially, live-action film is photographic while comics are iconographic.[13]

Comic book theorist and practitioner Scott McCloud's pyramid of the pictorial language once again proves useful (Figure 3.1). Recall that McCloud constructs his pictorial map on a two-axis system.[14] The horizontal axis, or "The Representational Edge," is defined by "Reality" and "Meaning." Thus, the realist film would stand on the far left side of the representational edge while pure iconography would be placed on the far right side of the spectrum. Moreover, as images ascend the vertical axis, or "The Retinal Edge," the images become neutral on the representational edge. Thus, the filmmaker of a live-action comic book (or strip, in this case) adaptation has a choice to make: to

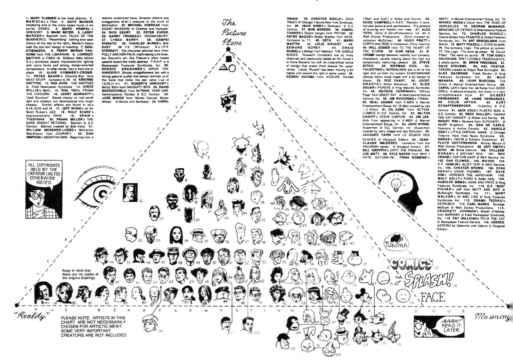

Figure 3.1. McCloud's pyramid of representation.

completely ignore the iconographic qualities inherent in the specificity of the comic medium (for example, Christopher Nolan's *Batman* films), or attempt to translate the graphical style of the original comic, compromising the two modes of representation. Beatty's film falls into the latter category by, in the words of Michael Cohen, deploying "a combination an 'aesthetic of artifice' . . . [and] 'cartooning.'"[15]

For Cohen, the film's "aesthetic of artifice" is derived from "exteriors [that] are noticeably clean and do not display the deterioration expected in a real environment, and the *mise-en-scène* of the interiors is also devoid of all surplus details and decoration beyond the denotation of the basic set dressing." As Cohen goes on to outline, Beatty and his production team utilized matte paintings, animation, and colored lighting to abstract the sets built on the studio back lot. The result, as the following three screenshots exemplify, is a stripped down world environment (in stark contrast to a film like Burton's *Batman*) that attempts to displace the photographic with the iconographic. Now, one might argue that Beatty is simply importing diegetic visual information into his adaptation, not necessarily remediating comics. After all,

Figure 3.2. The generic quality of warehouse mise-en-scène in *Dick Tracy* (1990).

Figure 3.3. The lack of detail of Tracytown in *Dick Tracy* (1990).

Figure 3.4. "Police" cars in front of the "police station" in *Dick Tracy* (1990).

almost every comic adaptation does this to a certain degree. For instance, even Nolan's realist Batman films are influenced by the diegetic material of the comics (for instance, the Caped Crusader's costume and logo). However, I would argue that diegetic influence and stylistic remediation can be placed on a continuous spectrum and that the latter categorization is to be found in elements that are stylistically excessive or stand at normative odds with the continuity system. Essentially, Beatty goes beyond the adaptation of diegetic material by embracing forms of artifice that go beyond and against the nature of cinematic language.

This becomes apparent when analyzing the above screenshots. First, notice the aforementioned "stripping down" of the detail in the mise-en-scène. The scene featured in Figure 3.1 is set in a warehouse. Yet the only visual markers that we are provided with are a bunch of wooden crates (lacking any sort of label painted or burned into the wood such as "Acme Exports") and the exposed structure of the building (most notably the steel girders running along the ceiling). The warehouse lacks any realist cues of being inhabited. We do not see any spilled crate contents or oil stains on the wood floor. Nor do we see as much as a forklift crammed into a corner of the space. The setting is dressed generically, the crates are iconographic and used in an almost metonymic sense, which illustrates a stylistic paradox embraced by Beatty: the set design of *Dick Tracy* grabs our attention because it is nondescript.

The same quality marks the mise-en-scène of Figures 3.2 and 3.3. In Figure 3.2, we are presented with one of the film's key settings: the Club Ritz, owned by antagonist "Big Boy" Caprice (Al Pacino). Yet compared to the other buildings on the block, the Club Ritz is given few external distinguishing marks (aside from a neon sign that remains unlit in the darkness). Figure 3.4 portrays another of the film's key settings: the police department where Dick Tracy (Beatty) works. Yet the cars, station, and lamp post are simply painted with the word "Police" (or "Police Station"). Unlike real police cars and stations, we are not provided with the name of the city the film is set in. Opposed to Bazin's formulation of photography and film, *Dick Tracy* does not ontologically affect us as being the product of a non-living agent.

Compare the above film stills to one of Chester Gould's strips (Figure 3.5). In this strip, we notice the roots of the film style Beatty and company embraced. The interior of the strip's main setting, a laundry truck, lacks any identifying detail and appears as a white background for the bulk of the strip. Notice the background of the two final panels as well. Like the mise-en-scène of the film, they are abstract and minimally defined. Moreover, the red of Breathless Mahoney's blouse matches that of Wetwash Wally. Essentially,

Figure 3.5. The iconographic qualities of Chester Gould's *Dick Tracy* (1951).

Gould, who produced episodes of the strip on a daily basis, could not afford to spend his time detailing the world of *Dick Tracy*.

For Cohen, the "aesthetic of artifice" involves both the stripping down of the mise-en-scène of any unnecessary details as well as the manipulation of the film's color palate. Comic strips and books were originally defined by their colors (hence the reason why Richard Outcault's "The Yellow Kid" became the known title of *Hogan's Alley*). The color of comics in the late 1800s was a novelty in the otherwise black and white pages of the newspaper. However, as printing technology evolved from the early to mid-twentieth century, it also became limited by the four-color printing process available at the time. According to McCloud, the four-color process "restricted the intensity of the three primaries [red, blue, and green] to 100%, 50%, and 20%, using black ink for the line work. . . . To counteract the dulling effects of newsprint and to stand out from the competition, costumed heroes were clad in bright, primary colors and fought in a bright primary world!"[16]

Similar to their philosophy of stripping down the level of detail in the mise-en-scène, Sylbert, Storaro, and company also embraced the color palate that had defined Gould's strip. Sylbert restricted the palate to six colors (red, blue, yellow, green, orange, and purple) in addition to black and white, all of which were held at the same shade. Thus, Dick Tracy's signature coat would be the exact same color as a passing Yellow Cab. According to Michael Lloyd, one of heads of the Buena Vista Visual Effects Group at the time:

> Warren was pushing a non-comic book look originally. Our problem was that we had something that was supposed to have somewhat of a comic book feel to it, yet with real live people and real physical things. In an ordinary picture, we would paint a real surrounding; but what we had to come up with for *Dick Tracy* was a stylized look that not only worked with reality but blended into a stylized world. We bent the rules in the use of color and architecture.[17]

While Beatty and his production team graphically remediated the iconographic minimalism of Gould's compositions and the limited color palate the writer/artist was bound to, they also attempted to remediate Gould's caricatures. Paying particular attention to the strip's peanut gallery of villains, the crew extensively utilized makeup and prosthetic devices to distort the visages of the cast. Cohen describes this process as "cartooning" and that it "complements the 'aesthetic of artifice' . . . [through] filming effects, such as sped up footage, or the outrageous behavior of the characters themselves. . . . [including their] design."[18] Focusing on the design of the characters, let us return to McCloud's pyramid in Figure 3.1 for a moment. Gould's Dick Tracy occupies the fourth line from the bottom, towards the middle-left of the representational edge. He is neither abstracted the point of just being pure lines and colors on a page nor a realistic representation. Tracy's face is defined by a series of rigid lines: chiseled jaw, a nose like the beak of an eagle, and a clean cut head of hair. Yet for the film, Beatty did not utilize Gould's visualization as a guide for his own character. In the film, Dick Tracy is simply Warren Beatty in a yellow coat and hat. Perhaps this was due to vanity, as actors, actresses, and studios are sometimes reluctant to undermine the physical qualities of what makes someone a star. On the other hand, Gould's design of his hero stands in stark contrast to how he portrays his villains. Compare Gould's depiction of Dick Tracy in Figure 3.5 to the chart of villains below (Figure 3.6).

Compared with his depiction of Tracy (which now appears to be fairly naturalistic!), Gould's design of the villains owes more to caricature. Their evil nature has manifested itself upon their physical form. Unlike Tracy, who is untarnished by unnatural flourishes and superfluous detail, Flattop is marked by his deformed trademark cranium, droopy eyes, and fish-like lips. Similarly, Pruneface's eyes and mouth blend into the disgusting crevices of his face, obscuring the two openings that serve as his nose. Moreover, unlike Tracy, Gould's physical depiction of the villains provides them with the source of their identities. The Brow has a large forehead; Flattop's skull looks like a

PRUNEFACE
1943

FLATTOP SR.
1944

MRS. PRUNEFACE
1943

SHAKEY
1945

LITTLEFACE
1941

THE BROW
1944

Figure 3.6. The villains of Gould's *Dick Tracy* (1941–1945).

deflated football. Essentially, Beatty was following essence of Gould's character design: Tracy is portrayed naturalistically (towards the lower left of McCloud's pyramid) while the villains are baroquely represented (towards the middle of the representational edge, but higher than Tracy upon the retinal edge, closer to the picture plane).

Compare Gould's character designs with this image featuring the main villains from the film (Figure 3.7). On the bottom left we see Flattop (William Forsythe), and on the far right, Pruneface (R. G. Armstrong). Forsythe's makeup, designed by John Caglione Jr., nearly matches the abstract caricature of Gould's strip. The signature crown of the character, the strange brow, and the freckles around the nub of a chin have been retained in the character design. Similarly, the canyons of Pruneface's face and his slicked back hair, not visible in the above picture, have made the transition to celluloid. While

Figure 3.7. The villains of Beatty's *Dick Tracy* (1990).

Caglione's makeup does not quite match Gould's elongation of the character's face and the lack of definition of eyes and nose, it effectively abstracts the gallery of villains from the reality that Tracy's representation embodies. Essentially, Beatty's film attempts to graphically remediate both the personal style of Gould (his caricatures and the generic representation of setting) and the general, medium specific, style of the comic at the time (the four-color printing process) through the use of the color palate, art direction, and make up design.

Despite Sylbert's public proclamations to the industrial trade the *Hollywood Reporter* that the remediation was a "very inexpensive way to do the picture" and that the film did not have the $60 million budget of *Batman* (which was actually budgeted at $35 million), *Variety* reported a very different story.[19] According to the other industrial trade, the production budget of *Dick Tracy* was nearly $101 million, initially leaving Disney with a $57 million dollar loss.[20] After a lukewarm domestic opening weekend of $22 million (*Batman* had grossed $40 million on its opening weekend one year earlier), Disney studio head Jeffrey Katzenberg expressed disappointment with the film's box office grosses, writing in a memo that the film "made demands on our time, talent and treasury that, upon reflection, may not have been worth it."[21] The film would eventually gross a total of $162 million, including both domestic and international territories, and would become the biggest home video rental of 1990.[22] Perhaps, in the end, the film turned a small profit after factoring in the enormous print and advertising budget of $50 million. However, unlike the *Batman* and *Superman* films that inspired the executives at Disney to grant the project a greenlight, *Dick Tracy* would not become a franchise; a sequel would not be made.

In retrospect, it seems self-destructive that Disney expected to rival *Batman* by allowing *Dick Tracy* to go so far over budget. Admittedly, both films are based on pre-established comic book properties, but that is a rather superficial analogy when we consider the value of both texts within the American cultural sphere. Quite simply, the two properties could not be further apart. While both comics debuted in the 1930s and remained visible into the 1980s and 1990s, *Dick Tracy* lacks the quality and extent of visibility of *Batman*. Admittedly, *Dick Tracy* is still a weekly, syndicated, comic strip. In contrast however, Batman appears in a handful of books that are published on a monthly basis, is a licensing cash cow, has a large fan base, and helped contribute to the cultural reevaluation of comics. Tellingly, in contrast to *Batman*, neither the *Wall Street Journal* nor the *Los Angeles Times* published any reports of fan anger regarding Beatty's casting choices.

Finally, in the horizontally integrated era of films that *Tracy* and *Batman* are a part of, many feature high tech gadgets (which are very helpful in selling toys and other merchandise) and either contemporary or fantastic/futuristic settings aimed at roping in the youth audience. *Dick Tracy* is set in the 1930s and—despite the cool two-way radio watch—retirees probably identified with the period more than American youth. Beatty seemed to acknowledge this rift in demographic appeal in his personal correspondence. In a response letter to a Ms. Broeske, Beatty writes that "I like [the strip] because it takes me back to a time in my childhood when . . . values seemed clearer."[23] Essentially, the casting of Beatty (who was 45 at the time), retro setting, and the music of Madonna and Stephen Sondheim seemed to be aimed at an adult audience while the centrality of a child protagonist and cartoonish aesthetic was aimed at children (and perhaps nostalgic adults). How could such a schizophrenically realized film attract a wide audience?

While the film's reception at the box office and general critical opinion of the film could be described as lukewarm at best, there was a significant amount of praise for the production design of the film. As Roger Ebert noted in his review of the film, "This is a movie in which every frame contains some kind of artificial effect. An entire world has been built here, away from the daylight and the realism of ordinary streets. . . . [The film] reflects the innocence of the comic strip. . . . [and] is one of the most original and visionary fantasies I've seen on a screen."[24] Richard Corliss came to a similar conclusion in his review, writing that the film is "comic strip art, a flip-book of impudent images that is faithful in detail to [Chester] Gould's boisterous graphics."[25] The film would be nominated for Academy Awards for Best Cinematography, Best Costume Design, and Best Sound, winning Oscars for Best Art Direction, Best Makeup, and Best Original Song. Essentially, film critics and trade organizations (like the Academy of Motion Picture Arts and Sciences) are receptive to stylistic remediation, and in some cases try to place it into larger discussions regarding film form for readers and potential viewers. Yet it is normally the economic success of these endeavors that spurs further formal exploration. For instance, *Dick Tracy*, followed by *The Dark Knight*, has the honor of being the comic book film with the most Oscar wins. This is an odd distinction considering, in the words of critic Keith Phipps, that the film has "become at best a hazy memory."[26]

The Remediation of the Multiframe in *Hulk* (2003)

Under the shadow of the Comics Code, Marvel and DC Comics solidified their positions atop the apex of American comic book publishing. According to comics historian Roger Sabin, "no American publisher was more adaptable to the new conditions than Marvel. . . . In a move intended to take on DC Comics at their own game, a new line was masterminded by editor-writer Stan Lee and artist Jack Kirby: between them, they decided that an interesting new direction would be to make the personalities of the heroes more of a focus than the plots."[27] Their first creation, *The Fantastic Four* (1961-), became the publisher's top seller and produced "an unprecedented barrage of fan mail."[28] Lee and Kirby followed up *Fantastic Four* with the creation of *The Incredible Hulk* (1962-) which, despite being a "damp squib at first," slowly became one of Marvel's most popular characters. [29] By the mid-60s, Hulk was ranked by an *Esquire* poll alongside Bob Dylan and Che Guevara as a favorite revolutionary icon.[30] The comic would eventually inspire a television series starring Bill Bixby (1977, 1978–1982).

After lukewarm box office receipts on *Dick Tracy* and the fan backlash against *Batman & Robin* (1997), stylistic remediation in comic book films largely disappeared until the release of Ang Lee's *Hulk* in the summer of 2003. The film, like *Dick Tracy* before it, spent several years in pre-production limbo. In 1996, *Variety* reported that producer Gale Anne Hurd was attempting to acquire financing of approximately $100 million.[31] One year later, the trade reported that Jonathan Hensleigh was working on the screenplay and Joe Johnson was attached to direct.[32] A few months later, Universal, faced with the actuality of a $100 million budget, pulled the plug. According to *Variety*,

CGI was to blame, as the "inherent . . . demands and subsequent costs" slowed production.[33] Moreover, according to Kevin Feige, head of production at Marvel Studios, "The technology hadn't been there."[34]

After dumping Johnson and Hensleigh, the studio went back to the drawing board and hired director Ang Lee in the winter of 2001. Lee was coming off his commercially and critically successful film *Crouching Tiger, Hidden Dragon* (2000). Yet the hiring of Lee was an odd choice, as the director had established a presence for himself in the art cinema with films like *Eat Drink Man Woman* (1994) and *The Ice Storm* (1997). When asked why she was drawn to Lee, Hurd replied that "Between the character work that is at the core . . . and the ability to create something visually that we've never seen before, there are not a lot of people who bring that to the table."[35] Budgeted at $137 million, the film went into production in spring of 2002.

As comic book scholar M. Keith Booker writes, "[*Hulk*] openly acknowledges its roots in the comics. . . . Its heavy use of split screens is especially effective as a sort of allusion to (though not really a recreation of) the look and feel of the comics, whose pages are divided into multiple panels."[36] Thus, one of the defining stylistic devices of Lee's film is his remediation of what comic book theorist Thierry Groensteen (drawing off the concept of Henri Van Lier) has described as what is "essential about comics": the multiframe, or the grid of the page that links together individual panels.[37] For Groensteen, who is reluctant to provide a formal definition of the comic, the multiframe represents two fundamental characteristics. First, comics are composed of interdependent images (or, as Scott McCloud has described, sequential images). Secondly, the first relationship that panels have with one another is that they occupy the same space of the multiframe.[38] This formal attribute tends to be oversimplified by some media studies scholars and industrial personnel such as Avi Arad, the chief creative officer at Marvel. For Arad, "Comic books are basically . . . highly detailed storyboards."[39] However, as *Maus* author Art Spiegelman has been quick to note and this analysis will confirm, "Comics are not storyboards for movies at their best."[40]

While both film and comics rely on sequential images as a means of producing a narrative, they are both presented by the filmmaker/author and engaged with by the viewer/reader in significantly different ways. The sequential images of film take the place of one another on a presented surface. Unless a filmmaker utilizes a split-screen, we are never presented with two separate compositions within the same space. Moreover, as David Bordwell, Kristin Thompson, and Janet Staiger have documented, the prevailing stylistic norms of both classical Hollywood cinema (1928–1960) and contemporary Hollywood cinema reflect a desire for continuity of space and time. For Bordwell

Figure 3.8. Stan Lee and Jack Kirby's *Incredible Hulk* (1962).

and his associates, analytical editing techniques like the 180-degree rule and establishing shot patterns produce a cinematic text that "conceal[s] its artifice" and relays a "comprehensible and unambiguous" story that "possesses a fundamental emotional appeal."[41] Essentially, when the system of classical norms is functioning at its ideal, the jarring effect of juxtaposing a new shot on the same space where an earlier one had appeared is negated.

The multiframe of the comic and the multiplicity of images it presents makes that sensation impossible to the comics reader. Admittedly, a similar set of classical norms—many of which have been drawn from Western reading habits and the visual arts at large—have been described by Will Eisner in his manual *Comics & Sequential Art*. For instance, reading order dominates the comic. Characters who "speak" first via dialogue balloons are placed on the left side of the panel. As Eisner notes, "The most important obstacle to surmount is the tendency of the reader's eye to wander."[42] The reader of the comic, unlike the spectator of a film, is entered into the role of a collaborator (that is not to say that the spectator of a film is passive, just that spectatorial activity differs) with regard to digesting the panels individually, placing them into a sequence, and inferring the spatiotemporal relationship between them. For instance, the 180-degree rule (and spatiotemporal continuity in general) is often neglected in comics due to the fact that comics, unlike film, define such relationships via space rather than time. Quite simply, if a comic book artist religiously followed the classical cinema norms that Bordwell and his colleagues have outlined, the industrial standard of thirty-six pages would quickly balloon to hundreds, if not thousands, of pages.

The definition of the reader as a collaborator who provides continuity to discontinuous sequential images intersects with Scott McCloud's definition of comics. For McCloud, the reader takes the individual panels (separated by the gutter), arranges them into sequences, and performs an act of closure that unites them spatiotemporally and determines their narrative significance. As he writes, "If visual iconography is the vocabulary of comics, closure is its grammar."[43] While McCloud is careful to note that film sometimes relies on the same techniques (the Kuleshov effect being a key example of cinematic closure), closure provides the glue to every multiframe of panels. In order to illustrate these stylistic principles a bit more concretely, here are five panels (Figure 3.8) from the first page of writer Stan Lee and penciler Jack Kirby's *Incredible Hulk* #1 (1962).

In the above panels, Lee and Kirby give us a dialogue scene that introduces three major characters: Bruce Banner (the hero), General Thunderbolt Ross (one of the title's antagonists), and Betty Ross (the hero's love interest/the daughter of the General). Moreover, we are introduced to the conflict between

Banner and General Ross. Bruce is ambivalent to test the gamma ray bomb, which displeases the General. Because the sequence takes place in the same setting, the break between the panels of the multiframe is largely temporal. We notice these temporal breaks both in how General Ross crosses the room during the transition from panel one to panel two and in how the dialogue progresses. If we are to assume that cinema has an engrossing quality for the viewer, as suture theory has gone on to explore, comics are fundamentally different from both formal and phenomenological standpoints. We are not folded into the action; there is no camera to align our identification with. Rather, it is our role, as the reader, to fill in those temporal gaps from panel to panel via the act of closure. Closure provides spatiotemporal continuity where none exists. Moreover, if we are putting the sequence in dialogue with cinematic norms, it is fitting to note those that Lee and Kirby ignore. While they begin the sequence with the equivalent of an establishing shot pattern, the entrance of Betty in panel four catches us by surprise (we do not see her in the first panel!). Secondly, there is a jarring break in the 180-degree rule, apparent in the transition from panel one to panel two. As noted above, strict adherence to the classical norms of cinema is not feasible in comics due to a shortage of space.

When Ang Lee was hired to direct *Hulk*, he attempted to match each unique device of the comic with a cinematic means of expression. As he notes at length in an interview with Brent Simon, the fundamental stylistic difference between the media forms of film and comics was not an artistic obstruction but an opportunity. Lee states that "The comic books give me a good excuse to try something I've always wanted to without being distracting. I think the time is right—-especially for kids, the way they grow up with television, cartoons, the Internet, and video games.... The principle is very similar to when you open up a comic book: your eyes go somewhere, you choose what you see—-not necessarily like a regular movie-viewing experience in which filmmaker's editing mandates that you watch it a certain way."[44]

It is odd, considering Lee's statement alongside his remediation of the multiframe, how much of the final presentation is the product of a media specific, formal, compromise. While the technique is glimpsed in an early montage of young David Banner (Paul Kersey) experimenting with genetic modification, its first prolonged use appears when Banner causes an explosion that kills his wife. Lee's use of the multiframe, in this instance, is limited to the two separate panels, as exemplified by the images below (Figures 3.9–3.10). As you can see, particularly in Figure 3.8, Lee's use of the multiframe is illusory, at least with regard to how it functions spatiotemporally. Rather than

Figure 3.9. David Banner starts the reactor in two "panels" of the *Hulk* (2003).

Figure 3.10. David Banner hears alarm bells across the splitscreen of *Hulk* (2003).

Figure 3.11. A barrage of simultaneous panels inhabiting the splitscreen of *Hulk* (2003).

giving us two images portraying separate instances of time (or space) as a comic book would, Lee gives us two images of one space that are taking place simultaneously. As he cuts from the same diegetic space (the laboratory) in Figure 3.8 to two separate spaces in Figure 3.9, the same temporal rule applies: the announcement that the guard is delivering on the left side of the screen is the same one Banner is hearing on the right side. Essentially, Lee's frames are not encapsulating separate moments in time that are structured by the multiframe. Rather, he is providing us with an embellished use of split-screen: a glimpse of two separate spaces at the same time.

This example is indicative of all Lee's uses of split-screen.[45] Even when the director adds additional "panels" to the multiframes in the film, they take place simultaneously rather than sequentially (Figure 3.11). The act of closure, which McCloud describes as the grammar of comics, is performed for the viewer by the soundtrack. Of course, the viewer may momentarily need to initially compromise the two frames but, as Bordwell notes, the overall style of *Hulk* can be categorized as "intensified-continuity."[46] Following Bordwell's implied argument (Bordwell is analyzing breaks of the 180-degree rule, not Lee's use of the multiframe), Lee's stylistic flourishes are both generically motivated and function within the normative practices of continuity style. First, with regard to generic motivation, the multiframe is a formal attribute of the comic book and given that *Hulk* is based on a superhero comic, it is fitting that it looks like one. Secondly, with regard to continuity style, the multiframe is used infrequently and the soundtrack smooths over any discontinuity between spaces. This is an antithetical conclusion, given Lee's ambition to move beyond "a regular movie-viewing experience in which filmmaker's editing mandates that you watch it a certain way."[47]

While Bordwell's analysis is often considered monolithic and overreaching (and, in some cases, it can be), his analysis of *Hulk* is reinforced by the direction Lee gave his creative team. Garson Yu, the visual designer for the film, noted in an interview that Lee

> wanted me to develop a new visual language incorporating multiple cameras to tell a story. In film, it's difficult to show multiple events simultaneously on one screen. Ang wanted to develop a concept that incorporated how we normally read comic strips. He wanted to present the film in one giant comic page.[48]

As Yu notes, Lee drew upon the design of the multiframe and its facility for presenting multiple images for multiple, *simultaneous* events. Quite simply, as the film's editor Tim Squyres observed, it is not stylistically feasible to fully remediate both the form and the function of the multiframe on film. As Squyres notes, "You can't just take the layout of a comic book and put that on a movie screen. It just doesn't work . . . You'd end up wasting all your screen."[49] Like the impossibility of comics mimicking the continuity system, media specificity still proves an obstacle when the relationship between the two forms is inverted, at least in the case of the multiframe. The filmmaker, despite the financial assistance of a media conglomerate (NBC Universal) who financed George Lucas's Industrial Light & Magic with a $1.5 million production budget for comic book transitions, could not escape from the norms of the continuity system.[50]

For digital theorist Lev Manovich, comics and the multiframe represent a type of spatial montage that was neglected by the cinema when the temporal montage of the continuity system became the norm. Manovich, writing in 2001, sees the possibility of a return to spatial montage thanks to the evolution of two factors. First, Manovich believes that the development and refinement of computer effects technologies will make live-action cinema a "raw material" that will become one of many elements in "digital cinema," held together via the tools and techniques of "animation."[51] Secondly, and as Lee notes in his interview with Simon, our relationship with the screen has evolved thanks to the computer's presentation of multiple windows. As Manovich writes, "I believe that the next generation of cinema—-*broadband cinema*, or *macrocinema*—-will add multiple windows to its language. When this happens, the tradition of spatial narrative that twentieth-century cinema suppressed will reemerge."[52] While Manovich's conclusions are, in retrospect, suspect (for instance, television could be argued to have predated digital spatial montage, a connection he does not explore), his theories serve as a main tenet of digital cinema theory and cannot be ignored. The question that will be briefly explored here is, given Ang Lee's remediation of the multiframe in *Hulk*, have we reached the era of broadband or macrocinema?

Given this stylistic analysis of the multiframe and its differing functions in both the comic and the film, the answer would be not completely. Lee's use of the multiframe not only follows the norms of continuity established by a cinematic device (the split-screen), but it is drawn upon briefly and infrequently. Yet does the spatial montage of Manovich's broadband cinema or macrocinema need to completely adhere to the norms of either form (film or comics) in order to have emerged? When he later describes spatial montage in depth, he writes that "The logic of replacement, characteristic of cinema, gives way to the logic of addition and coexistence. Time becomes spatialized, distributed over the surface of the screen. [Guided by the principles of the computer's graphical user interface (GUI), spatial montage] follows the logic of simultaneity."[53] Given this elaboration, it seems that—the case of Lee's *Hulk*—spatial montage is present to a degree. We are presented with simultaneous spaces that Manovich links with the GUI. However, the passage of time is not spatialized within the multiframe sequences of the film; the device functions as a capsule for spatializing two separate spaces. The beginning stages of an exploration of spatial montage may be present in *Hulk*, but it has yet to appear in the way in which Manovich describes.

While Lee's film may have established some important groundwork regarding the practice of spatial montage, it also crippled its development due to its financial failure. Universal had embraced Lee's unique stylistic approach by providing him with a production budget of $137 million which, after factoring in prints and advertising costs, was probably closer to $200 million.[54] According to Lee, "In a smaller movie you cannot afford that kind of freedom in creating images."[55] The film grossed $245 million worldwide. To put this in perspective, *Spider-Man* (2002) carried a comparable budget and grossed nearly $822 million worldwide.[56] While *Hulk* had a long list of factors that undoubtedly contributed to its lackluster opening, including Lee's attempt to cater to both of his audiences (the art house and the popular), his attempt to stylistically remediate the comic were scapegoated by the industry's trade press. Following the film's opening weekend, *Variety* editor Peter Bart wrote an editorial stating that the industry was ambivalent to engage with Lee's varietal of formal exploration. As the former studio executive noted, "I've talked to several of the studio production chiefs about all this and find myself empathizing with their reasoning. They know they have to deliver 'event pictures' but they dread sitting through dailies each afternoon that look like a series of comicstrips [sic]."[57]

Lee's innovations, like those of Warren Beatty and the team on *Dick Tracy* (1990), were applauded by critics. Richard Roper noted in a telecast of *Ebert & Roper* that "Much of the credit has to go to director Ang Lee for giving the story a dark elegance and, as Roger noted, jazzing it up with those dozens of creative cuts, wipes, split-screens, and dissolves. This is a superhero movie that really captures the essence of comic book pop art."[58] Similarly, Andrew Sarris wrote in his review that he "didn't particularly mind these ["editing tricks of simultaneity"] . . . because at the very least, they kept the movie from becoming tedious and turgid, a fate from which its recent rivals in the genre do not entirely escape."[59] Unlike *Dick Tracy* however, the creative team behind *Hulk* would not be recognized by the Academy of Motion Picture Arts and Sciences. Like Beatty's film thirteen years earlier, Ang Lee's *Hulk* would not spawn a direct sequel. When the character was revisited in director Louis Leterrier's reboot *The Incredible Hulk* (2008), the $150 million film did not exhibit stylistic remediation. However, the financial result was almost identical; the film grossed $263 million worldwide. Given the film's economic performance, Bart may have misplaced the blame when he placed the disappointing returns for *Hulk* on Ang Lee's doorstep. After all, the next film to be analyzed, Zack Snyder's *300* (2006), over performed at the box office . . . partially because it looked "like a series of comicstrips [sic]."[60]

The Economic and Formal Compromises of Stylistic Remediation

The taxonomy of the process of stylistic remediation between these two media has only begun to be elaborated upon. This chapter teased out the formal and ontological differences between the media forms of the comic book and the film and how two filmmakers, Warren Beatty and Ang Lee, attempted to stylistically remediate two defining factors of the old medium—graphical representation and the multiframe—in their adaptations for the new medium. These two case studies of remediation, as will be reenforced by the analysis in the following chapter, have brought us to some tentative conclusions. First, stylistic remediation is a relatively expensive process. The production budgets of both *Dick Tracy* and *Hulk* averaged $119 million. In 1990, when *Tracy* was released, the five top grossing films of the year (*Home Alone*, *Ghost*, *Dances with Wolves*, *Pretty Woman*, and *Teenage Mutant Ninja Turtles*) had an average production budget of $18 million. In comparison, the five top grossing films of 2003 (*The Lord of the Rings: The Return of the King, Finding Nemo, Pirates of the Caribbean: The Curse of the Black Pearl, The Matrix Reloaded,* and *Bruce Almighty*) had an average production budget of $111 million. Obviously, the production budgets of films has increased dramatically over the past twenty years, and as the budgets associated with the 2003 titles illustrate, a large factor in this increase is computer generated imagery. Essentially, any deviation away from cinematic realism—which stylistic remediation is—carries a large price tag.

Secondly, stylistic remediation is rarely a "clean" process. When the formal vocabulary of one medium is modified in order to represent the initial medium, the translation typically exhibits a degree of stylistic noise. Beatty's *Dick Tracy*, when analyzed along side *Hulk* and the case studies in the following chapter, is an anomaly. By blending makeup effects, cinematography, and mise-en-scène, Beatty successfully captures the representational gap between the normal looking hero and the grotesque caricatures that defined Chester Gould's strip. Essentially, the film form follows the functions of Gould's comic. On the other hand, despite Ang Lee's intention to experiment with the language of the continuity system, his stylistic remediation of the multiframe is the product of a compromise. Lee's split-screens are superficial multiframes; they look like them but they do not function in the same way. By avoiding compositions based around sequential images, the film merely showcases embellished split-screens. This conclusion should not be read as a value judgment (to borrow from adaptation terminology for a brief moment, it is irrelevant if Beatty's adaptation is more "faithful" with regard to form), but as a acknowledgement of the limits of the practice. After all, stylistic remediation does not exist in a cultural vacuum. As these case studies have attempted to account for, the objective is a product that appeals both to fans and a wider demographic (those budgets need to be recouped somehow!). And despite the proclamation of Rorschach in *Watchmen*, one of the case studies we now turn to, refusing to compromise simply is not a pragmatic approach when it comes to fulfilling that objective.

CHAPTER 4

"He Cared More about the Appeasement of Fanboys . . .": Spatiotemporal Remediation in *300* (2006) and *Watchmen* (2009) and Textual Remediation in *American Splendor* (2003)

Introduction: Further into the Taxonomy

Thus far, stylistic remediation has been established as being a means of formal experimentation tied to big budget, blockbuster, films. While the two often go hand in hand, they are not synonymous with one another. In fact, as this chapter will illustrate through analyses of *American Splendor* (2003) and *300* (2006), stylistic remediation can also be seen in films that occupy the lower to average side of the budget spectrum. Moreover, despite the economic implosions of both *Dick Tracy* (1990) and *Hulk* (2003), stylistic remediation can also prove to be an effective marketing hook that can lead a film towards box office glory. However, the analysis of *Watchmen* (2009) will also reenforce the *Hulk* hypothesis. When an expensive, formally experimental, film fails at the box office, style still becomes the scapegoat.

The taxonomy of remediation at the center of this analysis has been partially fleshed out through the analyses of two formal obstacles that stand between the vocabularies of both media. Graphical remediation and the spatial remediation of the multiframe have already been defined and analyzed. This chapter will delve deeper into the latter relationship by engaging in an analysis of the comic book panel and the film frame in terms of spatiotemporal construction and representation. Moreover, the central relationship between image and text in the comic will be considered in the remediations of Robert Pulcini and Shari Springer Berman's adaptation of Harvey Pekar's *American Splendor*.

The Remediation of Space and Time in *300* (2006) and *Watchmen* (2009)

Recalling Mark Rogers' helpful distinction between industrial and artisan comic book publishing, Frank Miller and Lynn Varley's *300* (1998), published by Dark Horse, would fall firmly into the latter. A limited series spread across five issues, the volume is noteworthy for featuring a shift from the super-hero genre to the historical epic and for its exploration of publication format. Miller, frustrated by the presentational format of comics, wanted to reimagine the space of the page. In conversation with Will Eisner, Miller noted that the seven by ten format "makes no sense. It's only tradition that keeps it alive.... I found when I did *300* that there was something that felt so much more organic about it, because as humans we tend not to look up and down as much as we do side to side. The horizontal image, I find, is much better for captur-ing landscape and detail."[1] Favoring a layout that is twice as wide as a typical comic (the book spawned a new, industry-wide publication format dubbed the "widescreen format"), *300* also defines its unique visual style through the representational juxtaposition of ink and watercolor.[2]

The first issue of *300*, retailing at $2.95 (opposed to the usual $1.99), sold 48,986 copies when it was released in May of 1998.[3] The title was ranked forty second on the Diamond Comic Distributors sales figures for the month (the month's top ranked title, *Uncanny X-Men*, sold 142, 959 copies).[4] While its initial sales were fairly modest, the title would go on to win the prestige of numerous Eisner Awards (Best Limited Series, Best Writer/Artist, and Best Colorist). Moreover, once the series was collected into a hardback volume, the title sold an additional 88,000 copies (the success of the film prompted an additional printing of 40,000 copies, retailing at $30.00 a copy).[5]

Filmmaker Zack Snyder was drawn to adapting the title. Like so many members of the contemporary generation of filmmakers (such as Michael Bay, Michel Gondry, Spike Jonze, David Fincher, and McG), the filmmaker began his career in music video and commercial production. He transitioned to feature filmmaking with a remake of George Romero's seminal horror film *Dawn of the Dead* (2004). Snyder's debut, budgeted at a modest $26 million, went on to gross $102 million worldwide. Moreover, despite its dubious cul-tural status as both a horror film and a remake, it attracted positive reviews. The success of the film prompted Snyder to turn to the adaptation of Miller's graphic novel as his next project. Despite the cultural legitimacy that came with Miller's name and the slew of Eisner Awards that *300* won, Hollywood was ambivalent.

As Snyder noted, "No one was really interested in making it into a movie. They just didn't get it. It was late 2002, and *Troy* was just in preproduction.... They had everything they needed [and] they said, 'Oh, what? You're going to come around with your crazy graphic novel?' I didn't know how hard it is to make a movie."[6] Despite the box office misfires of *Troy* (2004) and *Alexander* (2004), Warner Bros. and its associated production company Legendary Pictures changed their outlook towards the property when another Frank Miller adaptation, *Sin City* (2005), performed well. As Jeff Robinov, head of production at Warner Bros. noted, "The movie is all about Zack Snyder. Until he showed us his storyboards, I had no idea what the movie was. We already had our share of sword-and-sandal movies. Another one was not an obvious choice. But that's not this movie."[7] The film entered production in the fall of 2005 with a rumored production budget of $60 million.[8]

The spatiotemporal difference between the comic book panel and the film frame is the most difficult form of stylistic remediation to describe. This is because the spatiotemporal dimension of the comic book panel is contingent upon the subjective reading habits of each individual reader. For instance, consider the construction of time in the comic. A reader can take a few hours or an indefinite amount of time to read *300*. On the other hand, cinematic time progresses at a rate of twenty-four frames per second regardless of the viewer's presence (unless, of course, he or she is watching it on a piece of hardware that allows for viewer control of the experience). To complicate this further, the comic book panel does not exhibit a pre-defined amount of time. The time portrayed both within the panel and through the progression of panels, as Scott McCloud notes, can vary greatly. With this noted, let us first turn to the definition of two aspects of spatial remediation in *300* before engaging in a temporal analysis of *Watchmen*.

The first aspect of spatial remediation of *300* that we will consider involves movement through space. Returning to Avi Arad's proclamation for a moment ("Comic books are . . . greatly detailed storyboards."), we once again realize how misleading this analogy is. First, the comic book panel, unlike the storyboard, does not contain any movement vectors. Storyboards often contain arrows and notes regarding camera placement and movement. On the other hand, movement in an individual comic panel can only be portrayed via devices like action lines (the next chapter will define and engage with action lines in more detail). This dynamic between space and time, articulated via movement, is complicated in Miller and Varley's comic. First, Miller alternates between single panels that take up the space of an entire page, eliminating the multiframe altogether. Secondly, due to the lack of a comic book system of norms similar to that of the Hollywood continuity system, it can be incredibly difficult to determine what part of a space Miller's characters occupy. As Pascal Lefèvre writes, framing can limit "the scope for the viewer and therefore the available information, the artist can cause a reader to make wrong inferences" regarding the diegetic space.[9]

An example of this spatial ambiguity in Miller's *300* is evident in young Leonidas' battle with the wolf. Miller represents the battle in ten panels, which span across three pages. Yet the details of the environment that the man and beast are fighting in are at first a mystery to us. Miller alternates between panels depicting enclosed and wide open spaces. The first panel shows the young hero surrounded by what looks to be a cave and the wolf enters a small chasm in front of the boy. However, the subsequent panel portrays the two of them in what looks like a snow swept void. As the sequence progresses, Miller narrows the frames of his panels as Leonidas lures the wolf into another, previously unestablished chasm. Finally, the wolf gets stuck between the narrowing rocks and nimble Leonidas deals him a death blow with his spear.

Despite being described as a "shot-for-shot adaptation of Miller's graphic novel," it is illuminating to hear Snyder describe his approach to compromising the differing formal grammars of film and comics in this instance.[10] After photocopying panels from the book, Snyder planned the preceding and succeeding shots to the original panel. Essentially, he needed to fill in the ruptures of time and space that were initially closed by the reader and the multiframe. As Snyder notes, "If you look at the book, it's a montage, right? It's not a moment-to-moment experience, like a film is. So the challenge for me is to . . . get into [Frank Miller's moments]."[11] While Miller portrayed the battle in ten panels and interrupted the sequence with interlaced flashback panels, Snyder uses more than thirty shots and avoids cross-cutting between the time frames. Moreover, Snyder and his director of photography Larry Fong use a combination of static and mobile framing. Essentially, both storytellers portray young Leonidas killing the wolf through the same thrilling and visceral images. However, the way in which the artists structure the relationship between the individual images is drastically different. Miller uses cross-cutting, an ambiguous presentation of space, and a narrowing panel aspect ratio to elicit suspense. Snyder, on the other hand, utilizes camera movements and fast-paced editing to similar effect.

While Miller and Snyder's approaches to depicting movement through space are structurally different, there is a spatial quality of Snyder's remediations that affect the viewer in a similar fashion as Miller's work. Essentially, the reader of the comic is continually reminded of the constructed, artificial, nature of comics. This quality stems from both comics being rooted in a parodic tradition and the self-reflexive nature of the multiframe as well. With regard to Miller and Varley's style, the collage of techniques that the two artists bring to the material is both what makes the text both memorable and

Figure 4.1. Miller's two dimensional blood becomes marketing iconography.

artificial. According to Miller's artistic philosophy, "Doing realism in comics is really saying we are the poor man's film. . . . As time goes by, I find myself more and more in love with stuff that's closer to bigfoot cartooning. I want people's sweat to be *flying* off their heads when they're upset. It's something comics can do."[12] While sweat may not be a defining element of Miller's anti-realism in *300*, another bodily fluid—blood—certainly is.

Specifically, when hell is unleashed in the concluding chapter of *300*, the bloody carnage is rendered through splashes of ink and watercolor. The overlaid effect of the blood on the space results in a flattened image. For instance, the blood does not appear to occupy the same space as the characters, horses, and grit because the application of ink does not involve the use of spatial perspective. The absolute reds of the drizzled gore feel as if they are the product of a filter placed over the image. Moreover, Miller and Varley's unique rendering of blood became a defining element in the film's marketing campaign, as seen in the below marketing still (Figure 4.1), and the film itself.

In order to remediate the flattening effect of Miller's use of blood, Snyder distributed a "style guide" to ensure continuity across the film's various effects teams (which included ten vendors across four countries).[13] The guide included an entry describing the representation of blood as needing to be 2D and "designed and rendered in a way that audiences can clearly identify that what they're seeing is a deliberate exercise in style, rather than a mistake. It needs to be simultaneously brutal and beautiful. In the graphic novel, Miller

Figure 4.2. Clashes in representation in
300 the film (above) and the comic (below).

and Varley depict blood with a spattered ink effect, a technique that is car-ried over to the film in all the live-action battles."[14] In order to match this quality, the filmmakers went so far as to incorporate scanned blood spatters from Miller and Varley's book into the film.[15] These effects, again, flatten the space of film. The film's cinematic space, which is embellished on the z-axis via camera movements, has been re-rendered in two dimensions by Snyder's remediation of Miller's style.

Snyder and his team furthered the effect of artificiality by repurposing Miller and Varley's watercolored skylines. The comic book continually jux-taposes the stark pencil work that defines the characters with vaporous, tex-tured skies. To best visualize this concept, below is a panel of the comic placed aside its corresponding film frame (Figure 4.2). In the images, we can see how the representation of Leonidas clashes with the representation of the setting in both the film and the comic. In the comic, Miller's pencils define the character in a series of rigid lines (exemplified by his beard and hair especially). In contrast, the water colored skies embody a smoother aesthetic that verges on Impressionism. In the film, the photographic representation of the character stands in opposition with the unearthly skies behind him. As the film's visual effects supervisor Chris Watts and visual effects art director Grant Freckelton note, "Our skies are created using a blend of photographic and watercolor elements, giving the backgrounds a uniquely textured feel without being entirely painted."[16] The juxtaposition of styles in both versions affects the reader as being artificial. However, due to the comic's roots in caricature, the image is also tactile and attributable to an authorial personality, which returns us to Lefèvre's assertion that subjectivity is inherently to comics.

Leading up to the film's release, there was an abundance of news ink spilt on Snyder's remediations of the material and how similar the adaptation was to Robert Rodriguez and Frank Miller's adaptation of *Sin City* (2005) two years earlier. The *Los Angeles Times* noted that Snyder "uses actors on spare sets altered digitally in post-production. Only one shot in the entire movie . . . was actually filmed outside, and even then . . . [it was] digitally enhanced."[17] Fittingly, the story is complemented by a sidebar, pointing the reader to go online to access a feature entitled "The Match-Up," which tracks how closely "the movie follow[s] Frank Miller's graphic novel."[18] Building off of the buzz the film had created, Warner Bros. attempted to financially capitalize on the public's awareness of the film's unique style. On January 26, 2007, roughly six weeks before the film was to be released, the studio announced that the film would also be released in the IMAX format.[19] Four days later, Robinov announced to *Variety* that Snyder's visual style had prompted Warner Bros. to write up a two-year, first-look, production deal with Snyder's production company, Cruel & Unusual Films. It was also announced that their first project would be the long-languishing adaptation of Alan Moore and Dave Gibbons' *Watchmen* (1986).[20]

In contrast to Pascal Lefèvre's analysis that "Not only do these [stylistically embellished comic book] adaptations seldom please the critics, they seem to have little automatic appeal for comics readers," *300* was a tremendous success.[21] Despite the film's uncomfortable allegory, which equates equates the battle of the Thermopylae with the war on terror, worldwide box office figures were staggering.[22] Opening on 3,100 screens domestically, it became the third top grossing R-rated film in history. *300* grossed $70 million in its opening weekend alone, $5 million more than its disclosed production budget.[23] After worldwide box office figures were accounted for, the film totaled $456 million. The film split critics, many of whom lamented the film's meatheaded ideology and story while praising Snyder's style. In a quote that provided Warner Bros.' marketing and publicity department with some prestigious ammunition, film critic and *At the Movies* co-host Richard Roeper described the film as being "the *Citizen Kane* of cinematic graphic novels."[24] Obviously, Snyder's visual style was drawing favorable attention from critics. Yet it becomes difficult to gauge as to how much the audience was drawn in by the look as opposed to a macho action film. While far from being a definitive measure, the Amazon.com consumer reviews of the film can provide a small snapshot. Out of roughly two thousand consumer reviews, approximately 10 percent use the terms "style" (118 reviews), "stylization" (60 reviews), or "stylized" (60 reviews), while the "look" of the film is described in roughly 20 percent (409 reviews).[25] Essentially, the style may have been an area of interest for a small fraction of the audience.

Hoping to capitalize upon Snyder's status as a box office heavyweight and as a filmmaking "visionary" (as the *Watchmen* trailers describe him), Warner Bros., Paramount Pictures, Legendary Pictures, DC Comics, and Lawrence Gordon Productions gave Snyder a $130 million production budget and rushed the much-awaited adaptation of *Watchmen* into production. While the series had been optioned throughout the 1980s and 1990s by various studios, the plug was constantly pulled due to high production costs. Production began on the film in the fall of 2007, roughly six months after the release of *300*. Coincidentally, Warner Bros. planted a single-frame image of the *Watchmen* character Rorschach in a *300* trailer.[26] To say *Watchmen* was anticipated would be an understatement.

Watchmen, written by Alan Moore, penciled and lettered by Dave Gibbons, and colored by John Higgins, was a twelve issue, limited series. Like Miller's *The Dark Knight Returns* (published the same year), the text criticized the myth of the superhero through a cynical, revisionist narrative based upon Golden Age heroes. Moore and Gibbons's title is now considered a classic of the comic book form. The text was named one of the hundred greatest novels of the twentieth century by *Time* magazine in 2005 and ranked thirteenth on a listing of the fifty best novels of the past twenty-five years published by *Entertainment Weekly* in 2008. Moreover, it was one of the first comic titles to cross-over to a larger audience. As comic historian Roger Sabin writes, "Unprecedentedly for direct sales comics, they [*Watchmen* and *Dark Knight Returns*] received a great deal of critical attention outside fandom, and were even reviewed seriously in broadsheet papers."[27]

To give the reader a sense of how the readership of comic books has shifted over the past decades, the debut issue of *Watchmen* shipped in May of 1986 and sold 34,100 copies through the direct market distributor Capital City (there were several distributors at the time, so this number is only a small piece in a larger, unknowable puzzle) ranking fifth in their list of shipped monthly titles.[28] It is also significant that *Watchmen* sold "at a price point twice the going rate for the best-selling comics of the day: $1.50."[29] Moreover, the title did not feature franchise characters like Batman or Spider-Man. Despite these two significant variables, the title was a moderate success. Essentially, the economic success of *Watchmen* has gradually increased over the years due to its cultural status as one of the pioneering titles of a new age of comics. It was solidified when the individual issues were collected and published as a graphic novel available in both paperback and hardcover editions.

To approach this briefly from an anecdotal perspective, when *Watchmen* was presented at 2008 San Diego Comic-Con panel, the line to get into Hall H spiraled around the site. Tightly weaving its way through a grassy space the size of a football field, the line ended up crossing the street, and went one block past the facilities. Given the capacity of the hall, there were roughly 6,500 people in line with hundreds, if not thousands, turned away. As Snyder reiterated to fans, "We loved the book and we loved the images, and we really cared to make them come to life as much as we could, and make it respect-ful."[30] As Snyder's co-producer and wife, Deborah, also noted, "We feel a *great responsibility* [when it comes to the film's treatment of the book]."[31] Snyder attempted to put fan fears to rest in multiple ways. He claimed to be using the graphic novel as a storyboard and he attempted to earn the blessing of the book's anti-Hollywood scribe, Alan Moore. He also enlisted Dave Gibbons to serve as an advisor and to promote the film.[32] Moreover, Gibbons not only provided his endorsement of the film publicly ("[the screenplay was] as close as I could imagine anyone getting to [the book].") but "signed" the film's mise-en-scène.[33] The artist's trademark "G" is represented as a piece of graffiti on the wall's of the film's version of New York City.

One of Snyder's goals in achieving a favorable fan response was not only to attempt to adapt nearly every narrative event onto the screen (the most heated topic of contention was the film's altered ending which, while the-matically similar to the book, was dramatically revised) but to use the graphic novel as a set of storyboards. Similar to his approach on *300*, Snyder wanted to remediate Moore and Gibbons's compositions spatiotemporally.[34] As noted at the beginning of this chapter, describing the remediation of the spatiotem-poral aspect of the comic is difficult because so much of it, specifically with regard to time, is contingent on the practices of the reader. To put this into perspective, an individual's reading habits can vary from reading to reading. On the first encounter, our imaginary reader may read *Watchmen* quickly, carried along by the momentum of the mystery plot and the quest for resolution. The second time around, despite being familiar with the plot, the reader may take longer. Our imaginary reader may begin to pay increased attention to the book's visual motifs and how they intersect with the content (the fifth issue, entitled "Fearful Symmetry," exhibits a sprawling symmetrical multiframe layout structure). Essentially, the general reading habits of a comic book reader may follow this trajectory: the first reading is defined by narrative comprehension while subsequent readings allow for greater consideration of how style interacts with content.

Time in the comic is further complicated by the fact that, unlike cinema and its predecessor the photograph, the individual frame of the comic does not capture a single moment in time. As theorist Scott McCloud usefully describes comics in contrast to film, comics define time spatially and "The problem is there's no conversion chart!"[35] Unlike the cinematic frame, the comic panel does not capture a fraction of a second. The duration of the actions depicted in a comic panel is vague and subject to ellipsis. Yet to say that comic time is a fluid vector and unquantifiable is not to say that it cannot be focused by the writer/artist. For theorist Thierry Groensteen, the sequential panels of the comic perform what he describes as "the rhythmic function." As Groensteen describes, comics obey "a rhythm that is imposed on it by the succession of frames—a basic heartbeat that, as is seen in music, can be developed, nuanced, and recovered by more elaborate rhythmic effects stressed by other 'instruments' (parameters), like those of the distribution of the word balloons, the opposition of colors, or even the play of the graphical forms."[36] Groensteen, never one to make generalizations, is reluctant to go as far as McCloud with regard to the conversion chart between the dimensions of the panel and the length of time they represent. Groensteen writes that "All normative propositions do not do justice to the diversity of the expressive techniques and to the aesthetic of the authors."[37] However, a common belief is that larger frames correspond to a longer encapsulation of time.

Yet and this is perhaps a prime case against making such a generalization, the connection between panel size and time is not quite so simple in *Watchmen*. A worthy case study is the book's opening sequence, which chronicles a pair of police officers investigating the death of a former costumed hero, the Comedian. The sequence, told over the course of eight pages, is rendered in nearly identical multiframes. The pages alternate between seven, eight, and nine panel multiframes with the sole exception of the introductory

Figure 4.3. The fluidity of time as expressed by panel size in *Watchmen*.

page ("At Midnight, All the Agents . . . ," the sixth page of the issue). The third multiframe in the sequence, composed of seven panels, intercuts a flashback of the murder attributed to the detectives (Figure 4.3). The first six panels of the page are all roughly the same dimension, whether they cover the duration of the assailant kicking the Comedian (panel one), lifting him off the ground (panel three), picking him up (panel five), or a few lines of dialogue from the detectives (panels two, four, and six). The multiframe is punctuated by the largest panel on the page: the Comedian is tossed out a plate glass window to his death on the pavement below. Yet consider the concept of the correspondence between panel size and the expression of time. Does it take a shorter amount of time for two men to hypothesize how the Comedian went through the window than it took to actually throw him out? Does it take the same amount of time for the detectives to discuss the Comedian's identity as it did for his assailant to land a kick? The answer to both questions would be an overwhelming no.

The progression of panel sizes (small to large) in the opening of *Watchmen* does not express increasing periods of time. The layout of the page is not motivated by the expression of time but by the expression of an experience that binds the formal attributes to the narrative information. The final panel is the largest because it expresses the inciting incident to the story, the murder of the Comedian. Significantly, the layout of page three echoes that of the first page. The first multiframe features six identically sized panels, representing a zoom or dolly up the side of the building, and a larger, punctuating, panel at the bottom of the page depicting the two detectives looking out the window. The first page solicits narrative questions from the reader. Why is there blood in the gutter? It appears that a man has jumped out the window of his apartment. The third page answers those questions visually. The man was attacked and thrown out the window. This compositional technique is what Groensteen describes as "braiding," a unique formal property of the comic which prompts the reader to place separate multiframes in dialogue with one another. For Groensteen, the size of the panel may be used to express the duration of time, but that is only one of its many possible functions.

Despite Snyder's rhetoric about making a respectful, faithful, adaptation and his obsessive attention to doing so, his remediation of time in the film's opening sequence loses Moore and Gibbons's visual braiding. The opening of the film features a similar shot to the comic (a zoom out of the Comedian's smiley face pin). However, the final spatial location of the zoom does not reveal the two detectives looking out the broken window. Rather, we see the Comedian tending to a fuming teakettle and watching television, a few moments before being attacked. Moreover, Snyder abandons the flashback cross-cutting. He focuses on the murder in the first sequence, segues into a credit sequence, and then revisits the scene of the crime from the detectives' point-of-view. Finally, his interpretation of the Comedian's murder is temporally elongated. Occupying only ten frames in the book, the murder takes place over the course of five minutes in the film. To quantify this spatiotemporally, the sequence takes up less than 0.38 percent of the comic's approximately 2,688 panels. In the film, the sequence takes up 1.5 percent of the running length, an increase of nearly four times.

Despite this difference in narrative construction and emphasis, Snyder does capture the phenomenologically subjective temporal experience of reading a comic book via his manipulation of cinematic time. He does this by photographing the fight at varying shutter speeds. Aside from "real-time" shots (24 frames a second), the fight occasionally takes on a slow, poetic quality, reminiscent of Sam Peckinpah's innovative style. For instance, when the Comedian is thrown across the room, it takes nearly nine seconds for his body to make the voyage. At other times, Snyder decreases the shutter speed, making a knife fight appear as if it is taking place at superhuman speed (a point of frustration for many of the book's fans, as the Comedian and his assailant do not possess any superpowers). Finally, there are individual shots that include the representation of the act of varying the shutter speed. This technique, called "speed ramping," appears when a vicious punch landed on the Comedian's face begins in slow motion and progressively speeds up. One such shot, a reproduction of the final panel on page three, is the longest of the sequence (16 seconds). Thus, while the action contained may be one of the shortest in the sequence (a man falling a few dozen stories to his death), both the comic and the film give the action an added formal emphasis due to its narrative significance.

Snyder and Warner Bros. hoped that, through stylistic remediation and the various other actions already elaborated upon here, catering to fans of the novel would eventually translate into a greater, broader, awareness of the property. The *New York Times* reported that early reaction to the film's trailer encouraged the printing of an additional nine hundred thousand copies of the graphic novel.[38] However, the film failed to replicate the economic success of *300*. Carrying a production budget of $130 million and undisclosed print and advertising costs, the film grossed $185 million worldwide.[39] The underwhelming performance of the film can be partially attributed to its status as an R-rated superhero film and its three-hour running time. To make matters worse, the film's worldwide totals were compromised by a lawsuit. Twentieth Century Fox, who previously licensed the rights, sued Warner Bros., Paramount, and the film's other production companies and was awarded both an upfront payment (rumored to be $5–10 million) and a percentage of the film's worldwide gross (rumored to be between 5 and 8.5 percent, in addition to any grosses from sequels or spin-offs).[40] Critical reaction, like that to *300* two years earlier, was mixed. The mixed reception was compounded by fans, who had turned against the adaptation (the film carried an exit poll score of a "B").[41]

One anonymous Warner Bros. marketing executive proposed a theory as to why the film failed:

> Alan Moore always said that *Watchmen* the graphic novel couldn't be made into a movie. So, at the end of the day, Zack Snyder's slavish attention to detail in making this a literal translation is what ultimately doomed the film. He cared more about the appeasement of the fanboys than [about] a cohesive, coherent movie meant for everyone.[42]

Thus, just like *Hulk*, the style of a "literal translation" was scapegoated by the industry. However, stronger justifications for the film's failure can be made. First, consider the type of narrative *Watchmen* weaves: a deconstruction of the superhero myth. Arguably, one of the reasons why the comic resonated with readers in 1986 was because the medium had nearly fifty years of genre texts to deconstruct. In contrast, the superhero movie genre was still—to borrow from Thomas Schatz's generic categorizations—in its classical stage. Perhaps the uninitiated audience (those unfamiliar with the book and the history of American comics) were not quite ready for such a pessimistic portrayal of superheroes as being profoundly psychologically damaged. Essentially, the studio over-budgeted a niche-audience film.

While the graphic novel sold nearly a million copies in 2008, it sold only a hundred thousand the year before. While these numbers are an estimate, if the title sold a hundred thousand copies a year from 1986 to 2007 (2.1 million) and an additional million copies in 2008, that means only 3.1 million people were well-versed in the world of the property. Compare that level of awareness with J. K. Rowling's book *Harry Potter and the Half-Blood Prince* (2005), which sold nine million copies in its first twenty-four hours of release.[43] The results stemming from that saturated level of visibility are far from surprising. The film based on Rowling's book, budgeted at $250 million, became the second highest grossing film of 2009 with $933 million worldwide. In contrast, *Watchmen* failed to crack the top twenty-five when it came to worldwide box office grosses. Stylistic remediation may be a method of appeasing a property's fan base and it can occasionally encourage wider-awareness (*300*, *Sin City*). However, the costs, many of which are tied to CGI, must be kept in perspective, even when the film comes from a financially established multimedia conglomerate that wishes to capitalize upon the property synergistically.

Textual Remediation in *American Splendor* (2003)

In contrast with the previous case studies presented here, Shari Springer Berman and Robert Pulcini's *American Splendor* (2003), based on Harvey Pekar's comics (1976–2008), stands out. While the films of the previous three case studies were budgeted at an average of $110 million each and were released on thousands of domestic screens in their first week of release, *Splendor* had an unconfirmed budget of $2 million and was released to just six theaters (272 theaters during its widest release). Directed by two documentarians, produced by Good Machine (which, in 2002, had recently merged with USA Films at Vivendi SA to form Focus Features), and distributed by HBO Films and Fine Line Features (both part of the Time Warner conglomerate at the time) after winning the 2003 Sundance Film Festival's Grand Jury Prize, *Splendor* is an independent film. In the post-classical era of Hollywood that is often defined by two modes of filmmaking, the art house indie and the blockbuster, *Splendor* is one of the few films based on a comic book to be classified as the former (*Ghost World* would be another notable example).

Like the film, the *American Splendor* comics are, to return to Rogers's binary, an artisan production. Throughout its thirty-two year run, the title went through three publishers. The series was initially self-published before moving to Dark Horse Comics. Significantly, after the success of the film, the title ended up at Vertigo, an imprint at DC Comics in 2006. Moreover, given Pekar's self-professed inability to draw, the title went through a long roster of artists including Robert Crumb, Joe Sacco, Eddie Campbell, and Gilbert Hernandez. According to Pekar, he sold "very few comic books and lost money at it."[44] Looking at the title's sales performance from 1997 to 2008, the title averaged roughly 4,800 copies a month. Earning a Diamond Comic Distributor ranking of 287 (4,086 copies at $2.95 an issue) in 1997, the series experienced a slight increase (perhaps due to the film) and ended up ranking 270 (5,397 copies at $2.99) in 2008.[45]

One might ask that if the production context of *Splendor* is so radically different from the other titles analyzed here, why include it in this study? First, the film is one of the few to remediate the relationship between text and image of the comic, thus its inclusion is justified from a stylistic criteria. Secondly, as will be established, the production companies behind independent films like *American Splendor* and *Sin City* (2005) are also concerned with appeasing a

Figure 4.4. The thought balloon freeze frame in *American Splendor* (2003).

Figure 4.5. The thought balloon freeze frame in *American Splendor* (2003).

Figure 4.6. The animated thought balloon in *American Splendor* (2003).

Figure 4.7. The transition for balloon to the frame in *American Splendor* (2003).

Figure 4.8. Giamatti's Pekar vs. Animated Pekar in *American Splendor* (2003).

property's fan base, which stylistic remediation is very much a manifestation of. As the filmmakers note in the production notes for the film, "We really saw this as an adaptation of the comic books. . . . We tried to find a vehicle that was as rebellious as the way Harvey puts his comics together. . . . It wasn't random; we owed it to *American Splendor* to work like that."[46] Essentially, it is necessary to include *Splendor* both from a stylistic standpoint (rounding out the taxonomy of stylistic remediation) and from an industrial standpoint (to establish that stylistic remediation appears in both contemporary modes of filmmaking).

The role of text in the definition of comics is subject to passionate debate in comic studies. For historian David Kunzle, the definition of a comic strip includes "a preponderance of image over text."[47] Likewise, historian Bill Black-beard notes in his definition that comics regularly feature enclosed "ballooned

Figure 4.9. Pekar and Crumb's "Standing Behind Old Jewish Ladies . . ." (1986).

dialogue or its equivalent and generally minimal narrative text."[48] Theorist David Carrier goes one step further, asserting that the defining characteristic of modern comics is the speech balloon. As Carrier writes, "The speech balloon is a defining element of the comic because it establishes a word/image unity that distinguishes comics from pictures illustrating a text."[49] On the other hand, for theorist Thierry Groensteen, the central element of comics is "iconic solidarity" or "interdependent images that, participating in a series, present the double characteristic of being separated."[50] Essentially, Groensteen argues that the classical view that the text and the image are equal in narrative status is no longer the case and that the sequential image does not necessarily need "any verbal help."[51]

Groensteen's proposal that comics are defined stylistically by the presentation of sequential images juxtaposed in space is a sentiment largely shared by Scott McCloud. However, the use of text is an artistic norm utilized by the bulk of practitioners. Looking across a bookshelf of graphic novels and comic book trade paperbacks, it is difficult to find texts that feature more than a handful of pages with text-less panels. Even the largely "silent" tenth chapter of Alan Moore and Eddie Campbell's *From Hell* (1999), "The Best of All Tailors," features text on seventeen of its thirty-four pages. Alas, just like dialogue in film, text may not be one of the medium's defining elements. However, it is the pragmatic norm.

Berman and Pulcini's film is one of the richest examples of the stylistic remediation of comics into film. As Craig Hight writes in his essay "*American Splendor*: Translating Comic Autobiography into Drama-Documentary," the film is "a hybrid of drama-documentary combining conventional aspects of this form with elements of the graphic style of comic books."[52] Hight argues that the film's focus on mundane vignettes matches the structure of Pekar's original books. Furthermore, the film commonly incorporates panels from the books at transitional moments, a notable example being the graphically inspired credit sequence. Moreover, Hight writes that the film, like Pekar's comic, represents the author via differing modes. While Pekar himself appears in the film via a set of interviews (some archival, some produced for the film), he is represented in the reenactment sequences by Paul Giamatti while Donal Logue portrays the author (or, to be more specific, he portrays Giamatti portrayal of Pekar) in a stage play based on the comic. Finally, the writer is represented "within graphic and animation sequences derived from . . . the comic."[53]

For this case study, we will be focusing our analysis on two elements: the film's use of thought balloons and captions. With regard to the filmmakers' use of thought balloons, one scene is particularly illustrative: the "Standing Behind

Old Jewish Ladies in Supermarket Lines" scene. Adapted from an issue with art by Robert Crumb, the scene prompts the film's representation of Pekar to venture into writing comic books. As he suffers in line behind the old woman who happens to be "penny-wise," Pekar's quick stop at the grocery turns into an episode out of Homer's *The Odyssey*. Next to his head, a thought balloon forms (thought balloons are different from dialogue balloons insofar as they normally have a cloud-like texture, do not have the point near the character's mouth, and are placed near the head instead of the mouth). The balloon goes from being filled with text to manifesting an animated Pekar that provides a scathing critique of his social situation. Finally, the animated Pekar breaks out of the balloon via a two-step process that puts his imaginary form next to Pekar's stranded body. In order to better illustrate the scene under analysis, screenshots have been provided for the sake of clarity (Figures 4.4–4.8).

Now, compare and contrast the film sequence (Figures 4.4–4.8) with the actual Pekar and Crumb story below (Figure 4.9). The Pekar strip, unlike the film, involves a flashback device. In panel one, Pekar's character addresses the reader personally, beginning his story with a proclamation: "Man, I really hate t'shop for groceries . . . Especially when the store is crowded!"[54] These panels, differentiated from the supermarket sequences graphically by the spotlight effect around Pekar, turn him into an active character. He is speaking to us emotionally. Significantly, he is also controlling the story. In contrast, the supermarket sequences feature a largely "silent" Pekar. He whistles, quietly suffering in line, cursing when he returns to the supermarket. Significantly, the flashback is not relayed through thought balloons but through captions (see panels two, three, and four of Figure 4.9).

The film weaves the two separate spaces (Pekar telling the story and Pekar at the market) of the original story into the one scene. Instead of captions, Berman and Pulcini go through a range of representational strategies to remediate the unique textual experience of the comic. First, the filmmakers provide us with freeze frames and thought balloons. In contrast to the comic, Pekar's suffering in line his anger is captured within the same diegetic space. Eventually, the freeze framed thought balloons (Figures 4.4–4.5) give way to an animated thought balloon that becomes filled with an incensed Pekar (Figure 4.6). Then, his repressed emotions propel him into a neighboring frame (4.7) and, ultimately, into the same space as Giamatti's Pekar (4.8).

Berman and Pulcini's representational evolution of Pekar's thoughts is unique in how they mobilize film language to capture both the tone of the writing and the experience of reading a comic. While the sequence (animated by John Kuramoto and Gary Leib) does not graphically remediate Crumb's dirtier portrayal of Pekar, the text in the first two thought balloons and the dialogue that the animated Pekar delivers is abridged from the original comic. Not only do his observations remain intact, but Pekar's tendency to clip the endings off of words does so as well.[55] More significant to this analysis, Berman and Pulcini use the freeze frame to render the constant temporality of film into the reader defined temporality of a comic. We must pause to digest both the composition (which has also been digitally altered to carry the texture of newsprint) and Pekar's thought bubble. Significantly, instead of transposing the text into voice over narration, the filmmakers prompt us to acknowledge the representational function of the thought balloon.

Yet the role of Berman and Pulcini's remediation evolves as the sequence segues into its live-action/animation hybrid. Balloons in comics, according to Carrier once again, are unique insofar as they "bridge the word/image gap" because they are words presented within (and sometimes as) pictures.[56] The nature of this presentation is that balloons, unlike other elements depicted in the frame graphically such as the mise-en-scène, are only "visible" to the reader, not the characters inhabiting the frame. The surrounding characters sharing the frame may hear dialogue or may consider what the character producing a thought balloon is thinking about, but they are not aware of the stylistic device, as characters in a film are oblivious to voice-over narration. For Carrier, this produces a paradox in the image. In the schema of "reading" a comic, we often find ourselves grappling with the elements separately (the image, the text of the balloon, and the shape of the balloon) before we—pun intended—put them in dialogue with one another. However, this process does not mean that the form is completely neutral from a graphical standpoint, as its stylistic qualities can denote tone or its use.

Berman and Pulcini's evolving use of the balloon (from containing text to animation) captures this dynamic before ultimately moving beyond it. Once the sequence makes the transition from text to animation, the balloon no longer acts as the bridge between text and image but as a visual container for the film's voice-over, unifying the narrational elements. Moreover, once animated Pekar breaks out of the container and the balloon disappears, the traditional role of the balloon as being a non-diegetic element of the physical mise-en-scène becomes challenged. Animated Pekar physically confronts Giamatti's Pekar (Figure 4.8), forcing him to acknowledge both the thoughts being expressed by both his animated id and the formerly "invisible" element of the balloon as well. Essentially, the filmmakers initially engage with the passive qualities of the balloon in the freeze frames and text of their textual remediation. However, perhaps realizing that such a faithful remediation is not exactly cinematic, they shift towards an aggressive animation, producing a more dynamic form of interaction between the two media.

Furthermore, thought balloons are not the only textual form that Berman and Pulcini remediate in the film. Throughout the film, beginning with a dazzling credits sequence that takes the form of a multiframe with each panel presenting a new title card (some animated, some live-action, some photographs of the film's actual subjects), the filmmakers utilize the caption to inform the viewer of the time and the setting. For instance, one caption is superimposed on an establishing shot and reads "Meanwhile in Delaware." While these captions match the presentation Pekar's own, taking the form of a square box that hugs a boundary of the frame (normally the upper portion), they differ significantly in their contribution to the narrative. Specifically, as Groensteen writes, the caption is "equivalent to the *voiceover*, encloses a form of speech, that of the explicit narrator (who can be the principal narrator or the delegated narrator, intra- or extra-diegetic, etc.)."[57]

In Pekar's work, such as the "Standing Behind Old Jewish Ladies in Supermarket Lines," the caption is often an extension of his explicit narration. For instance, in "Standing Behind . . . ," the captions serve as the bridge between the present tense panels of Pekar addressing us and the flashback panels depicting his interactions at the supermarket. Essentially, the captions of Pekar's work are subjective and tied to the writer (both the character and the writer) as narrator. They serve, as Groensteen notes, as the equivalent to the voiceover. The captions of the film, however, are not subjective, as they are not attributed to any of the presented versions of Pekar. They do not belong to a diegetic narrator; they simply serve as the filmic equivalent of the captions used in most fiction films, presenting objective information that helps the viewer situate him or herself with regard to the time and place of the story. Essentially, Berman and Pulcini are—like the other filmmakers explored here—remediating a stylistic comic book device while adjusting its function towards cinematic norms. Stylistic remediation is again the production of formal compromise between the two media forms and, in these cases, the formal vocabulary of remediating medium—film—dominates.

Berman and Pulcini's film was incredibly successful by independent standards. As mentioned before, the film carried an unconfirmed budget of approximately $2 million and went on to gross nearly $8 million worldwide. Yet according to HBO Films President Colin Callender, who purchased the distribution rights, their distribution focus did not initially involve the theatrical market. Instead, the film was purchased as content for HBO's premium cable network.[58] After the festival prizes and positive word of mouth rolled in following the Sundance Film Festival, HBO gave the film a modest theatrical release with the intent of raising awareness. Not only were audiences and critics pleased with the film (Ebert named the film his third favorite film of 2003 and the film was nominated for the Best Adapted Screenplay Oscar) but so were the Pekars. According to an interview with Harvey's wife Joyce Brabner, the most important benefit of the whole experience was that "it gives Harvey an opportunity to do more work."[59] When Pekar was asked what he thought about the film, he gave a characteristically short response: "I think the film did a good job at capturing the spirit of my work."[60]

With Great Investment Comes (Potentially) Great Return

Given the breadth of time (1979–2009) and analysis (ranging from stylistic, industrial, and technological) covered in the previous chapters, it is worth recapitulating the conclusions that have already been substantiated. First, allow us to reconsider the role that horizontal integration and multimedia conglomerates have played in the process of stylistic remediation. As noted above in the analysis of *American Splendor,* the average budget of the films analyzed in the previous two chapters was roughly $110 million (not including print and advertising costs). According to the film industry website *The Numbers,* the average production budget on most contemporary films is $65 million.[61] As analyzed here, particularly in the cases of *Superman* (1978), *Dick Tracy* (1990), *Hulk* (2003), and *Watchmen* (2009), there appears to be a direct correlation between rising production budgets and the extensive use of physical and computer generated special effects. In the case of *Hulk,* Universal went as far to allot an additional $1.5 million to allow director Ang Lee to experiment with stylistic remediation. Obviously, multimedia conglomerates occupy a better position when it comes to capitalizing upon these properties because they often own them outright and because they have a diverse network of assets that, in turn, provides capital and minimizes financial risk.

To quantify this, a comparison between the number of comic book films released prior to 1989, the year the merger between Time Inc. and Warner Communications was announced, and after is useful. According to a keyword search for "based on comic books" on the *Internet Movie Database,* 154 titles were released prior to 1989 while 472 have been released since (this includes television shows and international productions, so it is not an exact number but it still illustrates the point).[62] The reason for this rise is obvious by now. Media conglomerates can capitalize upon the added visibility and cultural capital of comic books and their adaptations both directly and indirectly (through licensing rights). Returning back to the case of *Batman,* film industry scholar Douglas Gomery writes:

> There were more than 100 licensees for *Batman* products for 300 different items.... About a quarter of *Batman*'s 100-plus licenses were newly issued and covered goods specifically based on the movie, as opposed to the comic character.... The winner in the merchandising boom was clearly Warners, which in addition to reaping prodigious publicity benefits received a percentage of merchandising revenues.[63]

We also saw this trend with *Watchmen*, as DC Comics, a subsidiary of Time-Warner Communications, sold an additional one million copies of the graphic novel when the film was announced. Essentially, to provide a variation upon the Spider-Man maxim "With great power comes great responsibility," with great investment comes the potential for great return.

Now, the question may be raised as to the industrial logic behind stylistic remediation. Why would studios, in light of the success of Sam Raimi's *Spider-Man* films and Christopher Nolan's *Batman* films, attempt to grapple with the particular formal attributes of the original source material when they can just focus on story? First, most comic book fans, the main demographic for films based on comics, are just as interested in the art of the comic as they are in the story. This is particularly evident at San Diego Comic-Con, as fans flood "Artist's Alley" for both autographs and original sketches from their favorite artists. The sentiment from filmmakers practicing stylistic remediation acknowledges this interest, as evident in Zack Snyder and Warner Bros.' collaboration with Dave Gibbons in the production and marketing of *Watchmen*. To produce a comic book film without dealing with its unique formal devices is like adapting a musical and neglecting to include the music; it may work but it also fails to realize what is fully unique about the original form.

Yet while Twentieth Century Fox's Chief Marketing Officer John Hegeman continually pushes the philosophy of appeasing the core demographic, we have seen that, particularly in the case of blockbuster budgeted films, this fan service does not necessarily work out economically. *Dick Tracy*, *Hulk*, and *Watchmen* were all disappointments for their studios, and the reason for this is significant: comic book readers make up but a small percentage of the audience. They may be a knowledgeable, vocal, and visible demographic, but they are also in the minority. As Neil Rae and Jonathan Gray write, "While comic book adaptations such as *Spider-Man* and *X-Men* have grossed up to $820 million, and attracted millions of viewers worldwide, it is unusual for the global sales of the most popular American superhero comic books to rise above 150,000."[64] The Hollywood studios seem to be finally acknowledging this harsh reality, as costly failures (such as *Scott Pilgrim vs. the World*) have prompted a reevaluation of the genre.

Finally, let us consider the role of technology in the remediation of comic book style. Specifically, has it enabled a Manovichian shift in the language of cinema? Given the role that CGI compositing software has played in many of these films, most notably *Hulk* and *300,* stylistic remediation is very much bound to advances in graphics technology. However, despite a filmmaker's desire to remediate comic book form within the confines of cinema—even a cinema freed by relative economic restraint and representational constraint—the multiframe of *Hulk* owes more to the Classical Hollywood style than it does to either Manovich's definition of digital cinema or to its source material.

PART

REMEDIATION BEYOND COMIC ADAPTATIONS

THREE

CHAPTER 5

Derived from Comic Strip Graphics: Remediation beyond Comic Book Adaptations in *The Matrix* (1999), *The Good, the Bad, and the Ugly* (1966), and *The Dark Tower: The Gunslinger Born* (2007)

Introduction: Broadening the Scope

In the study of the stylistic remediation between comics and cinema, film adaptations of comic books are a logical place to begin the conversation. They provide case studies with a one-to-one formal correspondence. We are able to compare an artist's style with a filmmaker's interpretation of the ontological differences between film and comics. This interpretation involves decisions regarding representational mode, the spatiotemporal correspondences between the comic book panel and the cinematic frame, and the transposition of the word/image binary. Yet an analysis of stylistic remediation that limits its boundaries to the subcategory of adaptations misses the larger picture. As this chapter focusing on case studies beyond adaptation will argue, specifically through an analysis of "bullet time" in *The Matrix* (1999) and a comparison of the graphic and spatial presentations in *The Good, the Bad, and the Ugly* (1966) and *The Dark Tower: The Gunslinger Born* (2007), the integration of stylistic attributes from one medium into another has significant cultural and industrial implications.

Action Lines Become Bullet Time in *The Matrix* (1999)

Lilly and Lana Wachowski's film *The Matrix* has become one of the defining film texts of Generations X and Y. Spawning two film sequels, toys, video

115

games, comics, and an anime release, the immense economic and cultural popularity of the science fiction film almost immediately invited comparisons to George Lucas's *Star Wars Episode IV: A New Hope* (1977). As science fiction author David Gerrold writes in an introduction to one of the many academic volumes published in its wake, "*The Matrix* hit the film-going public by surprise, much like *Star Wars* a generation earlier, and for many of the same reasons. It had a breathless pace, astonishing eye-candy, a sense of mythic adventure, and an acid-tinged sensibility."[1] Similarly, Bob Rehak notes:

> Industrially, bullet time became a celebrity in its own right from 1999 to about
> 2003, organizing commercial, critical and technical discourses around *The
> Matrix*.... As shorthand for the visual excitement of its parent text, it anchored a
> blockbuster advertising campaign.... Seemingly overnight, its distinctive brand
> of slow motion spread to other movies, making guest appearances in Shakespear-
> ean tragedy ... a high-concept television remake ... a caper film ... a teenybopper
> SF ... and a cop/buddy film.[2]

Thus, the film's "eye-candy"—specifically the sequences featuring the film's heroes Neo (Keanu Reeves), Trinity (Carrie-Anne Moss), and Morpheus (Laurence Fishburne) performing the impossible by gracefully dodging bullets in slow-motion (bullet time sequences)—became one of the film's defining characteristics both for spectators and for the Warner Bros. marketing department.

Before delving into an analysis of the film's bullet time sequences in the context of the comic book stylistic convention of action lines, it is essential to note the tangled web of stylistic remediations that rest at the foundation of this visual technique. First, bullet time evolved from less-refined manifestations in music videos and advertisements throughout the 1980s and 1990s. Secondly, as Joshua Clover argues in his monograph on the film, the roots of the technique can be found in the martial arts and shooter video game genres. As Clover writes, "We recognise it as an explicit immersion effect. Shot from our point of view, the optical perspective swoops through a three-dimensional space, fully-rendered, 360 degrees, without ever revealing the apparatus of filmmaking; we could be inside the synthworld of *Zelda*, except that the graphics are incomparably higher resolution."[3] Finally, as visual effects supervisor John Gaeta explains the foundations behind the aesthetic, the Wachowskis were inspired by "literary SF, Japanese *manga* and *anime*, as well as kung-fu movies whose signature use of slow-motion, wire-based martial-arts."[4] Essentially, bullet time is the stylistic by-product of a ongoing, dialogical process of remediation.

Long before Gaeta and his visual effects crews were assigned the task of finding a technologically feasible way of capturing bullet time, the Wachowskis decided to have the entire film storyboarded in order to better explain the style they had in mind for the action sequences. "No one really understood the level of the action or the level of detail that we wanted in the action sequences," Lilly Wachowski notes in a rare interview in the documentary *The Matrix Revisited* (2001). Her sister Lana adds, "[The inspiration came from] comics and graphic type storytelling where you can freeze a moment, make an image sort of sustain, you can't really do that in a film."[5] Having started their careers as writers for the comic book title *Ectokid* (1993–1994), the Wachowskis approached their artistic partner on the title, penciller Steve Skroce, to aid them in visualizing bullet time. The duo also hired *Hard Boiled* artist Geof Darrow as a conceptual designer, tasked with designing the mechanical design of the ships and technology in the film. Skroce and Darrow allegedly storyboarded the entire first film and up to 80 percent of the film's sequels, *The Matrix Reloaded* (2003) and *The Matrix Revolutions* (2003).[6]

From Skroce and Darrow's meticulously designed storyboards and the Wachowskis' pastiche of inspirations, Gaeta created a bullet time rig that featured a combination of over one hundred still cameras and a handful of motion picture cameras. The cameras were organized in a circular fashion (within a green screen environment) that could easily be reshaped, depending on the sequence being choreographed. Essentially, the rig can be considered a descendant of Eadweard Muybridge's motion photography system taken to the extreme. As Gaeta states in *The Matrix Revisited*, "Bullet time was really the technical hurdle.... [The Wachowskis] showed their [story]boards [to a few effects houses]. Each time they [the Wachowskis] had done that, they [the effects houses] tended to have a similar reaction. Faces turned white [because of the complexity of the special effects needed]." With footage captured by the bullet time rig in hand, the filmmakers turned to Manex Visual Effects to refine the style in post-production. The result of the collaboration, both conceptually and technologically, is a hybrid of the graphic remediation of comic book's articulation of movement (via the stylistic device of action lines) and cinema's inherent ability to capture movement (via the progression of time).

According to Scott McCloud, comics—a medium constructed out of frozen, sequential images—have "the problem of showing motion in a static medium. How do you show this aspect of time in an art where time stands still?"[7] While motion can be deduced by the reader via the process of closure, such a representation of motion is problematic from a pragmatic standpoint. Comics are limited with regard to the space of the page and the space of the

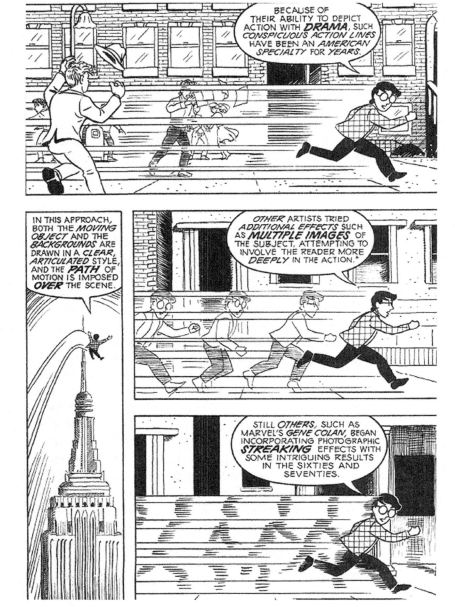

Figure 5.1. McCloud's discussion of action lines in practice.

book. If an artist relied only upon the process of closure to depict motion, the comic would be structured like a Muybridge motion study. Essentially, the spatial real estate offered by the page would be squandered on capturing subtle temporal transitions. Moreover, as McCloud also notes, such a representation of action would lack dynamism. Given the medium's reliance on the superhero genre, viewing action sequences represented by split-second progressions in time would become both tedious and boring to the reader (not that it cannot be used as an effective contrast). The solution to this limitation are action lines and their decedents such as the use of multiple images and photographic streaking, which became an "American specialty" of representing motion in a static image (Figure 5.1).[8]

As exemplified by the figure, motion lines (specifically exemplified by panels one and two) are a form of visual-metaphor. Unable to represent the temporal progression of movement and actions physically, comics represent such actions through the abstracted iconography of the lines. Motion lines suggest both a momentum and a trajectory of the force being represented. Moveover, the comic book artist can also underline the function of the lines with text or, in the case of the above example, other aspects of the panel's mise-en-scène. For instance, in the first panel of Figure 5.1, the thick parallel lines projected by McCloud's representation of himself are paired with three other notable aspects of the setting. First, the lines intersect with McCloud's form, which is posed as if he is running towards the end of the panel's depiction of space on the right side. Secondly, his speed is suggested by the ferocity of the action lines; at their furthest point away from McCloud, we are able to see the space "behind" them (the man with the papers is a clear example of this). However, as the lines converge closer to the author's running form, the space behind him becomes a void, unknown to us because the speed of his avatar is so intense. Finally, the two other men in the panel—the man with the hat and the man with the papers—are affected by McCloud's mad dash; both men lose their belongings due to the blast of air caused by the running author.

The stylistic devices of multiple images and streaking function similarly. In panel three, McCloud shows us multiple images, emphasized by the use of motion lines. The images spell out the previous locations of his figure (represented by the fainter, less detailed drawings), again voiding the background closer to the moving object. The similarities to Muybridge's motion studies are obvious: McCloud's drawings provide temporally short encapsulations of sequential movements (albeit within the space of one panel). Streaking, as McCloud notes in his exemplary final panel, is more photographic in nature. The artist does not render himself in detail. We are only given a haze of abstracted movement representing his previous position.

Figure 5.2. Streaking and multiple images as motion in *The Matrix*.

The special effect technique of bullet time draws upon all three methods of depicting motion lines. One of the film's most noteworthy examples occurs when Neo—who has recently discovered that the space of the film's matrix is a simulation that can be spatially and temporally manipulated at his will—is drawn into a gun fight with the film's sinister agents on the roof of an office building. Neo begins unloading his pistols on one of the agents, whose supernaturally fast movements are rendered via a combination of streaking and multiple images (Figure 5.2). Initially, the use of streaking and multiple images causes us to question the temporality of what we are seeing. Is the agent *really* moving that quickly? Or, due to the shot's status as a point-of-view shot taken from Neo's perspective, is the movement subjectively filtered?

When Neo is fired upon, the questions the first shot poses are answered. Bullet time is inverted and the viewer experiences time slowly. The fluid temporality of the matrix is the product of its manipulation by the agent and Neo. The bullets, moving at their proper velocity, mark the air around him through the motion line defined ripples (Figure 5.3).

Despite their reliance on motion lines, both shots also exhibit the hybridized nature of stylistic remediation. The first shot, a static shot taken from Neo's point of view, draws its inspiration from the static framing of the motion studies and the comic book. However, the progression of time—despite the agent's manipulation—is represented as passing before us (both Neo and the viewer) at twenty-four frames a second. Essentially, streaking

Figure 5.3. Bullet trajectories marked by motion lines in *The Matrix*.

and multiple images—unlike a comic—are not the only means of represent-ing action. The Wachowskis use them as an amplification technique. Then, the filmmakers formally contrast the shot exemplified in Figure 5.2 with the shot of Neo engaging in the same behavior (moving faster than the bullets). In Figure 5.3, the camera rotates in a circular motion around the character as he acrobatically dodges the bullets in a ten-second shot. Rather than being experienced at a natural frame rate, time is slowed while the space is simul-taneously dissected. Essentially, the second shot is the dynamic inverse of the first. We are presented with a utilization of comic book style that has been modified to fit the technologically evolving cinematic apparatus.

For comic theorist Robert C. Harvey, filmmaking that manipulates the essence of the medium in the service of remediating comics is a violation of film's ontological nature. In his discussion of how the formal attributes of film and comics differ, Harvey discusses the depiction of unnatural motion using speed lines in Will Eisner's *The Spirit* (1940–1952). Harvey subsequently asks, "Could film do as much? In slow motion, perhaps? Not likely. The cam-era would slow both movements. . . . It could be done on film through the use of special effects. Special effects in film can presumably accomplish anything. But special effects are just that—special; they are not the stuff of ordinary live action committed to celluloid."[9] For Harvey, as with André Bazin and Siegfried Kracauer before him, cinema's inherent ability to capture action and motion (via the automated chemical process of photography) places it at a debt to reality. According to Harvey, it is unnatural for a filmmaker to infringe on those specific properties.

Yet even Bazin noted that silent cinema had realized two oppositional stylistic paths: the tendency of directors to either put their faith in reality or their faith in the image (artifice).[10] For Bazin, the latter tendency disappeared with the advent of sound and the ability to stage in depth, producing "a much higher degree of realism."[11] Yet for most new media scholars, the refinement of special-effects technology has begun to lead to a reevaluation of film style, whether it be in the form of Lev Manovich's "spatial montage" or Garrett Stewart's analysis of the shifting temporal sands of what he describes as "postfilmic cinema" or "digital cinema."[12] For Stewart, "we have watched a filmic medium's original serial imprint yielding to computerized adjustments at every level, from the generation to the editing of projected images. Increasingly, the temporal transit (mechanical) of the image, frame by frame, gives way to its temporal transformation (electronic) within the frame."[13] In other words, digital cinema has given rise to an experience of time that no longer is beholden to the norm of twenty-four frames a second. Cinema has been ontologically redefined by technological shifts in its production, distribution, and exhibition processes.

While Stewart's overall conclusions are somewhat problematic (despite technological evolutions, film prints are still exhibited and both film and digital cameras feature variable shutter speeds), his conclusion that such technologies have given filmmakers the ability to manipulate time more precisely is a fair assessment. While Stewart goes on to tie this tendency in Hollywood filmmaking to the fantastic genres of sci-fi and mystery and analyzes *The Matrix*, he does not directly engage with bullet time.[14] Yet we can supplement his analysis (published in 2007, in the midst of the superhero boom of the 2000s) by noting that the manipulations of time he dissects commonly occur in one sub-genre of sci-fi films: superhero films. Moreover, the change in representation not only owes its manifestation to the software Stewart alludes to (Adobe Premiere and Final Cut Pro) but to comic books as well, as this analysis of bullet time has illustrated.

The Matrix franchise is commonly used as a seminal text in the critical literature of cinema and media studies, most notably by Henry Jenkins, addressing the industrial and narrative phenomenon of "transmedia storytelling." As Jenkins defines the concept, transmedia storytelling involves "stories that unfold across multiple media platforms, with each medium making distinctive contributions to our understanding of the world, a more integrated approach to franchise development than models based on urtexts and ancillary products."[15] As Jenkins describes the franchise specifically:

Its sequel, *The Matrix Reloaded* (2003), opens without a recap and assumes we have almost complete mastery over its complex mythology and ever-expanding cast of secondary characters. It ends abruptly with a promise that all will make sense when we see the third installment, *The Matrix Revolutions* (2003). To truly appreciate what we are watching, we have to do our homework. The filmmakers plant clues that won't make sense until we play the computer game. They draw on back story revealed through a series of animated shorts, which need to be down-loaded off the Web or watched off a separate DVD.[16]

For Jenkins, building off of Ivan Askwith's assertion that *The Matrix* franchise is best described as "synergistic storytelling," transmedia storytelling is a mul-tifaceted phenomenon that intersects with the social (collective intelligence), the technological (the evolution of production and distribution software and hardware), and the aesthetic (world building). Yet the practice is also strongly motivated by economics. As Jenkins quotes Mike Saksa, senior vice president of marketing at Warner Bros., "This [*The Matrix*] truly is Warner Bros.'s syn-ergy. All divisions will benefit from the property. . . . We don't know what the upside is, we just know it's going to be very high."[17]

In retrospect, Saksa's evaluation of the property's potential seems to have been sorely optimistic. The first film, budgeted at $63 million, grossed more than $463 million worldwide. While the economic success of the sequels was strong, they were also criticized upon post mortem for underperforming at the box office.[18] Specifically, *Reloaded*, carrying a production budget of $150 million, grossed $742 million worldwide. *Revolutions*, also budgeted at $150 million, dropped to a $427 million worldwide return. Essentially, *Revolutions* experienced a 43 percent drop in comparison to its direct predecessor and earned less than the original film. In the assessment of both Jenkins and prominent film critics at the time, the economic downturn of the franchise was tied to its ambitious narrative construction, which demanded too much from casual viewers and provided too little return for diehard fans.[19] Tellingly, during a transmedia panel put together by Jenkins and Denise Mann, comic book and television writer Javier Grillo-Marxuach (*Lost, The Middleman*) was asked for his views on transmedia storytelling, in which scholar Will Brooker posed the question by using *The Dark Knight* (2008) alternate-reality game (ARG) "Why So Serious?" as an example. Grillo-Marxuach noted, with a laugh, "If I had to do homework to understand Batman, I'd punch someone in the head."[20]

Not to digress too far off topic, but the lack of broader interest in *The Matrix* franchise appears to have caused Warner Bros. to ease off on the transmedia throttle. For instance, *The Dark Knight* ARG and straight-to-video animated film *Batman: Gotham Knight* (2008, released a week and a half before the feature) do not provide any information necessary to understanding the plot of the film. Any extra narrative information delivered by the other platforms is either commented upon in the film in its opening moments or inconsequential. Specifically, one of the main topics of discussion in the *Gotham Times* newspapers distributed via "Why So Serious?" campaign is the conflicted public sentiment regarding Batman. Yet this is depicted in the film during the scene in which Bruce Wayne (Christian Bale) dines with girlfriend (Beatrice Rosen), Harvey Dent (Aaron Eckhart), and Rachel Dawes (Maggie Gyllenhaal). Secondly, Batman encounters a character from *The Dark Knight*—the police woman Ramirez—in the *Gotham Knight* short "Crossfire." However, the encounter is never alluded to in the feature film. Despite the fact that these narrative events may take place in the same diegetic world, the transmedia texts of the ARG and the animated film do not make distinctive contributions to the narrative. Essentially, while they may be transmedia texts, they hardly participate in transmedia storytelling. Warner Bros. appears to have learned the hard way that transmedia is a gamble and a risk that is not necessarily worth taking (particularly when the production budget of the franchise's "mothership," the film, is $185 million).[21]

While Jenkins has begun to complicate his analysis with an added emphasis on "world building," a form of "transmedia entertainment" that is less defined by character and plot, most theorization of transmedia storytelling fails to account for the importance of style.[22] Sensory experiences can, in their own way, encourage active forms of fandom that involve deeper analysis of both the narrative and form of the central text under investigation. For instance, when the Star Wars video game *Jedi Knight: Dark Forces II* (1997) was released, players were drawn to the game because of one major addition to the weapons arsenal—a lightsaber. A similar reaction occurred when players discovered a cheat code that allowed access to the Millennium Falcon in *Star Wars: Rogue Squadron* (1998). These thrills had nothing to do with narrative and everything to do with engaging in an experience players had held dear to them: fighting like Luke Skywalker and flying like Han Solo.

This thrill of the sensory is also tied to stylistic remediation in all the forms analyzed here (comic book films, beyond comic book films, and the dialogical process of remediation) and also exemplifies of the cornerstones of transmedia storytelling: collective intelligence. As Jenkins describes, quoting Pierre Lévy, collective intelligence can give way to an environment in which "distinction between the authors and readers, producers and spectators, creators and interpreters will blend . . . [to form a] circuit," which will spur the involvement of others.[23] A prime example of this involvement with regard to stylistic remediation can be seen in *Solace in Cinema*'s "*300* Comic to Screen Comparison." The article collects a series of screenshots chronicling the correspondences between the panels of the comic and the frames of the film, a format which the author of the story claims to have borrowed from a similar project focused on *Sin City* (2005).[24] The story inspired nearly a hundred comments, some of which discussed the film's similarities to the graphic novel. Essentially, collective intelligence and pleasure in a transmedia property need not be bound to narrative.

To take this analysis back to bullet time and *The Matrix*, an analysis of the reception of the video game *Enter the Matrix* (2003) is enlightening. The review site *IGN.com* gave the game a lukewarm review (7.2 out of 10 for the Playstation 2 incarnation of the title), lodging a major complaint at the video game's form (its ludic properties). Most notably, the player's avatar takes the form of two supporting characters (Niobe and Ghost) and the player is never given the chance to play as one of the film's three lead characters. As reviewer Chris Carle writes, "It's nice that *Enter the Matrix* does not follow the same tired license formula of recreating a mini version of the movie within the game, but damn! It would have been cool to take off through the city as Neo, or shoot it out with agents as Trinity. How about giving Morpheus that samurai sword and seeing what he can do?"[25] More significantly, Carle adds in his conclusion, "That said, it's worth a play to see the extra footage and experience the bullet-time and focused hand-to-hand combat. . . . This effect is not new to video games. . . . but it was often more than a gimmick than anything."[26] Oddly enough, Carle barely mentions the story and how it relates to the film series. For the reviewer of the video game, one of the seminal tests in the transmedia universe established for *The Matrix*, the experience of not getting to play as Neo in the bullet time sequences trumps the ability to connect narrative dots.

We have returned to terrain explored by Bob Rehak in the quote that introduced this case study. As Rehak notes in his analysis of bullet time, the technique appeared in a range of genre spanning films over a four year period (even the video game *Max Payne* utilized bullet time as a core game mechanic). Thus, the argument can be made that transmedia storytelling was not the real cultural gift *The Matrix* franchise bestowed upon the entertainment industry; it was bullet time, the stylistic remediation developed by two comic book artists and a special-effects technician. After all, as noted in the analysis of the "Why So Serious?" campaign, there still appears to be ambivalence around the embrace of transmedia storytelling. Let us begin to consider style as a characteristic capable of uniting multiple platforms, without running the risk of alienating a casual consumer. Essentially, we can call the formal migration of bullet time—particularly when limited to *Enter the Matrix* and *The Matrix*

Comics (2003–2005)—an example of transmedia style: narratives delivered across multiple platforms that are united by stylistic remediation.

Comic Book Space and Caricature in the Spaghetti Westerns of Sergio Leone and Stephen King

For Spaghetti Western scholar Christopher Frayling, director Sergio Leone's films exhibit a visual style that relies "on cutting effects derived from comic-strip graphics."[27] Scholar Adrian Martin appears to agree with this analysis, writing in his monograph on *Once Upon a Time in America* (1984) that the gangster film differs from Leone's Westerns insofar as "it is not as purely comic book-like."[28] Unfortunately, both scholars leave their assertions drifting, lacking a proper analysis to ground them. Leone's films are often described as having a "comic" quality, but this is normally directed towards his use of violence as a means of producing a comic or absurd effect. In this light, the use of "comic" in describing Leone's work can be incredibly vague. Are Frayling and Martin describing the gag as a structuring mechanism or a remediation of the medium itself?

Before attempting to elaborate on Frayling and Martin's description, a brief consideration of Italian historical and cultural context is needed to move this argument beyond circumstantial evidence. Born in 1929, Leone was a child during the 1930s when, as Italian comics scholar Simone Castaldi posits, "American adventure comics such as *Flash Gordon, Mandrake,* [and] *The Phantom*" were "especially successful" in Italy.[29] As American comics took off in Italy, Castaldi argues that they appear to have:

> "stimulated local production. In fact, Italian authors absorbed their form and content then reformulated them in an all-but-Mediterranean fashion (a similar trend emerged again in the '60s and '70s with the phenomenon of Italian genre cinema—especially with spaghetti westerns and crime movies). . . . Italian comics of the post-war years were mostly adventure comics, reflecting—and often— rewriting—many popular American genres, especially westerns [such as *Tex Willer*]."[30]

Despite the popular establishment of Italian western comic books, Leone appears to have been more interested in the American titles. According to Frayling, Leone found Italian comics "abominable" and once remarked that "Luckily, there was a thriving black market, where you could buy all that was forbidden. American novels and comics were sold under the counter, or from suitcases."[31] Frayling, in his biography on Leone, claims that the language barrier was not an issue for the filmmaker, as "the graphics were much more interesting in any case."[32]

While we cannot be sure which American comics or which graphical aspects of those texts captured Leone's attention, we can begin to analyze his work's debt to its sister medium in sequential images in how the filmmaker subverts the classical conventions of spatial construction. To summarize Bordwell, Thompson, and Staiger once again, the classical Hollywood mode of storytelling (which was not limited to Hollywood in terms of its definition or practice, merely solidified and stabilized) presents space in a progression of long-shots to close-ups. The introduction of a new location normally begins with an establishing shot before providing a closer dissection of space. For example, when introducing two characters at a coffee shop, a filmmaker would normally begin with a shot of the coffee shop's exterior and then cut to a medium shot of the booth that the two characters occupy, Then, the filmmaker could segue into a close-up, shot/reverse-shot sequence of the characters involved in a dialogue exchange. This normative system exists for the sake of narrative and spatiotemporal clarity; the classical system keeps ambiguity at a minimum in order to emphasize story over style.

Film and comics differ greatly with regard to their individual systems of norms, specifically in the presentation of space. While film and comics have many formal affinities (the use of sequential images to establish a narrative, the use of a frame or panel as a window into a world, and the use of montage), the differences in their physical form produces medium specific differences. As discussed in the previous chapters, comics cannot engage with the classical Hollywood system's presentation of space due to spatial limitations. A comic book that attempts to present space in such a way would burn through its industrial standard of thirty-two pages very quickly if a writer/artist decided to bow to continuity rules. Therefore, spatial discontinuity is simply inherent in the form as an additional variable that the reader must provide closure to during the process of reading. Thus, due to the limitations of the form and to the fact that it being completely fabricated by the artist, the spatial reality presented in comics is malleable.

As comic theorist Thierry Gronensteen describes, "In cinema, the frame is, from the moment of shooting, the instrument of an extraction, of a deduction . . . The frame assigns limits to the profusion of the represented elements, and it elects a privileged fragment. The frame of a comics panel does not remove anything" due to the panel being composed within the frame, not composed around it.[33] Groensteen is correct, if we limit his interpretation of film form to the classical system of spatial articulation. For Groensteen, the physical reality that is filmed as cinema is the product of compromise: any choice of framing is affected by reality, limiting the filmmaker's compositional choices. However, the work of Leone owes more to the comic than to the classical mode, complicating Groensteen's simplification and providing a specific analysis to ground Frayling and Martin's conclusions.

Leone undermines the classical continuity system in *The Good, the Bad, and the Ugly* (1966) in two specific instances worth noting here. The first occurs in the film's opening sequence. The film begins with a long-shot of a valley, encroached by a rocky ridge, in the middle of the desert. The viewer reads the shot as an establishing shot because of its scope. However, after a few moments, we quickly realize that it does not establish anything. The ridge lacks any buildings, characters, and landmarks to distinguish it from its surroundings. Suddenly, from off-screen left, the face of a man (Al Mulock) swoops into frame. His entrance alters the shot; it evolves from a long-shot to an extreme close up (this shot is paid homage in the opening page of *The Dark Tower: The Gunslinger Born*, which will be analyzed shortly). In the second shot, we are provided with an establishing shot of a village from the man's point-of-view. The village appears to be largely abandoned; its sole inhabitant is an old dog that runs across the mid-ground of the frame. Slowly, two figures emerge from the horizon line. However, Leone keeps them at such a distance that we are unable to notice any distinguishing characteristics. Again, the purpose of the establishing shot is undermined by Leone's staging of the action. When he cuts into the space to give us those details, he skips the long-shot to medium-shot progression and goes straight into a close-up. The space of the film is ambiguous to the point that it becomes an indicator of baroque self-consciousness.

As the sequence continues, the staging suggests that the three men will be engaging one another in a gunfight. The man seen in the opening frame is filmed as being at the far end of town while the other duo approaches him through the village. It feels like a classic showdown set-up. Once again, Leone films the sequence in a combination of extreme close-ups and extreme long-shots. Once again, he undermines their functions because he does not depict the three men within a medium-shot frame until the last possible second, just as they veer off and approach a building on the left side of the space.

As the sequence comes to its conclusion, Leone once again breaks with the function of the classical system. The three men storm the building and we hear the gunshots of an ensuing gunfight. However, Leone keeps the camera outside the building during the violence, which keeps the viewer in narrative darkness the entire time. Eventually, the camera tracks away from the building's door towards the window. Suddenly, Tuco (Eli Wallach)—with a pistol and ham hock in hand—jumps out of the window. His entrance shocks us because Leone's spatial construction has kept the existence of a fourth character a complete mystery. Again, Leone introduces a character outside the formal norms of the classical system. Essentially, the entire opening sequence works to subvert our expectations of both the Western narrative (the potential duel becomes a one-way slaughter) and our typically unambiguous understanding of cinematic space.

A similar depiction of space occurs later in the film when Tuco and Blondie (Clint Eastwood) ride off in search of a cemetery to find a hidden cache of gold. The duo rides towards the camera across a wood-lined trail, Ennio Morricone's score keeping pace with the horses. Suddenly, the music stops and the duo dismount their steeds and walk towards the camera. Tuco, consulting a map, points to off-screen right, and says "There should be a bridge across that river." Again, Leone does not allow the viewer to fully read the space. Instead, Tuco's assessment performs the task for all of those involved (both the characters and the viewer). The men look out towards the space of the bridge and the camera tracks them as they continue their walk towards off-screen right. When Blondie expresses his concern over a daylight crossing, Tuco boasts "I've got a good sense of where I'm going!"

As he continues to brag about his knowledge of the space at the crossing, the team is flanked by a man with a rifle. The man emerges from the left-side of the frame, creeping up from behind them. The man with the rifle's entrance is quickly followed by the emergence of two swords in the foreground—from the camera's position in space—directly in front of Tuco and Blondie. Realistically, our antiheroes would have seen the men ahead. The swordsmen are on the path directly in front of them, uncovered by foliage. However, this is not a realist depiction of cinematic space. Leone further undermines both Tuco's assessment of the space and the classical system of editing when the camera reveals that there is—surprisingly—an entire military encampment established at the bridge.

In these two examples, the reality of cinematic space is treated by Leone as being malleable. The space, to return to Groensteen, does not limit or determine the camera's dissection of the geography. In Leone's usage, the camera is liberated, brazenly constructing barriers around the viewer's understanding of the geography. As Roger Ebert writes in his essay on the film, "Leone established a rule that he follows through *The Good, the Bad, and the Ugly*. The rule is that the ability to see is limited by the sides of the frame. At moments in the film, what the camera cannot see, the characters cannot see, and that gives Leone the freedom to surprise us with entrances that cannot be explained by the practical geography of his shots."[34] Frayling makes similar note of Leone's unorthodox composition of space, writing:

Objects appear from out of frame, originating *beneath* the camera's field of vision.... The whole of *The Good, the Bad, and the Ugly* can be interpreted, or 'read,' in terms both of the cinematic exploration of spaces or shapes, and of the experimentation with a form of pure iconography.... [He] uses space geometrically, operating in terms of the possibilities of the wide screen; in other words, he manipulates spaces *cinematically*—a technique which reveals a profound knowledge of the possibilities of cinema (and of the uses to which the wide screen can be put), at the same time as a *celebration* of the 'codes' of the Western. Often, the flattening effect of the wide screen image, and the emphasis on the geometry of spaces, rather than their depth, achieves a kind of unity with the action itself—where a set of cinematic mythologies are being acted out.[35]

Given how Leone subverts the codes of classical cinematic spatial construction, the adverb "cinematically" (given emphasis by Frayling) is perhaps ill-chosen. However, this may have been the track he was alluding to when he (and Adrian Martin) noted the influence of the comic strip upon the Spaghetti Western. The frame in Leone's world is not—to return to Groensteen's contrast of space in film and comics—an instrument of extraction or deduction. The filmmaker, like the comic artist, is composing space within the frame rather than allowing the space to dictate his presentation. In this sense, the films of Leone owe more to the plasticity of spatial construction taken by the comic artist than the adherence to reality embodied by the classical system.

Now that we have established Leone's unorthodox construction of space, let us now turn to the areas where Leone's comics-informed style overlaps with a contemporary Spaghetti Western comic series: the Marvel Comics adaptation of Stephen King's *The Dark Tower* novels. First, both Leone's film and the Marvel comics rely on the graphic design of caricature to establish their characters. Secondly, both texts utilize the dimensions of the frame, temporal duration, and spatial abstraction in order to solicit suspense. Before continuing with a formal analysis of how these two texts overlap, a brief note of context regarding King's series is helpful. While the author has made a name for himself in the horror genre with such titles as *Carrie* (1974), *It* (1986, winner of the British Fantasy Award), *Misery* (1987, winner of the Bram Stoker Award), and *Under the Dome* (2009) over the span of his thirty-year plus career, one of the author's most noteworthy literary achievements has been his fantasy-Western series *The Dark Tower* (1982–Present).

The Dark Tower series, which launched with *The Gunslinger* (1982), has become a linchpin in a mythological universe King has spread across many of his titles. Characters like Randall Flagg (the antagonist of *The Stand*) and the Crimson King (who also appears in *Insomnia*) and locations like Derry and Castle Rock make appearances both in the *Dark Tower* books and in other tangential titles. Essentially, the structure of King's literary universe owes much to the comics. There is a core series that provides the basis for the author to draw readers towards cross-over titles (think of Batman and his appearances in both monthly *Batman* titles and *Justice League* titles). As King notes in an interview, the comic book medium was a natural home for his *The Dark Tower* series because "The four-color world . . . has always had a strong influence on my work."[36]

When Marvel Comics acquired the rights to the series in 2007, the publisher tasked King (who serves as Creative and Executive Director on the project), Marvel editor Ralph Macchio, writer Peter David, and artists Jae Lee (pencils) and Richard Isanove (color) with the extensive adaptation.[37] The first issue had an astonishing debut, selling 172,116 copies, and ranked second for the month of February 2007. Moreover, the debut of the title is noteworthy because it was outsold by the seventh issue of the Marvel "event" title *Civil War* (2006–2007), which pitted Capt. America against Iron Man (*Civil War* sold 265,886 copies). Essentially, despite the fact that the *Dark Tower* carried a steeper cover price ($3.99, opposed to $2.99) and did not feature any of the popular established heroes from Marvel's stable of stars, it still provided stiff competition.[38] Eventually, the title became the twenty-third bestselling comic book of the 2000s.[39]

The first visual aspect worthy of analysis in the stylistic overlap between *The Good, the Bad, and the Ugly* and *The Dark Tower: The Gunslinger Born* is how the Western landscape physically marks the characters according to their moral code (King did, after all, base his protagonist on Clint Eastwood's "Man with No Name").[40] Specifically, both texts are linked insofar as the desert has left physical scars on the characters that also serve as iconography that establish their individual positions on the moral compass. As film scholar Patrick McGee writes with regard to Leone's film, "In the opening sequences of the film, each character is labeled by a moral or aesthetic term that appears on the screen over a freeze-frame of his image. The last to be identified is the Good, Eastwood's character; and it can be inferred from his role in the film that the word 'good' applied to him can be read as both an aesthetic and a moral category and probably is meant to represent the confusion of the two in the modern Nietzschean world."[41]

The ugliness of Tuco is foregrounded both by a similar titled freeze-frame and by his character's facial features. Most notably, he has a discolored, dead, tooth that stands out at the front of his smile. Moreover, Leone often directs and shoots Wallach as if he were a rabid dog. For instance, when Tuco is first caught and tried from his crimes against humanity (including "raping a virgin of the white race"), he shoots a devilish sneer at an elderly woman that causes her to audibly gasp. Furthermore, the character's ugliness is frequently commented upon (often ironically) and linked to his career as a criminal. As one bounty hunter informs him while holding a wanted poster with his image on it, "Hey, amigo! You know you have a face beautiful enough to be worth $2000?" Essentially, the graphic presentation of characters in *The Good, the Bad, and the Ugly* represents their own moral worth, much like the caricatures of Chester Gould's *Dick Tracy* comic-strip.

Lee and Isanove's work on *The Gunslinger Born* also draws upon caricature to the point that the characters almost literally wear their morals on their sleeves. Roland, the book's protagonist, is iconographically similar to Eastwood's Blondie. Both men wear the same color duster and cowboy hat, which conveniently casts a mysterious shadow over their faces. Yet when both Leone and the comic artists show us bodies unmasked of clothing, both are physically flawless. Both men are lean in form, have healthy tans, and are unmarked (at least at the beginning of both texts) by the desert and the resulting scars of dastardly deeds. Like Tuco in Leone's film, the villains of King's series—Cort, Rhea, and the Crimson King—are depicted as being physically deformed. Cort, a physical threat to the young Roland, exerts his power via his obese form. He is bald and his body is baby-like, embellished with fatty haunches. His face is scarred, wrinkled and—after he attacks the young protagonist—only houses one eyeball. Similarly, Rhea, the witch who casts a malicious spell over Roland's love, is physically branded by her evil ways. Her face, best depicted on the cover of issue five and the final page of issue six, appears mummified, wrinkled by the tendons of muscle that lie underneath her paper-thin skin. The only part of her face that appears to have any "natural" quality is her nose, which is represented as a deep, rusty-colored beacon on her otherwise alabaster face. This is a fitting visible attribute, considering that Rhea's character is essentially a blatant opportunist who attempts to use her gifts (as a brown noser) to solidify her position with the evil Coffin Hunters. Essentially, Frayling's analysis of Leone's world can double for that of *The Gunslinger Born*: "They are brutal because of the environment in which they exist. And they make no attempt to change that environment. They accept it, without question."[42]

The most obvious example of caricature in *The Gunslinger Born* is exemplified by the design of the Crimson King, the main antagonist in King's Mid-World. A hybrid of man and spider, the Crimson King is described by writer Peter David as being "the devil . . . the Antichrist . . . the Lord of Spiders" who—when he speaks—causes "a slumbering, dreaming infant" to shudder and die in its crib.[43] When the Crimson King is introduced in the second

Figure 5.4. Caricature and the Crimson King in *The Gunslinger Born* (2007).

issue of the series, we watch as he sits on his throne, the remainders of a human body hanging from his dagger-like legs as he feasts (Figure 5.4). Like Leone, the team behind *The Gunslinger Born* uses the device of caricature to make it abundantly clear which characters the reader is to align his or her sympathies with. The inhabitants of Leone's Civil War America and King's Mid-World have been physically defined by their deeds, both good and bad. There is nothing subtle or naturalistic about such a presentation. It is a form of stylization taken to baroque heights.

Considering the inspirational roots of *The Dark Tower* (the Westerns of Leone and, as King describes it, "the four-colored world"), it is fitting that caricature plays such a large role in the presentation of *The Gunslinger Born*. E. H. Gombrich, art historian and scholar of the caricature, writes that the art form is "the conscious distortion of the features of a person with the aim of ridicule. . . . [It shows] more of the essential, is truer than reality itself."[44] Unlike the caricatures of Chester Gould, Leone and Lee's depictions are not defined by the art of simplification. However, what unites both approaches is the desire on behalf of the artist to move away from a naturalistic representation of the human form towards a representation that links both external reality (the actual physical form of the person being depicted) with the internal reality of the subject. As Gombrich describes it, caricature penetrates "through the mere outward appearance to the inner being in all its littleness or ugliness."[45]

Leone's film and *The Gunslinger Born* also carry on a dialogue through two of the latter's stylistic remediations. The comic remediates both the dimensions of the widescreen frame and the use of temporal duration and spatial abstraction in order to solicit suspense. Specifically, Leone's compositions are often described (see the Frayling block quote as an example) as an exploration of the widescreen cinematic canvas. At times, the director may use the scope of the widescreen to lull the viewer into a false sense of spatial security (as he does with the Tuco and Blondie scene described above). After all, we experience the widescreen image as being all encompassing, a cinematic device that can capture and represent peripheral vision. At other times, Leone uses the widescreen image to focus in on incredibly small details, as he does in the shot which opens the film.

Similarly, David, Lee, and Isanove have structured the multiframes of *The Gunslinger Born* around horizontally orientated images (with the few notable exceptions being panels that span an entire page). Most comics are composed with vertical multiframes in order to conserve space. Essentially, the layouts of *Watchmen* (1986) are motivated by a publishing format that features a page that is taller than it is wide. In contrast to most comics, the panels of *The*

Gunslinger Born are all widescreen compositions (yet, unlike *300*, the comic is not published in the "widescreen format"). This compositional decision adds a cosmetic touch to David, Lee, and Isanove's remediation of Leone's style, especially his unique approach to cinematic violence.

Specifically, Leone often emphasizes the prelude to violence over the act itself. For instance, let us return to the opening sequence in *The Good, the Bad, and the Ugly*. The sequence clocks in at three minutes, which feels like an incredibly grueling and stress inducing amount of time (although, in temporal comparison with the opening of *Once Upon a Time in the West*, it pales in comparison). The first two and half minutes of the sequence are composed of a long walk of preparation as the bounty hunters ready themselves to confront Tuco. As film scholar Howard Hughes writes, "This scene [the opening ghost-town shootout] is a familiar Leone duel, but presented in an unusual way. Here the shots of boots, close-ups of eyes and guns being loaded add tension to the scene."[46] These graphical details, as already described, are abstracted from the larger space of the scene. We are unsure of their spatial relationship to one another and Leone's emphasis is not put on spatial cohesion but on the actions as part of an elaborate, masculine, ritual. When Leone finally reaches the shootout, it takes place over the span of seven seconds, 3 percent of the sequence's total running time. For Frayling, Leone turns the Western into an exercise in iconography, another stylistic attribute of the comic as Scott McCloud describes it.[47] Obviously, Leone's emphasis on the preparation for violence provides the sequence an incredible amount of suspense in which the act itself becomes an inevitable conclusion.

David, Lee, and Isanove partially borrow from Leone's spatial abstraction and pacing in the sequence in which Cort and Roland engage in a duel. Depicted over the course of nine pages and forty-three panels, the lead-up to the duel is given a similar amount of emphasis. The first page, prior to Cort's arrival, is visualized over the span of four panels, each narrowing in dimensions as Roland prepares and Cort approaches. When Cort finally does emerge to face Roland on the second page of the sequence, the creative team gives us a page layout featuring the most panels in the sequence, twelve. The first eleven panels are extreme close-ups of the faces of Roland and Cort as they announce their choice in weapons. Significantly, it is not until the page reaches the final panel that we are given a medium shot of where the two figures are in spatial relation to one another. The following five pages (and nineteen panels) depict the battle between the two characters, which ends in the full-page image of Roland standing over his fallen foe. In contrast with Leone's depiction of the showdown, David, Lee, and Isanove visualize the violence over the course of 62 percent of the sequence (if we are gauging it by the number of panels) in contrast to Leone's 3 percent. Yet the fragmentation of the preparation across the smaller panels of the page takes elongates the temporality of the reading experience. It takes us longer to read the eleven extreme close-up panels than it does to read the battle. Moreover, the multi-frame's presentation of time and space as an iconographic abstraction elicits suspense in a similar way. Leone's style, which remediated many stylistic aspects of the comic medium, is now being re-remediated in its initial form by King, David, Lee, and Isanove.

Conclusions: Beyond Adaptations

The purpose of this chapter was to engage in a discussion of stylistic remediation beyond comic book films and to look at the industrial practice beyond case studies in adaptation. In the case of *The Matrix*, we traced how the stylistic flourish of bullet time drew its inspiration from a tangled web of inspirational sources (video games, anime, Muybridge's motion studies, comic books) and was subsequently developed via a partnership between comic book creative personnel and cinematic special-effects artists. Moreover, the case study of *The Matrix* illustrated both how the norms of the comic have been ported over into the medium of film and where the phenomena of transmedia storytelling and stylistic remediation intersect.

As the name of the concept implies, transmedia storytelling is often theorized with regard to world-building or separate but overlapping narratives, offered up by various, cross-platforming texts. Yet despite the discussions about *The Matrix* as being a key text in the development of transmedia storytelling, we tend to underestimate the stylistic experiences that transmedia experiences can offer. For instance, as described in the reaction to the video game *The Matrix Reloaded* (a text commonly cited as being a milestone in transmedia storytelling), critics were more likely to voice disappointment at not being able to experience bullet time from the standpoint of Neo or one of the film's main protagonists over discussions regarding the video game's narrative complexity. Investigations into and alterations of a medium's style can lead to incredibly potent personal experiences. We have already begun to see this in the pleasure that comic book fans take in describing, comparing and contrasting comic book adaptations to their original sources. The difficulty inherent in this line of investigation for scholars is the need to begin to articulate their own pleasures and to acknowledge the subjective experiences that they bring to textual analysis.

In the second case study of this chapter, focusing on the stylistic intersection between *The Good, the Bad, and the Ugly* and the comic book adaptation of *The Gunslinger Born*, we have analyzed how Leone's style may have been—as suggested by Christopher Frayling and Adrian Martin—influenced by the form of the comic. Moreover, we discussed how Leone's remediations have been subsequently remediated by the creative team behind the comic. In short, this case study provides a relevant bridge to the next chapter, which will further investigate stylistic remediation as being a dialogical process. Essentially, a remediation does not necessarily end with one manifestation; it can be an ongoing and organic process.

CHAPTER 6

"There, That Looks Much Better": The Joker, *Sin City, The Spirit*, and the Dialogical Process of Remediation

Introduction: "I Want Us to Do Something like That."

In Michael Chabon's fictionalized account of the Golden Age of comics *The Amazing Adventures of Kavalier & Clay* (2000), Jewish writer Sammy Clay and his artist émigré cousin Joseph Kavalier create the successful comic book superhero the Escapist in 1939. During the beginning of their tenure on the series, they use the American comic book form to take out their aggression on the antagonists of all the Jews of the world: Hitler and his Nazis. However, after suffering editorial censorship, the duo shift their objective towards the formal exploration of the comic medium. Their inspiration for formal exploration does not come from the pioneering work of Winsor McCay, the titles being published by DC Comics, or the seminal work of Hergé. The motivator Chabon provides for Kavalier and Clay's experimentation in *Radio* #19, which caused "nine million unsuspecting twelve-year-olds of America" to want "to grow up to be comic book men," is Orson Welles's *Citizen Kane* (1941).[1] As Kavalier tells his American cousin after coming out of the New York City premiere, "I want us to do something like *that*."[2]

For Kavalier, as Chabon writes,

> *Citizen Kane* represented, more than any other movie Joe had ever seen, the total blending of narration and image that was—didn't Sammy see it?—the fundamental principle of comic book storytelling. . . . Without the witty, potential dialogue and the puzzling shape of the story, the movie would have been merely an American version of the kind of brooding, shadow-filled Ufa-style expressionist stuff that Joe had grown up watching in Prague. Without the brooding shadows and

bold adventurings of the camera, without the theatrical lighting and queasy angles, it would have been merely a clever movie about a rich bastard. It was more, much more, than any movie really needed to be. In this crucial regard—its inextricable braiding of image and narrative—*Citizen Kane* was like a comic book.[3]

Chabon's version of Welles (or at least Kavalier's interpretation of Chabon's version of Welles) is vaguely inspired by comic book form and practices stylistic remediation within *Kane*. Kavalier sees the film, and inspired by what he perceives as Welles's cinematic remediation of comics, decides to use the comic book form to re-remediate Welles's initial remediation of comics. In so doing, Chabon gives us an example of formal remediation as a dialogical process.

Chabon's case study is beautiful, poetic, and rewarding for both the cinephiles and comic book fans who read his book. However, it is also primarily a work of fiction. Kavalier, Clay, and the Escapist did not exist within the historical moment of the Golden Age of comics.[4] Yet Welles did acknowledge that his films were inspired by comic books. When discussing his film *The Stranger* (1946), Welles claimed that it "was pure *Dick Tracy*. I had to fight for it. Everybody felt, 'Well, it's bad taste and Orson's going too far,' but I wanted a straight comic-strip finish."[5] However, while Chabon's case study is largely fictional, the concept of dialogical formal remediation is not.

Take, for instance, one of the most memorable relics to emerge from the midst of 1989's Batmania. While the craze gripped much of America with movie tie-in merchandise for the young and old alike (including trading cards, toys, a Wayne Manor playset that turned into a batcave, and two film soundtracks), the comic novelization by Dennis O'Neil, Jerry Ordway, and Steve Oliff's *Batman: A DC Movie Special* (1989) is particularly noteworthy. Essentially, the *DC Movie Special* is a comic book adaptation of the Tim Burton film. It is not unusual for such products to exist (examples from the time period include comic books based upon *Terminator 2: Judgment Day* and *Robocop*). However, what makes the the *DC Movie Special* different than most comic book adaptations of popular films is how the title remediates the style of both the original comic and the film.

Specifically, the first image we are presented with is the cover (Figure 6.1) featuring Ordway and Oliff's graphical remediations of Michael Keaton's Batman and Jack Nicholson's Joker. Notably, we are not shown versions of the two seminal characters taken from O'Neill's own history on the title. Since this is an adaptation of the film, it is expected to look like the film . . . for the most part. An odd addition has been made to the lower left-hand corner of the cover: a black and white penciled Joker card. The card is a recreation a piece of Jerry Robinson's original concept artwork of the Joker, whom

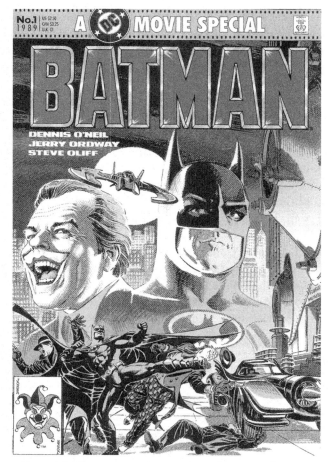

Figure 6.1. The cover art to *Batman: A DC Movie Special* (1989).

the artist co-created. It also appears on another important cover, *Batman* #1 (Spring 1940).

Yet the stylistic remediation continues! The introductory page of the issue begins with a caption: "It's just a movie, for Heaven's sake." The text block stands over a background of people watching a film in a movie theater, shrouded by the glow of the screen (Figure 6.2). The image of the audience is obstructed by an upper image layer that features a vertical column of panels depicting the opening images of the film. However, these panels are not presented in the usual grid-like multiframe of the page. The creative team behind the *DC Movie Special* has embellished them in a particular fashion: the panels are actually individual frames on a spool of motion picture film.

Figure 6.2. Cinematic remediation in *Batman: A DC Movie Special*.

The movie the audience is watching is Tim Burton's *Batman*, which means that the book we are reading provides the same experience as the film. As writer Denny O'Neil noted in a personal interview, "What I was trying to do is simply telegraph that this is not a comic book in the continuity. We're not going to play be all the rules of the comic books. This Batman is going to be a little different."[6] Thus, the comic book reader is equated with the cinemagoer and we expect both experiences to be roughly the same. This is not so much an early exercise in transmedia storytelling but an instance of a media conglomerate using two different forms to tell the same story by using the formal attributes of the culturally dominant medium (the film, in this case) to draw consumers to related ancillary products. As Eileen Meehan observes in her study of Warner Communications Incorporated, the average comic book reader in 1989 was a twenty-year-old male spending ten dollars a week on comics.[7] The film, according to Meehan, stood as a means of widening the audience and providing the "basic infrastructure necessary for manufacturing a line of films, albums, sheet music, comics, and novelizations."[8]

The focus of this chapter is on the dialogical aspects of stylistic remediation and how it has been used both historically and contemporarily to fuel the perpetual motion machine of synergistic properties. In the first section section on Batman's arch-nemesis the Joker, we will analyze how graphical representations of the character have been altered in response to the success of other titles in the franchise. In the second section of this chapter, the career trajectory of comic book writer/artist Frank Miller from a very successful film adaptation (*Sin City*) to his critical and economically disappointing follow up (*The Spirit*) will provide an illustrative case study of the limits of stylistic remediation. Specifically, both films heavily remediated the stylistic devices of film noir. Yet despite being visually and stylistically similar, only one of the films was culturally accepted. Overall, the purpose of this chapter is to analyze how stylistic remediation can result in an complex aesthetic dialogue.

There's Nothing Funny about a Clown in the Moonlight: The Graphical Remediation of the Joker

DC Comic's second hero in its stable of stars, Batman, made his comic book debut in *Detective Comics* #27 in May of 1939. The character, as Les Daniels notes in his study *Batman: The Complete History*, was assembled by writers and artists Bob Kane and Bill Finger from a collage of inspirational sources, including Roland West's film *The Bat Whispers* (1930).[9] Allegedly one of Kane's favorites, the film stars Chester Morris as a detective who disguises himself as a bat in order to kill off treasure hunters. Another popular piece of entertainment produced in 1920 provided some further defined the character: the Douglas Fairbanks film *The Mark of Zorro* (1920). According to Kane, the Fairbanks film "left a lasting impression . . . it gave me the dual identity [Bruce Wayne/Batman]. You're influenced at one point by another character, but then you embellish and bring your own individuality to it."[10]

Following the successful launch of the title, Kane and Finger decided it was time to flesh out their Batman production, both on and behind the panel. Additional artists were hired, such as Sheldon Moldoff and Jerry Robinson, and Batman's sidekick Robin made his debut in *Detective Comics* #38 (April 1940). By spring of 1940, Batman had become such an attraction that DC Comics promoted him from being part of the ensemble of characters featured in *Detective Comics* to his own title, *Batman*. The first issue of the title is also noteworthy for introducing Batman's most infamous villain, the Joker, a character who has not only become the cloaked hero's arch nemesis but his antithesis as well.

In creating the Joker (an act which has become its own source of controversy as Kane, Finger, and Robinson have all claimed to have created the Clown Prince of Crime), the creative team behind the title followed the approach that had worked so well for creating their hero: homage. Jerry Robinson allegedly based his initial designs off of the playing card (as seen on the front of the *DC Movie Special*). Moreover, according to Bill Finger's son, the graphic design of the character was inspired by a flyer for George C. Tilyou's Coney Island attraction "Steeplechase." According to Fred Finger, the "white-faced, evil clown" pictured in the flyers gave his father the idea for the character.[11] Moldoff, on the other hand, claims that Kane's own facial features (a lean face and mischievous smile) informed the design of the Joker. Yet as Daniels notes (and, as illustrator Brian Bolland coyly notes in his introduction to Alan Moore's *The Killing Joke*), the undisputed source for the Joker came from Conrad Veidt's character in *The Man Who Laughs* (1928).[12] According to Robinson, Finger saw his initial artwork and said "That reminds me of Conrad Veidt in *The Man Who Laughs*."[13] This prompted Finger to bring Robinson production stills from the film as he continued his work.

Looking at the work Kane and company present in *Batman* #1, the character of the Joker appears to owe more to Veidt's Gwynplaine than to Robinson's playing card. The playing card artwork pictures a heavy-faced clown dressed in red and black jester regalia, including a jingle bell hat. The final character, however, sports bushy green hair, slicked backwards. Dark circles run under his eyes, an elongated nose adds emphasis to his thin face. He is deformed by a grotesque grin and a violently pointed chin. As these two images present, the similarities between Gwynplaine (Figure 6.3) and the Joker (Figure 6.4) are particularly visible. Coincidentally, Kane and his team acknowledge the source of their homage in the final panel of the issue, in which the Joker proclaims "They can't keep me here! I know of a way out—the Joker will have the *Last Laugh!*"

Yet what deepens this fairly obvious remediation is Bob Kane's character design, which seems to be functioning on two different representational registers. Essentially, Kane's representation of Joker also remediates Gwynplaine and film through, for lack of a better description, a higher resolution representation. Kane's pencil work on the issue gives the character of the Joker more lines of definition than it does any other character. Take, for instance, the first page introducing the character holding up the playing cards that

Figure 6.3. Veidt as Gwynplaine (1928).

Figure 6.4. The Joker in *Batman* #1 (1940).

feature Batman and Robin. Joker's face features more than twenty lines (most of which define his wrinkled brow and his signature smile). The faces of Batman and Robin, on the other hand, feature less than ten.

Perhaps this difference in representation is a product of Kane's composition. The Joker dominates the multiframe while Batman and Robin are relegated to the background. Given this compositional choice and the fact that the issue introduces the villain, perhaps it is only logical that the Joker be given graphical emphasis on the opening page. However, the disjunction in definition continues into the issue. When Joker gets punched out by Batman towards the end of the issue, the Caped Crusader is once again rendered in just a few elegant pencil lines (less than ten) while the Joker has nearly as many lines on his forehead. Essentially, the Joker's face—to return to Scott McCloud's pyramid once again—occupies a position closer to reality than that of his heroic counterparts. The increased detail and the disjunction between Kane's representational styles becomes an illustration of the ontological differences between the hero's defining medium of the comic and the medium of film that inspired the villain's graphic design.

Throughout the subsequent decades, the essence within the initial design of the Joker became solidified. The purple suit, the slicked toxic green hair, the bleached skin, and the chilling rictus remained fairly constant. Similarly, Batman's suit would remain a graphically fixed commodity (grey with a black logo) until DC editor Julius Schwartz presented Carmine Infantino and Joe Giella's "new look" in *Detective Comics* #327 (May 1964). Joker's look, on the other hand, remained consistent into the 1980s, where it would be briefly challenged by Frank Miller's feminine portrayal in *The Dark Knight Returns* (1986). In Miller's design, the Joker has the signature hair and skin tone but not the fixed grin. In one sequence, he is shown to be applying his own lipstick, completing the look.

Despite the already documented success of Miller's book, his "overly gay" depiction of the Joker was not as nearly influential on the subsequent films and books as his dark and fascist portrayal of Batman was.[14] On the other hand, Alan Moore, Brian Bolland, and John Higgins' representation of the classical Joker in *Batman: The Killing Joke* (1988) gained a great deal of traction. The book, which tells one of the most cited origin stories of the character (the origins of Joker, unlike Batman, remained a mystery for the first eleven years of his appearance), presents the Joker as a more elaborate version of the initial design: the permanent grin, the pointed features, and the fang-like teeth (Figure 6.5). According to artist Brian Bolland, his inspirational source was the same as his predecessors. He writes, in the introduction to a reprint of *The Killing Joke*, that "I'd become a bit obsessed with the rictus grin of the

Figure 6.5. *The Killing Joke* Joker (1988).

character. I'd even recently been to see the wonderful 1928 film *The Man Who Laughs* ... a film which, lawyers advise me to say, played no part in the creation of the Joker. I think I had been limbering up to draw the Joker for some time."[15]

Moore's one-shot, which features the Joker shooting a woman at point blank range in order to paralyze her, worked with Miller's text in ushering in the adult portrayal of Batman that Tim Burton and Warner Bros. would find ideal for their film adaptation. According to Burton, who testified to not being a comic book fan, his admiration of Moore's seminal title led to its influence on the 1989 film. As Burton notes in an interview, "[*The Killing Joke* is my] favorite. It's the first comic I've ever loved. And the success of those graphic novels made our ideas more acceptable."[16]

The success of Burton's film and the Batmania it created during the summer of 1989 has already been touched upon: the massive box office grosses, the licensing deals, and both the revitalization of a property and an entire medium in American culture. While the Batmania eventually lost some steam in the hands of Burton, whose *Batman Returns* (1992) was deemed too dark for youngsters, the films brought forth a beloved entry in the Batman media franchise: *The Animated Series* (1992–1995). As television critic Leonard Pierce writes in his retrospective on the series, "Many people have (correctly) observed that *Batman: The Animated Series* defined the Batman of the '90s, in much the same way that Frank Miller's *Batman: The Dark Knight Returns* defined the character in the '80s and Christopher Nolan's films defined him in the 2000s. This carries special weight when you consider that it was Tim Burton's films that were meant to fulfill that purpose."[17]

Airing on Fox, the series found a balance between the best of the many incarnations of the superhero (including Burton's films, Miller's comics, and other sources). For instance, animators Bruce Timm and Eric Radomski decided to use black backgrounds—instead of the traditional white—in order to keep the style in dialogue with Burton's film noir mise-en-scène. Moreover, the unique blend of 40s art deco and advanced technology that helped define Burton's vision (Timm and Radomski describe it as being "otherworldly timelessness") was a guide for the animators.[18] Furthermore, the show's main musical theme was ported over from Danny Elfman's work on the Burton films. Finally, like Burton's film, *Batman: The Animated Series* aimed to attract both children and adults with its dark and fun approach to the superhero. Initially scheduled as an afternoon cartoon, the show was later moved by Fox into the prime-time schedule. A success, the show would go on to win three Emmy awards (Outstanding Animated Program, Music Direction, and Sound Editing) over its tenure. However, while the series defined itself with and in relation to the diegesis and tone of Burton's films, it also found itself on stable enough ground with fans and the Fox network to set out on its own path. One of the main sources of stylistic inspiration came from the original comics. As DC editor Denny O'Neil notes, the show runner went into the DC library and "photocopied thirty years of Batman" for stylistic cues and "got paid for it! That had never happened before."[19]

The depth of this remediation is best exemplified by the late run episode (which was broadcast under the revised title *The New Batman Adventures* from 1997 to 1999), "Legends of the Dark Knight." "Legends" focuses on three children who share stories about their encounters with the Caped Crusader. The most relevant sequence in this complex remediation is the second story, which depicts Batman and Robin in a fight with the Joker. The fight features a complete remediation of the characters provided by Golden Age writers and artists, most notably Dick Sprang. The stylistic shift is jarring in its emphasis on bright colors (the show is stereotypically dark, like Burton's films), the minimal use of shadows, and the overhauled design of the Joker. The overhaul jettisons the triangular features that the show had already established for the character, giving him a spherical chin and rounder features overall. Moreover, the filmmakers cast aside the menacing voice work provided by regular Mark Hamill, replacing him with comedian Michael McKean. Notably, the final, Joker-less, tale, adapts and remediates Miller's *The Dark Knight Returns* both graphically and with regard to vocal performance (Michael Ironside replaced series regular Kevin Conroy as the voice for Batman in this short).

As the animated series established itself, it spawned its own tie-in merchandise ranging from toys, novels, video games and its own comic, *The Batman Adventures*. *The Batman Adventures* is notable for multiple reasons, including how it remediated the graphical presentation of Timm and Radomski's series. According to Timm, who developed the look of the animated series, "One of the things I learned over the years . . . is that every time we were doing an adventure cartoon, there was always the drive to make the cartoons look more like comic books, and it really worked against what animation does best. The more lines you have on a character, the harder it is to draw over and over. I knew that simplicity would be better."[20] As you can see illustrated in this comparison between the Joker of the animated series (Figure 6.7) and the Joker of *The Batman Adventures* (Figure 6.6), the similarities in character design are indistinguishable, despite the shift in medium. The sharp crests of the Joker's hair, the trademark grin (slightly yellowed teeth, vividly crimson lipstick), and taunting eyes (yellowed and enclosed by thick black circles) are apparent in both representations. As Timm notes, both character designs of the Joker are stripped down to the bare essentials (compare the minimal Joker of *Batman Adventures* and *The Animated Series* with Bolland's above work). The comic book stylistically remediates animation design principles.

The look of the series, in dialogue with Burton's but also differentiated by its own stylistic attributes, became a bankable and defining characteristic of its tie-in comic book. As the comic progressed, characters were introduced in the comic that later appeared in the television show (the most notable example is the Joker's girlfriend Harley Quinn, first introduced in the one-shot *Mad Love*). According to Timm, the fluidity between media forms aided his creative ambitions: "I always wanted to be a comic book artist. I figured I'd just work in animation until I got better."[21] According to comics scholar Jean-Paul Gabilliet, Timm's style (influenced by Japanese *manga* as well) "gave birth to a 'school' of disciples" through the success of both the animated series and the comics.[22] As the comic and its contributions to the narrative presented in the television show gained traction, straight forward adaptations of the comic's story arcs were brought to the television screen.

The classical representation of the Joker initially presented by Robinson, Kane, and Finger in 1940 experienced a major renovation between 2007 and

Figure 6.6 and Figure 6.7. Joker in *The Batman Adventures* and *The Animated Series*

2008 from three textual fronts: Grant Morrison's run on the *Batman* tent-pole comic title, Heath Ledger's portrayal in Christopher Nolan's *The Dark Knight* (2008), and Brian Azzarello's graphic novel *Joker*. After Christopher Nolan teased the audience with the forthcoming appearance of the Harle-quin of Hate at the end of *Batman Begins* (2005), fans were rabid for a fresh embodiment of the Joker (he had been killed off in Burton's first entry into the series). This revised portrayal began with Grant Morrison's tenure on the *Batman* comic title. Morrison, who had made a reputation for himself in the Batman universe in the 1980s with his cerebral and grotesque *Arkham Asylum: A Serious House on Serious Earth* (1989), was coming fresh off of his successful miniseries *All Star Superman* (2006–2008). His first effort on the title, issue #655, began controversially with Batman shooting Joker in the face with a handgun. His series eventually climaxed with the "Batman R.I.P." arc, which featured the long-publicized death of Batman, and was brought to a close by comic legend Neil Gaiman's funerary tribute "What Ever Happened to the Caped Crusader?" in 2008.

Yet it is Morrison's ninth entry into the monthly series, issue #663, that stands out. Entitled "The Clown at Midnight," #663 is an issue structured unconventionally for a comic book, let alone a mainstream superhero title. For the issue, Morrison jettisoned the panel and multiframe format so elemental to the medium. Instead, the author structures the text like an illustrated prose manuscript. At the standard monthly issue length of thirty-two pages, the story is divided into ten chapters and told in blocks of text with the occasional illustration. Further undermining the conventions of the medium, artist John Van Fleet traded traditional pencils and inks for illustrations fully constructed on a computer. The issue, released in February 2007, ranked sixteenth for the month with 83,152 copies sold (Marvel's *Civil War* won the month with 265,886 copies sold).[23]

Appropriately, the narrative of #663 centers on how the Joker redefines himself, both mentally and physically. After being shot in the head, Joker is shown recuperating in Arkham Asylum, fresh out of having facial reconstructive surgery. In one scene, the bandaged bandit meets with Batman and, according to perceived differences in his nemesis's body language, the Caped Crusader notes that "The Joker's different."[24] A few pages later, when the Joker finally removes the facial bandages, he notes "There, that looks much better" and presents his freshly altered grin to us (Figure 6.8). Morrison's reinterpretation of the Joker is uncannily similar to the representation Nolan would utilize for Heath Ledger's depiction in *The Dark Knight* due to a very significant alteration of his facial appearance: the Glasgow grin.

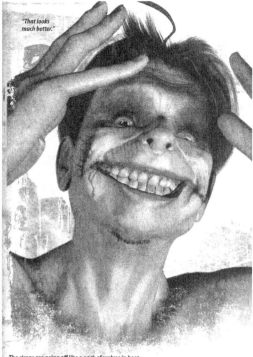

Figure 6.8 and 6.9. Grant Morrison and John Van Fleet's (2007) and Heath Ledger's Joker.

Opposed to the Joker's portrayal in the bulk of the comics and *The Killing Joke*, the character's trademark grin, often portrayed as the result of his chemical bath, has been replaced by a Glasgow grin. The demented, artificially produced grin (sometimes called the Chelsea smile), is the product of bodily mutilation that is said to have originated through the particularly violent practices of British gangs. Essentially, and this is alluded to in *The Dark Knight* when the Joker kills the African American gangster Gambol (Michael Jai White) by reenacting how he got "these scars," the Glasgow grin is produced by sticking a knife, utility blade, or blade of glass into the victim's mouth, between the cheek and the gum, and extending the lines of their natural grin with a series of cuts.

When Warner Bros. and Nolan provided fans with a teaser image of the character, only available after a photo scavenger hunt was completed via the alternate-reality game described earlier, it stirred quite a bit of controversy amongst fans. Nolan's *Batman Begins* had been much beloved at the time for trimming away the excesses of the Schumacher films and bringing the hero back to a noir reality. However, fans viewed the depiction of the Joker as artificial. The Joker was supposed to find actual joy in the sadistic torment of his victims. Thus, it was a betrayal to depict that joy as being something artificially produced by cutting one's face open like a jack-o'-lantern.[25]

The anxiety of the fan community was silenced when the film was released and Ledger's portrayal became incredibly popular. Nolan's *Dark Knight* (budgeted at $185 million) went on to gross more than $1 billion dollars worldwide and became the top grossing film of 2008. In an attempt to further capitalize upon the success of the villain, DC Comics solidified the revamped depiction with its publication of Brian Azzarello and Lee Bermejo's *Joker* (2008). Like its textual predecessors, *Joker* redefines its subject. This revision occurs both at the level of characterization (he is a sociopathic gangster in Azzarello's book, which is in line with Nolan's depiction) and his visual appearance.[26] Like Morrison's and Nolan's Jokers, Azzarello and Bermejo's boasts a horrific Glasgow grin, which conveniently provides a close-up for the volume's cover art.

It would be tempting to read this as all part of a coordinated artistic effort in remediation, but the production context of *Joker* suggests that such a conclusion is not so cut and dried. While the graphic novel appeared on bookshelves a few months after the release of Nolan's blockbuster, Azzarello and Bermejo had actually been at work on the title since 2005.[27] The team had been handed the project following their work on another villain centered title, *Lex Luthor: Man of Steel* (2005).[28] Essentially, despite being the last title released, Azzarello and Bermejo's was in production one year *prior* to Nolan's film (2007), coinciding with Morrison's run on *Batman*. Moreover, Bermejo released sketches of his take on the Joker to the fan website *Batman on Film* while Nolan's film was still in pre-production.[29] The Glasgow grin graphical remediation of the character appears to be less an instance of a conglomerate synchronizing different artistic teams in the redefinition of the Joker and more of post-production marketing move to utilize the momentum and success of a primary text (*The Dark Knight*) to fuel the sales of ancillary texts (*Joker* and other reprints/reissues like *The Greatest Joker Stories Ever Told*).

This interpretation is solidified by interviews performed with Azzarello and Bermejo. When asked about the similarities between the appearances of the Joker and whether or not he consulted with the filmmakers at all during production, Azzarello notes "I think [the similarities are mostly a coincidence]. I mean they were so secretive with that film. So no, we had no idea what was going on with any of this. But it's a good coincidence. I don't think you can ask for a better project to follow that film than this. It's almost like a sequel."[30] In other interviews, the questions became less about how *Dark Knight* influenced the look of *Joker* to suggestions of the converse. When Bermejo was asked if he felt his concept art had been drawn upon in the design sessions for Ledger's character, he responded,

> I think that it's impossible to know these things unless you're Nolan and Co. I DO think that there are some similarities but all in all, someone once told me (and I find this VERY true) that ideas tend to 'float' around at the same time. It depends on a lot of things . . . pop culture of the moment, social conditions, trends in fashion. . . . All in all, I think that they probably would have done the same thing even if I hadn't been drawing him this way. . . . I'm proud of my interpretation of the character and IF it had any effect I can be nothing but flattered."[31]

According to Nolan, he and Ledger took inspiration from the paintings of Francis Bacon (whose art, coincidentally, appears in Burton's first entry into the series), the punk aesthetic, and Alex DeLarge (the protagonist of Stanley Kubrick's *A Clockwork Orange*). They then tasked make-up designer John Caligone (who also worked on Beatty's *Dick Tracy*) to come up with a prosthetic device that would showcase those influences.[32] Nolan has never gone on the record about Bermejo's concept art or Grant Morrison's work. However, Ledger did keep a "Joker Diary" filled with images ("AIDS, landmines. . . . blind babies . . . really horrible stuff") that Morrison's texts had informed.[33] As Morrison noted, after reading Ledger's diary, "I can see there's a lot of [*Arkham Asylum* and "Midnight"] in his Joker. . . . David Goyer [one of the screenwriters on Nolan's trilogy] has said they owe a debt to us. And it's really easy to see our influence. But at the same time, they created something quite new and extraordinary."[34]

According to these sources, the Glasgow grin Joker does not appear to be an instance of intentional or conscious stylistic remediation performed during the production stage. It did, however, become an overt remediation in the marketing stage. Specifically, both *The Dark Knight* and *Joker* were marketed in an identical fashion by emphasizing the drastically altered of appearance of the villain. As mentioned before, Ledger's character overshadowed the hero in many of the marketing campaigns. Early promo photos, many released alongside the news that Nolan was shooting portions of the film on IMAX cameras, featured the Joker behind clouded glass. After months of speculation, the viral "Why So Serious?" campaign disclosed the first image of the Joker (Figure 6.9) after fans provided their emails. Azzarello's title, as mentioned, also capitalizes upon the adjustment in Joker's representation: the cover features a close up of his Glasgow grin, the back of the dust jacket features another close up of the grin, and the first two introductory pages offer two more extreme close ups.

With the Joker's Glasgow grin, Warner Bros. and DC Comics offered up the latest incarnation of what Justin Wyatt dubs "high concept" or "a product differentiated through the emphasis on style in production and through the integration of the film with its marketing."[35] The unique look of the Joker, like the films and coordinated marketing campaigns Wyatt analyzes, provided the studio with "a *visual* form, presentable in television spots, trailers, and print ads. The high concept films therefore depend upon the visual representation of their marketable concepts in advertising."[36] Moreover, for Wyatt, the simpler the image (the revamped Batman logo in the Burton's film for instance), the easier it is to establish the film with potential consumers. In other words, with a visual device like the Glasgow grin, the film appropriated the visual grammar of advertising in order to simplify the task placed in front of the studio's marketing division. For Wyatt, these images have the potential to work against classical Hollywood narrative conventions by emphasizing style over story. Yet in the case of Nolan's film, the image, the marketing, and the narrative (the Joker's repeated, differing interpretations of his scars add to his characterization) work in perfect unison. Regardless of if it was an intentional remediation during the production stage, the Glasgow grin and the new interpretation(s) of the Joker offered up by Morrison, Nolan, and Azzarello completed the same objective Eileen Meehan noted in the construction of the original franchise: a means of widening the audience and providing a "basic infrastructure necessary for manufacturing a line of films, albums, sheet music, comics, and novelizations."[37]

The Curious Case of Frank Miller

While the graphical remediation of the Joker illuminates how the dialogical process of stylistic remediation can be an effective means of introducing and marketing ancillary titles (similar to what Justin Wyatt describes in his book *High Concept: Movies and Marketing in Hollywood*), the case of Frank Miller illustrates its limits. According to comic historian Bradford Wright, Miller's over-the-top, noir infused style made him the greatest influence on the comic book form since Stan Lee's work in the 1960s.[38] His success in the medium drew the attention of both those involved in comics and those working in its often aligned medium of film. Specifically, Hollywood executives, independent filmmaker Robert Rodriguez, and moviegoers were all eager to bring Miller's work to the big screen. Yet while Miller's signature style drew a great deal of praise when it involved his own properties (*Sin City*, *300*), his process of remediation quickly alienated the same audience it established when it was applied to his production of a film adaptation based on the work of another comic auteur: Will Eisner's *The Spirit*.

Miller's career at the drawing board began in the late 1970s when he began working for Marvel Comics on a revamp of Daredevil with artist Klaus Janson. In the words of Wright, "Preceding creators had already developed the blind superhero . . . alias defense attorney Matt Murdock, into a brooding, isolated soul. Miller went even further in this direction, portraying him as a deeply tortured soul, torn apart by his own internal contradictions as a lawyer and extralegal vigilante. . . . Miller's plots were tight and absorbing, his scripts, terse and ironic. The art by Miller and Janson was stripped-down, yet atmospheric, verging on a crude expressionism."[39] By 1983, Miller's work with Marvel earned industry-wide recognition and he was approached by rival DC Comics to pen a six-issue miniseries entitled *Ronin* (1983–1984). The series featured its own form of remediation, reflecting "the influence of Japanese and European comics on the new American comic books."[40] Three years later, Miller would cement his legacy with another miniseries for DC: *Batman: The Dark Knight Returns* (1986).

Driven by an upswing in sales and the cultural redefinition of the comic book in America, new publishers and product lines quickly began to spring up in order to capitalize upon the expansion. DC launched Vertigo Comics, a line that historian Roger Sabin describes as being "a new imprint designed to encompass titles devoted to horror and fantasy. In the now-established fashion, comics would first appear as single-issues, with a 'Suggested for Mature Readers' label, and would later be collected as graphic novels."[41] Slowly, as Randy Duncan and Matthew J. Smith describe, "publishers would once again overtly tap into the marketing power of their creators' names" (creators were often only credited on an opening splash page of an issue, not on the cover) and the industry began to change its position regarding the ownership of creative rights.[42] Gone were the days when creators like Jerry Siegel and Joe Shuster would sell the rights to their characters to the publisher for a measly $130. As Duncan and Smith note in their overview of the contemporary comic book industry, "Today comics creators have more opportunity for ownership of their properties and can enjoy more of the profits that their work can generate."[43] One noted publisher to rise during this era was Dark Horse Comics, a company that had established itself on licensed properties (most notably comics based off of *Star Wars*, a license which had kept Marvel Comics afloat throughout the late 1970s) and began to push towards what Duncan and Smith term "creator-owned properties that would go on to feature film development."[44]

Miller, following the release of *Dark Knight Returns* and *Batman: Year One*, left DC Comics after a disagreement with the publisher regarding censorship and property management. Miller noted that the publisher was "problematic because they don't like noise. There's always been a tension in my relationship with them because I want noise every time out."[45] He went on to sign with Dark Horse, which would release his properties *Hard Boiled* (1990–1992, with *Matrix* artist Geof Darrow collaborating), *Sin City* (1991–2000), and *300* (1998). According to Miller, his work with Dark Horse was significantly different from his tenures at Marvel and DC: "The whole thing about the first *Sin City* is that I was rediscovering the love of drawing on that job. I had absolutely no boss and it was the first thing I completely did from head to toe myself. . . . I can go off and do *Sin City*, we can do anything we want to, and they'll smile at us and nod. But the minute I turn around and dent the Batmobile, they [DC Comics] go out of their minds! They have such a precious view of these fantasies!"[46]

It was during his tenure at Dark Horse that Miller first became involved with Hollywood. Shortly after Paul Verhoeven's ultraviolent action film *Robocop* (1987) became a box office success with $30 million in domestic gross revenue (on a $13 million dollar budget), Orion Pictures announced its intent to make a "funnier, more satirical, and less violent" sequel.[47] Despite this early enthusiasm, it took Orion nearly two years to get the project off the ground. In the winter of 1989, producer Jon Davison had signed Peter Weller to reprise his role and Tim Hunter to direct (the director's seat later went to *The Empire Strikes Back* helmsman Irvin Kershner). Significantly, the project also marked the "screenwriting debut" of Miller.[48] Budgeted at $50 million, the film went on to become a critical and box office flop when it was finally released in the summer of 1990, grossing $45 domestically.

According to the clipping files available at the Margaret Herrick Library, Miller (and the project in general) received little press attention during pre-production. After the film was released however, both Kershner and Miller spoke about the failure of the film in the popular press. Specifically, Kershner wrote a piece for the *Los Angeles Times* while Miller was interviewed by *Time Out*. In his interview with *Time Out*, Miller expressed his dissatisfaction with the pre-production process, noting that his original script went through "eight major drafts" and that "rewrites reached such a pitch that sometimes actors would get their lines ten minutes before saying them."[49] For Miller, this resulted in a plot that "simply no longer made sense."[50] According to the writer, Orion put his script through the production wringer because "There is a tendency in film, with millions of dollars in the balance and nothing but words on paper, to change the words every ten minutes because you get worried about them. Fear is the main motivator."[51]

Despite the negative reaction of both the public and critical community to *Robocop 2* (1990) and Miller's less-than-desirable experience with Orion, the comic book pioneer was still willing to give the franchise another try. However, the production the second time around was rockier for all those involved. First, lead actor Peter Weller dropped out in the fall of 1990 after being disappointed with the second film, and according to *The Hollywood Reporter*, "Script problems finally convinced everyone to throw in the towel on it."[52] Two days later, the paper published a report to the contrary, in which producer Patrick Crowley claimed the film was "definitely on" and "there's never been a moment . . . when anyone has been dissatisfied with the script."[53] Despite the opposing stories offered by the *Hollywood Reporter*, Weller did not wear the trademark metal suit for the third outing (he was replaced by actor Robert Burke). Moreover, the $22 million film was originally scheduled to be released in summer but "awesome competition" and exhibition space scarcity pushed the film to November.

When it was finally released, the film grossed a mere $10 million domestically and was once again panned by critics. This time, Miller would remain silent in the press and his dissatisfaction with his work on the franchise would later manifest itself in his medium of choice. Frank Miller's *Robocop* (2003–2006), a comic series based off of his original scripts for the two sequels and supervised by Miller (the title was written by Steven Grant and illustrated by Juan Jose Ryp) was published by Avatar Press. Initial reviews were far from complementary and the title's introductory issue sold a meager 21,566 copies (ranking 104th behind Neil Gaiman, Andy Kubert, Richard Isanove, and Scott McKowen's first issue of *Marvel 1602*, which sold 152,528 copies the same month).[54]

During the decade following his negative experiences on the *Robocop* series, Miller veered away from working in Hollywood and retreated to his workshop to finish *Sin City* and *300*. In 2000, he was initially enlisted by director Darren Aronofsky to script an adaptation of *Batman: Year One* with the goal of revitalizing the fallen franchise.[55] The project was shelved and eventually evolved into Christopher Nolan's series. Still dissatisfied with Hollywood, Miller "rejected many offers" to turn *Sin City* into a film.[56] According to the author, the mentality of Hollywood was that "your screenplay is a fire hydrant with an awful lot of dogs lined up behind it. And I wasn't interested at all in directing—-I just wanted to draw my comics."[57] His combative stance towards Hollywood began to change when he was approached by Robert Rodriguez, who was planning on completing a short film based on the *Sin City* story "The Consumer is Always Right." Rodriguez flew Miller out to his base of operations in Austin, Texas and introduced the comic artist to both his "digital backlot" and actors Josh Hartnett and Marley Shelton. While shooting the film, Rodriguez informed Miller that he felt that they did not need to produce an adaptation. Rather, they could use advances in technology to make a translation. Moreover, the filmmaker wanted the creator to co-direct the film with him.[58] The author/artist, impressed with Rodriguez's "tree fort," ultimately agreed to work with Rodriguez and "special guest director" Quentin Tarantino.[59]

In order to complete the translation, which Rodriguez billed "Frank Miller's *Sin City*," Rodriguez utilized extensive green screen sets at his Troublemaker Studios so that he and Miller could "take cinema and try to make it into this book."[60] Miller, on the commentary track for the film, remarks how "I was always told that my skills as a cartoonist and the writing I do wouldn't relate to film" but that the green screen process essentially allowed him to draw on film. While the green screens allowed Miller and Rodriguez to use CGI to fill in backgrounds and to construct the mise-en-scène to match the style of the original book, it also had more pragmatic benefits. While CGI is typically an expensive filmmaking asset, extensively utilized only in large budget filmmaking, Rodriguez and Miller used it to lower costs. Filming their ensemble of stars (Bruce Willis, Elijah Wood, Jessica Alba, Clive Owen) separately, the filmmakers later composited them into the same space. For instance, "The Hard Goodbye" features a climactic battle between Marv (Mickey Rourke) and Kevin (Elijah Wood). However, due to a short and conflicting shooting schedule, the actors never met one another. Thus, despite all of its star power and visual flourishes, *Sin City* carried a relatively low production budget of $40 million. In comparison, the largest grossing comic book film of 2005—*Batman Begins*—was budgeted at $150 million.

In order to discuss the style of *Sin City* and Miller's overall approach, we will be conflating the graphic novels and the film for the sake of brevity. The focus will be solely on graphical remediation or remediation that addresses the difference between film's representational roots in photography and the comic's representational roots in the graphic arts.[61] Before proceeding, it is important to note that noir had stylistic roots in the graphic arts, including—arguably to the point of overestimation—the German Expressionist movement that extended across painting, literature, theater, dance, film, architecture and music. Moreover, this movement had stylistically influenced comics, particularly the wood engraved proto-graphic novels of Lynd Ward who—according to comics writer, artist, and historian Art Spiegelman—"became steeped in German Expressionist art, and learned wood engraving from a German master."[62] It is unclear to what degree Miller may have been influenced by Ward's woodcuts or by German Expressionist art in general. Looking at his compositions in *Sin City*, it certainly seems feasible that Miller was familiar with Ward (who experienced the beginnings of a reappraisal in 1972 when an anthology of six of his novels was published, complete with prologues written by the artist). However, given Miller's avid and vocal affection for film noir proper, it is safe to say, as comics historian Jean-Paul Gabilliet claims, that "Frank Miller . . . brought ['film noir' inspiration] back into fashion."[63]

In order to define how Miller embraced film noir style, we first need to define noir style. Two solid starting points in defining film noir style are the seminal articles authored by Paul Schrader ("Notes on *Film Noir*") and Janey Place and Lowell Peterson ("Some Visual Motifs of *Film Noir*").[64] For Schrader, whose essay also discusses the historical context and narrative themes of the movement, noir defines itself visually through scenes "lit for night," a preference for "oblique and vertical lines . . . [that] splinter a screen, making it restless and unstable" (Venetian blinds), equal emphasis lighting (this characteristic seems to overlap with "lit for night"), "compositional tension" (the mise-en-scène drives the action rather than characterization), and finally, "an almost Freudian attachment to water . . . (even in Los Angeles)."[65] The first volume of Miller's *Sin City* series, "The Hard Goodbye" (1991–1992), is essentially an illustrated accompaniment to Schrader's discussion of noir visual style. The arc never once features a scene that takes place during the daylight hours (we sometimes wonder if Sin City is a snowless metropolis located in Northern Alaska during winter). The inhabitants of Sin City are like the noir characters Schrader describes insofar as "One always has the

Figure 6.10. Noir equal emphasis lighting in *Sin City*.

suspicion that if the lights were all suddenly flipped on the characters would shriek and shrink from the scene like Count Dracula at sunrise."[66]

Similarly, Miller continually relies upon equal emphasis lighting to compose his panels. As the arc is rendered minimally in black and white, scenes and characters tend to reflect the setting they are placed within. A sublime example of this occurs when a captured Marv gazed out his cell window at one of the book's protagonists, Kevin (Figure 6.10). All five panels on the page are rendered with black backgrounds, with Kevin's emergence from the darkness accentuated by a reflection of light in his glasses or a thin-white line tracing his silhouette (courtesy of a nearby automobile headlight). In the one panel that features him on the page, Marv is represented as by a dark shape whose only features come from his vaguely defined eyes and mouth. Otherwise, he melts into the background.

A notable sequence of the novel illustrates numerous compositional tendencies that Schrader discusses. In fact, Miller's style tends to render the noir aesthetic more absolute—sharper, cleaner—than film. For instance, Miller's use of a hard line in Marv's long walk through the rain illustrates the fixation with water, compositional tension, and oblique and vertical lines is perhaps only rivaled by the chiaroscuro cinematography of Robert Krasker (*Odd Man Out*, *The Third Man*) and John Alton (*The Big Combo*). When the sequence begins, Marv remarks that he loves the rain because "it helps me think."[67] Yet the way Miller presents the rainfall is in tension with Marv's dialogue. The torrents of water, like the bars of the jail cell Marv will later inhabit, confine him. Fittingly, Marv begins to psychoanalyze himself (he is depicted as being a mentally imbalanced character who needs medication to remain mentally stable) as he continues his walk through the storm. He establishes that he has "a condition," is perhaps "imagining things," and it may turn out that he is "a maniac, a psycho killer."[68] Despite Marv's initial suggestion that it is a liberating force, the rain slowly begins to become just the opposite. He is a character whose fate is locked in thanks to his mental imbalance, causing him to be ostracized by the inhabitants of Sin City (Figure 6.11).

While Place and Peterson's analysis of noir style no doubt takes its lead from Schrader's essay (which was published two years earlier), it also makes significant contributions to the discussion of noir visuals that are worthy of discussion here. For Place and Peterson, noir's reliance on deep focus cinematography and wide-angle lenses results in a "certain distorting characteristics" and the style, as a whole, is defined by "antitraditional mise-en-scène" or a combination of off-angle compositions. These compositions are "symbolic representations of fragmented ego or idealized image" (the use of mirrors and portraits) and provide "no means of spatial orientation" (shot patterns that undermine spatial continuity).[69]

While Miller's work is produced by ink and pencils and not the photographic apparatus (making the visual distortion that comes from deep-focus cinematography and its wide-angle lenses an impossibility), he does draw upon the characteristics of caricature and, in one notable arc, color to lend his characters a similar type of distortion that serves the same narrative function. In the arc "That Yellow Bastard" (1996), Miller introduces us to Junior Rourke

Figure 6.11. Miller's Marv, lost in the psychoanalytical rains of *Sin City*.

(played in the film by Nick Stahl), a rapist of prepubescent girls that is being pursued by police officer John Hartigan (Bruce Willis). When he is initially introduced, the villainous Junior is depicted much like the other characters of Sin City: abstractly, nearly feature-less, in minimalist black and white. However, after being shot by Hartigan, Junior's form becomes marked and contorted. He becomes the Yellow Bastard of the title. Confronting the cop in his jail cell, the visually redefined Bastard now boasts an electric yellow skin

Figure 6.12. The grotesque distortion of the Yellow Bastard in *Sin City*.

tone that is beyond jaundice. Wrinkled dark circles emphasize his large, yellow, eyes and an obscenely large, bulbous nose takes up more facial real estate than his chin. Junior, like Orson Welles' antagonist Frank Quinlan in *Touch of Evil* (1958), is expressively differentiated from the rest of the characters by the tools of the medium (Figure 6.12).

This sequence also depicts Miller's embrace of the "antitraditional mise-en-scène" that Place and Peterson describe. Hartigan's cell is continuously depicted in canted frames (as seen in the first panel in the figure above), underlining the theme that Sin City is saturated with corruption and that the world of Hartigan (the one good cop in the system) is as unbalanced as the justice system. Moreover, the sequence undermines the classical rules of spatial orientation already discussed. When the space of the cell is initially introduced, Hartigan is depicted as being its only inhabitant (an overhead, canted, establishing shot begins the sequence). However, after Hartigan falls into a depressed psychological state, both the reader and the fallen cop are surprised by the entrance of the Yellow Bastard. On the page before the Yellow Bastard's introduction, Hartigan is seen alone in his cell, lying on the floor, when he cranes his neck and expresses a note of confusion: "Hnh?"[70] After the page flip, which is used masterfully by Miller to draw out the suspense and mystery of the scene, we find the Yellow Bastard sitting in the previously vacant space. Since we are not shown his entrance into the space with the panel equivalent of an establishing shot, and because Miller depicts even the smallest space of a jail cell ambiguously, the Yellow Bastard surprises both Hartigan and the reader.

In discussions regarding the classical period of noir (Schrader defines the classical period as 1941–1958), scholars are often quick to note that the visual motifs that define the movement or genre have been retroactively applied to other genres, such as the melodrama, thriller, and drama.[71] As historians are keen to note, noir was a French concept applied to American film. It was not widely received until 1955 with the English translation of Raymond Borde and Étienne Chaumeton's A Panorama of American Film Noir: 1941–1953 was first published in America. Essentially, critics question the existence of a cohesive noir style because its actual practitioners were unaware of any such concept. Miller's case sidesteps this potential critique, as his works were produced after the rise of noir as a debated category (Schrader, Place, and Peterson all published their essays in the 1970s). Moreover, he prides himself on being a scholar of noir, appearing in the documentary Film Noir: Bringing Darkness to Light (2006) with filmmaker Christopher Nolan, writer James Ellroy, and Paul Schrader. Essentially, Miller is more than aware of noir's influence on his work, and despite his insistence that comics are movies on paper is a "really corrupt" concept "because it makes us sound so inferior," he is not above stylistic remediation.[72]

Both of Miller's noir remediation texts, Sin City the comic and Sin City the film, were critically and commercially successful. The single issues tended to rank between numbers thirty and fifty in the Diamond Comic Distributors monthly listing, selling 49,000–53,000 copies per month (about 25 percent of the copies that a top ranked title would sell). The comic series was awarded numerous Eisner Awards, including Best Short Story (1995), Best Limited

Series (1995, 1996), Best Graphic Album: Reprint (1993, 1998), and Best Artist/ Penciller/Inker (1993). Moreover, the series was awarded two Harvey Awards for Best Continuing or Limited Series (1996) and Best Graphic Album of Original Work (1998). Finally, the series was voted by the readers of the *Comics Buyer's Guide* as their Favorite Limited Series of 1996. The film was also a success, grossing $158 million worldwide and winning Miller and Rodriguez a Technical Grand Prize for "visual shaping" at the 2005 Cannes Film Festival (the film was also nominated for the Golden Palm). Moreover, one month after the release of the film, all seven collected volumes ranked amongst the top hundred trade paperbacks.[73]

Spurred by the success of *Sin City* and Zack Snyder's adaptation of *300* (2007), Miller decided to give filmmaking another try. In an interview with *Variety*, the writer-artist remarked that "The fear is fading. Rodriguez said: 'Don't be nervous. All the stuff you've done throughout your career is the same thing you're doing now—-you're just using different tools.'"[74] Instead of bringing one of his own projects to the screen this time around, Miller chose to adapt a work by his late colleague Will Eisner (the two men published a book of interviews under the title *Eisner/Miller* in 2005). Eisner, one of the forefathers of the comic book and graphic novel forms, launched his career with the weekly strip *The Spirit* in 1940 and Miller felt it was time to bring it to the big screen. According to Miller, "I want to do him [Eisner] proud. [The film] is true to the Will Eisner that I know."[75] Miller completed the deal after meeting film producer Michael Uslan (producer of the *Batman* films) at Eisner's memorial where the producer told him "There's no way I can let anybody *else* do it."[76] With a production budget of $60 million, Miller began casting *The Spirit* in 2007 with Samuel L. Jackson in the role of the villainous Octopus and relative unknown Gabriel Macht as the lead.

Drawing from his work on *Sin City*, Miller decided to film the bulk of *The Spirit* on a digital backlot. According to producer Deborah Del Prete, the decision to use green screen derived from a desire to bring a comic book movie closer to the art that makes the native medium unique. As she notes, "We've always been telling comic stories but we've never actually been able to show the art in the way we are able to now. That's one of the great reasons for using the whole green screen technique because marrying art with the actual live action, you will get the experience as a comic fan that you got reading the books."[77] Despite the similar production method and nearly-identical style, Miller tried to distance the two films during interviews leading up to the release of *The Spirit*. When speaking to the *Los Angeles Times*, Miller noted "It's very different than the look and feel of *Sin City* and *300* because the source material is different."[78]

Yet fans of Eisner's original were dubious of Miller's interpretation. When footage was screened at 2008 San Diego Comic-Con, many attendees turned to one another with a look of concern. Something did not feel right with the footage being screened. As best articulated by reporter Geoff Boucher, "Eisner's humanistic and often gentle, Capra-like approach to his character has many comics fans wondering why Miller—famous for spilling vats of blood-red ink in his comics—is taking the old man's winking Spirit into a Sin City."[79] When confronted by this concern, Miller simply replied "I like to shake things up and tell the story the best way possible. And I can tell you first hand, that's what Will Eisner liked too."[80]

Despite Miller's assurances and the proclamation that his style was in dialogue with Eisner's, the interviews conducted between the two artists provide an illustration of how different the stylistic philosophies of both men are. Specifically, the two had passionate disagreements regarding the form of comics. Even Miller notes in the introduction to the interviews that "Will Eisner and I argued a lot. . . . What you're about to read is the climax of our several-decade debate. I bet he wins."[81] In a discussion about imitation, Miller notes that Eisner's work "is more like theater and mine is more like film."[82] When Miller admits he attempts to imitate other forms of visual media, Eisner pointedly notes that he has

> absolutely no intention of capturing the essence of any other medium. I'm in pursuit of a connection between me and the reader. The only entertainment form that provides a real, live, connection between the viewer and the actor is theater. In live theater, you are sitting there and watching a real thing happening. On film, you're just the camera. There's no sense of contact between you and the actors. It's an experience that you immerse yourself in. You're a spectator and comics is [sic] a participatory form.[83]

As the dialogue progresses, it becomes clear that Eisner is willing to embrace the essence of other media forms, but only in the vaguest possible ways (comics as participatory like theater, comics as grappling with the "visual language" of film, and the necessity to "use the same language"). As he notes in *Comics & Sequential Art*, Eisner is not above using the compositional principles of the graphic and visual arts as a guide for his work. However, he is not keen on homage, direct imitation, or, in terms of this study, stylistic remediation.

Eisner's philosophy becomes complicated when it is put in dialogue with his work on *The Spirit* (1940–1952). While the title may take some narrative and stylistic cues from noir (which, at the time, was not a historical or critical designation) such as the femme fatale and the protagonist who oscillates between law and lawlessness, Eisner's style and tone are far-less "hardboiled" than Miller's remediations. Placing his first entry in the series ("The Origin of The Spirit," 1940) in dialogue with Schrader's description of noir, approximately half of the panels are evenly lit. Moreover, Eisner's work with blooming colors owes more to Chester Gould's *Dick Tracy* (1931–1977) than Schrader's definition of noir (despite the fact that all the sequences seem to take place at night). In addition, Eisner's first entry lacks "an almost Freudian attachment to water" and shadows are used only sparingly to initially conceal the Spirit's identity (he would later be given a mask).

Moreover, while Randy Duncan and Matthew J. Smith are correct to a degree when they note that "Eisner was one of the first artists to bring the mood and the danger of the big city at night to the comic book page by simulating the low-key lighting of the film noir genre," the artist's work on the series went beyond noir. Some entries provide glimpses of low-key lighting and the compositional tension Schrader describes ("Meet P'Gell," 1946, Figure 6.13) while others exhibit colorful, comedic set-pieces ("The Story of Gerhard Shnobble," 1948, Figvure 6.14).[84] Quite simply, Eisner was a writer and artist whose *Spirit* was not defined by a specific genre, both in terms of style and narrative. The strip itself was marketed as offering three genres of entertainment: action, mystery, and adventure. Tellingly, comic historian Michael Barrier describes Eisner's Gerhard Scnobble story as being "playful ... serious ... [and] sentimental ... all at once."[85] Moreover, Eisner was dubious of the crime drama genre and Miller's reliance upon it. As Eisner noted despairingly to his colleague, "I guess crime dramas ... are form ... some have content.... The comics that I see are all generally about pursuit and vengeance—with vengeance being the primary motive of the pursuit."[86]

Finally, Eisner's reliance on color, despite his remark that it "is used essentially as a packaging device," distances it greatly from the noir tradition.[87] As Schrader describes color cinematography, it was "the final blow to the '*noir*' look."[88] While we should be cautious in claiming that color and noir are fundamentally incompatible (Miller and several neo-noir filmmakers have found a balance), to describe Eisner's *Spirit* purely in terms of noir is not only a simplification but a simplification that verges on being ahistorical. To borrow from genre theorist Rick Altman, noir was more of an adjective than a noun during Eisner's tenure on the series. Borde and Chaumeton's seminal introduction to the movement was released (in French) three years after *The Spirit* concluded. Essentially, how could Eisner's work fully embody an inconsistent aesthetic that spanned genres that had yet to be recognized, let alone defined?

Analyses of Miller's adaptation tend to come down into two camps when it comes to dissecting its failure which was, at the time, equated by the fan

Figures 6.13 and 6.14. Eisner's diverse style ranged
from low-key noir to colorful comedy in *The Spirit*.

site *Ain't It Cool News* with that of *Battlefield Earth* (2000).[89] A film scholar at the review site *Pajiba* suggested that the filmmaker was unable to grapple with Eisner's varied tone, writing "Miller has tried to reproduce the strip's mash-up of noir, slapstick, fantasy, and social reportage, but his mix doesn't cohere."[90] Also noting the adaptation's tone deafness, Nathan Rabin wrote that "*The Spirit* feels like the follow-up to *Batman & Robin* no one wanted. Main bad guy Samuel L. Jackson even spends much of the film indulging in egg-themed wordplay that almost inspires nostalgia for Arnold Schwarzenegger's avalanche of ice puns in the unloved third *Batman* sequel."[91] The hypothesis proposed earlier, that moviegoers are willing to accept stylization without the faintest hint of camp, appears to have held true for the few patrons who saw *The Spirit* in theaters (it grossed a mere $39 million worldwide).

The other camp of reviewers, consisting of many viewers who were familiar with Eisner's version, felt betrayed by Miller's interpretation. *The Spirit* was, in that much-maligned tenet of adaptation theory, unfaithful. Unlike Eisner's compositions, Miller drained most of the film of color by rendering his shots through the chiaroscuro that made *Sin City* memorable. Producer Deborah Del Prete even went so far as to describe the look of the film as being "contemporary noir."[92] Moreover, instead of dressing Eisner's femme fatales in actual clothing, Miller brought his signature obsession with the female form to the forefront by showcasing his actresses in leather bondage gear and Nazi paraphernalia. Yet there were other graphical betrayals that Miller was held accountable for: changing the color of Denny Colt's trademark trench coat and fedora from blue to black and showing the visage of Eisner's faceless villain, the Octopus.

However, the biggest shift was Miller's insistence on stylistic remediation, despite Eisner's hardline philosophy against it. Reaching beyond his re-remediation of noir style for a moment, Miller also remediates anime. In one scene, Octopus speaks with Silken Floss (Scarlett Johansson) and the objective space of the scene changes abruptly into one formed by the Octopus's deranged subjectivity. As Del Prete notes in the film's commentary track, "This whole . . . scene, when Frank told me about it, I had no idea what he was talking about. He wanted to do it like an anime and I kept going 'OK, fine, I'm sure you know what you mean."[93] As one self-described fan of Eisner's comic and Miller's work assessed the film, "everything about it was an insult to the memory of Will Eisner. . . . I believe once he admits these wrong doings to himself he can move on to another step that I feel should be a public apology."[94]

The marketing of *The Spirit* reiterates the the fact that Will Eisner's *The Spirit* has been redefined by Frank Miller. Featuring a stark black and white

Figures 6.15, 6.16, and 6.17.
The high-concept marketing of
Frank Miller's graphical remediation.

composition with the title character (red neck tie flailing in the wind) standing atop bricks spelling out the film's tagline ("My city screams."), the poster
promises everything that filmgoers loved about the other movies Miller had
been associated with. The hardboiled tagline is similar to that for *Sin City*
("Walk down the right back alley in Sin City and you can find anything.") and
the pointed, red, inky font appears to be a mash-up of those used on the marketing materials for *Sin City* and *300* (Figure 6.15, Figure 6.16, and Figure 6.17).
Frank Miller's graphical remediation, like bullet time and the Glasgow grin
Joker before it, had become a commodity born from an intersection of the
creative process and movie marketing. This time however, damned both by
tone and by the film's conflicted authorship, the concept crashed and burned
with critics and general audiences. As Nathan Rabin notes, "The hard-boiled
visual style of *Sin City*, with its comic book compositions, noirish black-and-
white, and impressionistic splashes of color, now feels shopworn. . . . In comics, it took Miller decades to devolve into embarrassing self-parody. In film,
he's made that leap over the course of a single disastrous film."[95]

Moreover, Miller and Lionsgate overestimated the cultural value of the
property. While Eisner's work has established him as one of the founding
fathers of American comic art and he has become an incredibly influential
figure, his books never topped the sales charts. As comics scholar Jean-Paul
Gabilliet notes, "Over a twelve-year career, the strip never experienced large-
scale popularity (only a limited number of Sunday newspapers carried the
Spirit section). . . . [Yet] In terms of artistic achievement *The Spirit* stands out in
America as the most worthwhile counterpart to the Belgian cartoonist Hergé's
Tintin in the mid-twentieth century."[96] Thus, considering the small readership
that *The Spirit* had and the canonical status that Eisner and the strip held with
that demographic, Lionsgate and Miller made an expensive and misguided
film that attempted to capture a wider audience with style rather than retaining the original fan community with narrative and stylistic fidelity.

In the years that have passed since *The Spirit* disgraced screens, Miller's
working profile has gone from high to low. From 2005 to 2008, Miller revisited the character who helped make him famous, Batman, for DC Comics' *All-
Star Batman and Robin the Boy Wonder*. Yet the series, scheduled to run for
twelve issues, never reached its conclusion. In 2010, DC issued a press release
announcing that the series would be rebranded as *Dark Knight: Boy Wonder*,
would finish the narrative begun in 2005 in six issues, and would "ship on
time, every month" (the original title had release date problems, allegedly due
to artist Jim Lee's full schedule).[97] As of 2015, the title has yet to be scheduled
for release. Also rumored to be on Miller's desk is a prequel to *300*, tentatively
titled *Xerxes*. His only film projects since *The Spirit* were a commercial for the

fragrance Gucci Guilty and the disastrous sequel to *Sin City* (2014). He is cur-rently in the midst of completing another sequel to *The Dark Knight Returns* —*The Master Race*—with the assistance of Brian Azzarello, Andy Kubert, and Klaus Janson.

Conclusions: Lines vs. Circles

The objective of this chapter has been to trace stylistic remediation as a potentially ongoing occurrence, widening the scope of analysis by providing a nuanced account that details the complex stylistic shifts that an art form experiences when it encounters other art forms. This can often result in a form of aesthetic dialogue that we have seen in the two case studies analyzed here. In the example of Frank Miller, we have established film noir influenced his work on *Sin City* nearly forty years after the fact. Moreover, Miller brought this stylistic sensibility beyond the comic book page, back to the film frame, and applied it to an adaptation of his predecessor.

Miller's remediation and the critical and fan reaction it inspired also begs questions about authorship, comics, and film. Authorship has been a defining force in the comic book industry since the rise of the graphic novel and adult print friendly lines, making Miller, Alan Moore, and other writers and artists commodities in themselves. Yet when those artistic sensibilities clash like Eis-ner's and Miller's, whose Spirit wins out? When the dust settled with critics, fans, and the box office, it appears to have been Will Eisner's original vision. Ultimately, the dialogical remediation of noir (from film, to comics, back to film) distanced the adaptation from its source material.

Yet dialogical stylistic remediation and the formal evolution it inspires are not always received poorly. As exemplified by the first case study of this chapter focusing on the Joker, the graphical remediation and redefinition of the character over the past decades has drawn from a range of media. His ini-tial design in the comics was informed by film. His cinematic representation was informed by the comics, which in turn influenced an animated series, which existed in dialogue with a comic book. Moreover, while the Glasgow Grin Joker was originally met with skepticism in some fan circles, the trifecta of comic and film texts produced by Morrison, Nolan, and Azzarello helped fans embrace the new look and provided Warner Bros. and DC Comics with the fuel for a perpetual motion marketing machine. Ultimately, the revamped design of the Joker unified the three texts which, despite taking place in three separate diegetic spaces, provided the studio and publisher with a high con-cept image to market the texts both seamlessly and simultaneously.

CONCLUSION: COMICS ARE IN RIGHT NOW?

In order to offer up a proper conclusion to this study, let us return to the three questions guiding this investigation that were first proposed in the introduction and offer answers based upon the research and analysis performed since their proposal. The first two research questions are closely related. What role have horizontal integration and multimedia conglomerates had in the process of stylistic remediation and what is the industrial motivation behind stylistic remediation, both in films and comics?

With regard to stylistic remediation, the role of horizontal integration and multimedia conglomerates has evolved towards greater influence throughout the past thirty years. A summarization of one of the central case studies here, the Time Warner media conglomerate (behind the production of comic and film titles ranging from Superman and Batman to film productions of *300* and *Watchmen*), is a prime example. During the production of their subsidiary's (DC Comics) film adaptation of *Superman: The Movie* (1978), the conglomerate left independent producers Alexander and Ilya Salkind, for the most part, to their own creative devices. In the early 1970s, Warner Bros. lacked confidence in the value of the property as a film franchise, licensing the rights for a mere $3 million. While the studio's licensing agreement came with a first look stipulation, the studio was not initially involved in the production.

The major stipulation that the Salkinds were required to honor as part of the licensing agreement was to accept input from a DC Comics creative executive liaison. However, given the reports in the trade papers and cited disclosures from the talent and personnel involved, this liaison merely requested that casting decisions be clean and family friendly. Essentially, DC Comics did not want to see their property defaced if an actor or actress with ties to questionable content (softcore or hardcore pornography being chief concerns) was cast in the film. Warner Communications remained uninvolved in the day to day production of the film until the film began to go over budget. Then, depending on the source, Warner Bros. provided $15 million in exchange for partial ownership rights (this is based on Jake Rossen's assumption that they liked the footage the Salkinds had provided and wanted to leverage the property back in the Warner Communications stable) or a film negative that was being held hostage (according to the *Los Angeles Times*).

Warner Communication's initial disinterest towards *Superman* can be attributed to both an unstable comic book industry and the cultural context of the comic book at the time. As comics scholar Jean-Paul Gabilliet writes, the 1970s "proved problematic for the large publishers [like DC]. They had to cope with dropping revenue, increasingly rebellious employees, and a society in permanent change necessitating a permanent evolution in the content of their magazines."[1] Moreover, American society, at this point in time, still viewed comics as being a mass medium of low cultural status. This belief was sustained by the legacy of Fredric Wertham and the child friendly content that was produced under the self-regulatory Comics Code that came in his wake. This cultural belief and the Comics Code were only beginning to be challenged during the 1970s. After arriving in Los Angeles, former DC and Marvel Comics editor Denny O'Neil notes that his manager encouraged him not to talk about "comic books. Talk about your science fiction stories and your journalism. Now, any connection with comic books will get you in the door."[2]

According to O'Neil, this perception began to change in the mid-1970s when DC hired editor Jeanette Kahn. Kahn "insisted we be proud in what we did. . . . Most of the time we said we worked in publishing or magazines. Part of the attraction for me was that it was so disreputable. It wasn't supposed to be good, it was supposed to be done by Thursday."[3] In contrast, when comics began to gain the cultural high ground during the 1980s, Warner Communications began to involve itself in the production of licensed content. Specifically, the conglomerate was forced to take drastic steps during the production of *Batman*. Driven by negative fan reaction to the casting of Michael Keaton (which was covered at length by newspapers ranging from the *Los Angeles Times* to the *Wall Street Journal*), the company hired Batman creator Bob Kane as a creative consultant, issued public statements from director Tim Burton regarding the tone of the film, and rushed release of a trailer in an attempt to placate disgruntled fans.

Moreover, after the first film became a box office success, DC Comics was reevaluated by the conglomerate. As O'Neil notes, "Anything that makes a billion is respectable. . . . In 1989, it seemed that the studio [Warner Bros.] did not want to use the word comic book. . . . The studio was a little uneasy about it but those attitudes did gradually change."[4] When the darker sequel began an economic slide (a 40 percent slide, to be exact, against a 225 percent increase in budget) and drew criticism from parents, endangering licensing rights with such companies as McDonalds, a new director was hired and a new tone for the series was established. To put the importance of licensing in perspective, comics scholar Mark Rogers writes that "The 1989 Batman film grossed $405 million worldwide . . . and sold over a billion dollars in merchandise. It is estimated that Warner Communications, then DC's parent company, netted at least $390 million, some $90 million more than the sales of the entire comic book industry that year."[5] As intellectual property licensing has become both more lucrative and more exploitable thanks to the vast and diverse holdings of media conglomerates, increased involvement at the larger corporate level has become both common and necessary to ensure the longevity of a tent pole franchise.

Yet despite the tremendous rise in the cultural and economic value of comic book franchises in media conglomerates at the time, Warner Communications and Warner Bros. did not exert pressure on DC and O'Neil. According to former Batman editor, "Initially, Jeanette and my immediate boss would go over proofs with me. . . . As far as editorial direction, my understanding was that I was hired to redo the Batman franchise, which consisted of only two titles at the time. So I thought, 'Ok, that's my job.' They were pretty much hands off, right up to the end."[6] Yet O'Neil noticed a marked shift when he retired from his role as editor in the late 1990s. He notes, "I still have a lot of dealings with DC and I would not be comfortable with the way comics are being done now. They aren't being done wrong, it's a personal thing. . . . Now, they've [comics and film] become virtually the same business. . . . Both comic book companies are serving as R&D arms for the movies."[7]

Similarly, stylistic remediation can serve as a research and development function by allowing multinational conglomerates to experiment with CGI and form in a way that, in the best instances, can be spread across multiple properties (like "bullet time" in *The Matrix*). In the case of a mid-budget project, aesthetic experimentation may also provide a "high concept" marketing hook that can differentiate a project (*300*) from its generic siblings. Moreover, corporate involvement in not just limited to tent pole franchises, as the analysis of the Scott Pilgrim Experience illustrated. As formal properties have become a lucrative means of drawing fans and potential readers towards both synergistic and transmedia texts, conglomerates have, for the most part, increasingly allowed and nurtured stylistic remediation. Normally, this allowance appears to be on the condition that production costs are kept low (as such big budget disasters as *Dick Tracy* and *Hulk* have provided very significant examples of how this technique, no matter how marketable, can backfire economically). By doing so, multimedia conglomerates, like Time Warner and *Scott Pilgrim*'s parent company NBCUniversal, can rely on the image and the style as an alternative means of product marketing to unite ancillary and transmedia texts. While transmedia scholars often discuss the phenomenon from the standpoint of narrative or storytelling, transmedia style, as discussed throughout this study (specifically the case studies on *The Matrix* and *Scott Pilgrim*) can be equally successful without running the risk of consumer alienation that transmedia storytelling can produce when a reader or viewer feels out of the textual loop.

However, due to the tremendous economic failure of *Scott Pilgrim vs. the World*, media conglomerates are in the process reappraising the cultural and economic field of comic books, comic book adaptations, and both transmedia storytelling and style. In June 2011, the *New York Times* reported that the bulk of Hollywood studios would be avoiding the year's biggest marketing event, San Diego Comic-Con. Tent pole releases like Disney and Marvel's *The Avengers* (2012) and Warner Bros.' *The Dark Knight Rises* and *Man of Steel* (2012) were absent from the proceedings. The 6,500 seat Hall H did not host panels or footage of the newest Batman or Superman films. Rather, the massive room provided an arena for science fiction and fantasy television programming. As the *New York Times* reported, "Comic-Con, as a growing number of movie marketers are realizing, has turned into a treacherous place. Studios come seeking buzz, but the Comic-Con effect can be more negative than positive. The swarm of dedicated fans—many of whom arrive at the convention in Japanese anime drag or draped in Ewok fur—can instantly sour on a film if it doesn't like what it sees, leaving publicity teams with months of damaging Web chatter to clean up."[8]

One of the most illustrative examples of this reevaluation is to be found in the transmedia production of Stephen King's *The Dark Tower* that was briefly explored by Universal. The project, during the span of a few months, went from greenlight to redlight. Initially envisioned as a transmedia story that would have spanned across three feature films, comic books, and two limited run television series, Universal Studios rushed the franchise into pre-production. After Javier Bardem had been cast in the lead, the studio was faced with rising costs. Initially, Universal attempted to scale down the budget. By July 2011, they pulled the plug altogether.[9] The ambitious project recently found a home at Sony Pictures and casting has begun with an early 2017 release date in mind. As of this writing, it remains unclear whether or not transmedia storytelling will play a role in this incarnation of the project.

A major factor that tends to be overlooked in these discussions is how many people read comic books (including more specific demographic information like gender and age) and what books they are reading. As Gabilliet notes in his essential cultural study of the medium, a 1999 American Library Association (ALA) survey found that only 33 percent of children between ages 11–18 (42 percent of boys and 27 percent of girls) read comic books. As Gabilliet writes, "More revealing was the marginal position occupied by comic books in the reading priority of the everyday cultural universe of young Americans: seventh position for boys, far behind magazines about sports, music, computers, and show business . . . and eleventh position for girls."[10] Gabilliet notes that tracking adult readership has become increasingly difficult, and cites with caution a 1997 survey conducted by comic book retailers. The results are shocking: the audience was only made up of approximately 1.25 million people (94 percent men, 6 percent women) at an average age of twenty-six.[11] Finally, the best-selling comics in the United States tend to be Japanese manga.[12]

One industrial concern regarding comic book publishing has been that of narrative complexity. Specifically, the universes that have been established over the past decades span hundreds of issues and titles, making them too complicated and intimidating to new and casual readers. In order to deal with this growing problem, DC Comics decided to reboot their line of titles in 2011. Entitled "The New 52," the various titles (distributed both physically and digitally) feature new character designs, writers, artists, and significantly, "#1" stamped on each cover. Due to the uncertain financial outlook for both comic books and comic book films that came in the wake of major failures like *Scott Pilgrim* and *Kick-Ass* (2010), the double-edged marketing sword of San Diego Comic-Con, and Universal's swift pulling of the production plug on a major transmedia adaptation of *The Dark Tower*, the future of stylistic remediation and transmedia style remains bleak.

Finally, is the remediation of comic book stylistics into films fundamentally a by-product of technologies and an indication of a Manovichian shift from cinema to digital cinema? Judging from the work of comics scholars Julia Round (2010) and Jochen Ecke (also 2010), their outlook towards stylistic remediation is positive. As Round writes, "A movie-inspired aesthetic has also redefined the [comics] medium in some respects. . . . Comparisons with the movies therefore seem more relevant to today's industry and likely to continue."[13] Similarly, Ecke notes,

> The thorough intermedial negotiations that the film industry has entered into with comics in the recent years have greatly helped to enrich the cinematic language. . . . The formal experiments of films like *300* or *The Hulk* [sic] can be regarded as the avant-garde products of this new, serious interest in comics as a medium.[14]

For both scholars, the intertwining businesses of comics and film have resulted in a formal influence and interchange between both media that will

continue into the coming years. Yet both writers approach the question of stylistic influences from the standpoint of formal and cultural analysis, avoiding
the industrial context.[15] However, the economic realities of the film industry
have seriously hampered the contemporary incarnation of the stylistic practice, much like the box office failures of *Dick Tracy* (1990) and *Hulk* (2003) did
earlier. However, the history of this trajectory has exemplified that stylistic
remediation is a trend defined by exploration, embrace, overgrowth, gradual
decline, and eventual rebirth. Stylistic remediation is also capable of producing a formal dialogue in which stylistic elements ping pong back and forth
between media, with each strike leaving its own formal imprint. This dialogue
can progress to the point that we are left unsure of where one medium leaves
off and the other begins.

Yet it is not just the economic and industrial realities driving stylistic
remediation at this current moment that encourage this pessimistic assessment. While the ties between stylistic remediation, digital technology, and
computer generated imagery can result in larger budgets, there also appears
to be a cultural fatigue towards the experience. This fatigue is best exemplified by the gradual decline of Zack Snyder and Frank Miller in the eyes of
both fans and general moviegoers (a sentiment traced here via the continuous
citation of movie reviews and industrial trade articles). Moreover, there are
creative limitations to how much the style of comics can be embraced by film
and vice-versa.

Accepting the premise that stylistic remediation is the result of evolutions
in both hardware and software, we should return to Lev Manovich's concept of spatial montage or the involvement of "a number of images, potentially of different sizes and proportions, appearing on screen at the same
time. . . . Spatial montage represents an alternative to traditional cinematic
temporal montage, replacing its traditional sequential mode with a spatial
one."[16] For Manovich, the possibilities of spatial montage are the result of evolutions in both technology and our perception of the image as influenced
by technology. Manovich writes that "Traditional film and video technology
was designed to fill a screen completely with a single image; thus to explore
spatial montage a filmmaker had to work 'against' the technology."[17] Manovich's thesis is historically dubious. He rightly considers comics and animation
proto practitioners of spatial montage, a stylistic practice that was marginal-
ized by classical modes of representation before digital tools and media made
a representational logic of simultaneity possible. However, he also overlooks
developments in television, specifically television news, which has engaged
in spatial montage since the staging of weather reports and the use of blue
screen throughout the 1980s and 1990s.

Yet despite the evolution of software and hardware and our increased ability to decipher multiple images simultaneously, Manovich's claim that we have transitioned into a new era of cinema in which "the diachronic dimension is no longer privileged over the synchronic dimension, time is no longer privileged over space, sequence is no longer privileged over simultaneity, montage in time is no longer privileged over montage within a shot" is overly optimistic.[18] After all, if spatial montage is upon us and if it had a precedent within the medium of the comic, is it not safe to assume that it would be apparent in comic book adaptations that practice stylistic remediation?

Yet even in the case of Ang Lee's *Hulk*, stylistic remediation and spatial montage are utilized by the filmmakers in a classical, Bordwellian, sense. The moments of spatial montage are incredibly brief in the grand scheme of the film. Moreover, they do not function in the same way spatial montage in comics does (wherein each panel embodies a different moment in time). Rather, the multiframe of *Hulk* embodies the spatial montage logic of split-screen cinema (where each image embodies a different portion of space during the same time; they are images of different spaces during the same, simultaneous, moment). Essentially, stylistic remediation bends to the rules of continuity editing that David Bordwell, Janet Staiger, and Kristin Thompson described as taking root in 1917, and as later refined by Bordwell and Thompson, continue into the present moment.

Bordwell has been the most vocal proponent and rigorous scholar of classical style. Recently, he published a pseudo-sequel to *The Classical Hollywood Cinema: Film Style & Mode of Production to 1960* entitled *The Way Hollywood Tells It*. In his expansion, Bordwell traces the stylistic evolution of Hollywood cinema since the 1960s and argues that despite the changes in film style Hollywood filmmakers still favor the "intensified continuity" of the classical norms embodied by the continuity system.[19] Bordwell has become a straw man for media studies historians and theorists because his theory is sometimes interpreted as being monolithic. Specifically, he attempts to account for every deviation from classical Hollywood normative style as still being, nonetheless, part of the normative style because they are motivated by the text. To a degree, Bordwell does overreach. Every normative system has outliers, some of which cannot be accounted for. As digital cinema scholar Sean Cubitt rightly objects, "Bordwell's strategy . . . is to establish as normative the practices of the North American film industry, and to derive all other filmic styles from that norm . . . thus leaving space neither for film styles independent of the North American industry nor for dialectical currents within the normative style itself."[20]

Bordwell attempts to justify these normative outliers within what he describes as "the bounds of difference." In order for Hollywood to continue to remain a profitable business enterprise, the classical system must be guided by standardization while also allowing for differentiation. As Bordwell describes, in the historical content of the Hollywood studio system, "Novelty and originality were taken to be valuable qualities, and scriptwriters evolved an entire vocabulary for describing variation. . . . Cameramen likewise claimed to see each story as requiring a unique visual style."[21] Yet for Bordwell, "The principle of motivation gives the classical paradigm a great range of non-disruptive differentiation."[22] Essentially, Bordwell argues that deviations from classical normative style can be motivated by the text in numerous ways. Film form can be generically motivated, realistically motivated, artistically motivated, causally motivated or, with the help of scholar Kristin Thompson, transtextually motivated.[23]

Bordwell cites film noir, a stylistic mode that would initially appear to be the most antagonistic to his system, and accounts for all the ways in which its formal attributes are motivated by the text. First, Bordwell writes that noir is commonly described as assaulting psychological causality (characters are incapable of logical action because they are deranged, thus muddling the viewer's conception of the character's motivations). Bordwell justifies this by writing that these outliers can be understood and justified within the wider umbrella of popular literature conventions (incomprehensible character motivations have been "conventionalized in psychological thrillers").[24] The assault of psychological causality by film noir is thus generically motivated. Moreover, Bordwell justifies low-key lighting as a stylistic device that is often motivated by a conception of cinematic realism that could "be plausibly motivated as coming from a single, harsh source."[25] The other two types of motivation Bordwell considers briefly are artistic (an example would be using symbolism, an intersection between imagery and theme/content) and casual (an example would be a flashback that is motivated by one character is telling another character a story). In the end, for Bordwell, noir remains "codified [formally and technically]: a minority practice, but a unified one. These films blend causal unity with a new realistic and generic motivation, and the result no more subverts the classical film than crime fiction undercuts the orthodox novel."[26]

Bordwell's theory—as later elaborated by Kristin Thompson—would attempt to account for the practice of stylistic remediation in comic book adaptations as being transtextually motivated. For Thompson, transtextual motivation "involves any appeal to conventions of other art works, and hence it can be varied as the historical circumstances allow. In effect, the work introduces a device that is not motivated adequately within its own terms, but that depends on our recognition of the device from past experience."[27] Essentially, the remediation of the multiframe in the film adaptation of *Hulk* is motivated by its comic book predecessor. As Thompson continues, "Transtextual motivation, then, is a special type which preexists the artwork, and upon which the artist may draw in a straightforward or playful way."[28] This assessment would be correct; stylistic remediation is transtextually motivated, and when it does appear, largely conforms to continuity editing norms. Thus, while it may be tempting to overestimate the special quality of this "special type" of motivation, the case studies analyzed here do not come anywhere close to being a form of Manovichian spatial montage or digital cinema (despite often being digitally produced, it simply does not function in the same way he describes). Perhaps we will find the outliers and dialectical currents that Cubitt describes when stylistic remediation finds itself rejuvenated by another string of box office successes (Zack Snyder's forthcoming film *Batman v. Superman* may mark a return to the stylistic practice!). Until then, we wait and look up to the sky.

NOTES

Introduction

1. Dudley Andrew, *Concepts in Film Theory* (Oxford: Oxford University Press, 1984), 98.

2. Undated memo from Whitney Bolton found in the comic strip clipping file at the Margaret Herrick Library at the Academy of Motion Picture Arts and Sciences. Judging from the films referenced in the memo, I would assume the memo dates from the mid-1940s.

3. For the most part, I am ignoring a discussion of these live-action serials and animated shorts because they fall outside the temporal boundaries of this project as discussed in the section "Limits of Investigation." To briefly summarize, I would argue that the production and cultural contexts between the two periods would make such an all-encompassing investigation unwieldy.

4. David Bordwell, *The Way Hollywood Tells It: Story and Style in Modern Movies* (Berkeley: University of California Press, 2006), 54.

5. M. Keith Booker, *May Contain Graphic Material: Comic Books, Graphic Novels, and Film* (Westport: Praeger, 2007), xii.

6. Matthew P. McAllister, Ian Gordon, and Mark Jancovich, "Blockbuster Meets Superhero Comic, or Art House Meets Graphic Novel?: The Contradictory Relationship between Film and Comic Art," *Journal of Popular Film and Television* 34 (Fall 2006), 110.

7. Eileen R. Meehan, "'Holy Commodity Fetish Batman!': The Political Economy of the Commercial Intertext," in *The Many Lives of Batman: Critical Approaches to a Superhero and His Media*, eds. Roberta Pearson and William Uricchio (London: Routledge, 1991), 48.

8. Ibid., 325.

9. On March 5, 2009, the *New York Times* started their own best seller list of "Graphic Books" that is now considered supplementary to the DCD ranking.

10. Valeria D'Orazio, "What Makes a Comic Book a Success Nowadays?" *Comic Book Junction*, 9 March 2009, <http://www.comicbookjunction.com/2009/03/09/what-makes-a-comic-book-a-success-nowadays/> (9 April 2010).

11. Roger Sabin, *Comics, Comix & Graphic Novels: A History of Comic Art* (New York: Phaidon, 1996), 68.

12. Ian Gordon, "Making Comics Respectable: How *Maus* Helped Redefine a Medium," in *The Rise of the American Comics Artist*, eds. Paul Williams and James Lyons (Jackson: University Press of Mississippi, 2010), 189.

13. *Taking Flight: The Development of Superman*, dir. Michael Thau, 30 min., Warner Bros., 2001, DVD.

14. Carol Blue and Al Delugach, "*Superman*: Rare Look at Film Finances," *Los Angeles Times*, 3 April 1980.

15. Randy Duncan and Matthew J. Smith, *The Power of Comics: History, Form, & Culture* (New York: Continuum, 2009), 71.

16. Ibid., 71–72.

17. Kathleen Hughes, "Batman Fans Fear the Joke's on Them in Hollywood Epic," *Wall Street Journal*, 29 November 1988, 1.

18. Bill Barol, "Batmania," *Newsweek*, 26 June 1989, 70.

19. David Glanzer and Gary Sassaman, *Comic-Con 40 Souvenir Book* (San Diego: San Diego Comic-Con International, 2009), 60–116.

20. Booker, ix.

21. "Forget the Stars; Studios Pay Most for FX," *IMDB.com*, 15 May 2006, <http://www.imdb.com/news/sb/2006-05-15#film1> (28 March 2011).

22. Richard George, "*300* in Film," *IGN.com*, 8 March 2007, <http://comics.ign.com/articles/771/771698p1.html> (28 March 2011).

23. Ibid. Note that one of the major shifts in the comic book industry during the past decades has been increased creator rights. Depending on the company—and this is how independent publishers like Dark Horse and Image were able to rope in major comic book auteurs—creators and personnel are often offered profit-sharing contracts and the possibility of retaining ownership on titles developed at their publisher. This was the case for *300* and *Sin City*, both of which were published by Dark Horse and owned by Frank Miller. When I spoke to *Red* (2003–2004) artist Cully Hamner about the terms of his legal agreement with di Bonaventura Pictures, DC Comics, and Summit Entertainment on the rights to his comic once it became a film (2010), he told me,

> I still own my artwork, and Warren and I still own the published comic; DC still owns the rights to publish it, since they've kept it in print. If it had been out of print longer than a certain license period, those rights would have reverted to us eventually, but the movie (and possible sequel) have made sure that DC will keep it in bookstores for a long time. But my art is my art, and actually, even that gets complicated. DC owns the rights to publish that art, as I said, for a period defined by keeping it in print. I, on the other hand, own the physical artwork itself, and can sell it to collectors as I wish. Summit Entertainment has the right to use art from the comic in the film or to market it. They can also hire me to do new art, but that would be . . . a separately paid and negotiated agreement.

24. Julia Round helpfully describes the difference between the comic book and the graphic novel as follows:

> The graphic novel (also known as a "prestige format" single issue) is defined as a "permanent" comic: it is often longer than the usual single-issue comic (with 20 to 24 story

pages) and consists of new material printed on higher-quality paper. Trade paperbacks use the graphic novel form to collect and reprint single stories (either reprinting entire mini-series, or typically runs between four and twelve issues from longer, ongoing series).

See Julia Round, "'Is This a Book?' DC Vertigo and the Redefinition of Comics in the 1990s," in *The Rise of the American Comics Artist: Creators and Contexts*, eds. Paul Williams and James Lyons (Jackson: University Press of Mississippi, 2010), 14–15.

25. Scott McCloud, *Understanding Comics: The Invisible Art* (New York: Harper Perennial, 1994), 81.

26. Sabin, 19.

27. Duncan and Smith, 291.

28. Greg M. Smith, "Shaping *The Maxx*: Adapting the Comic Book Frame to Television," *Animation Journal* 8, no. 1 (1999): 32–53.

29. Peter J. Boyer, "Film Clips: As Batman, West is Out of Movie Lineup," *Los Angeles Times*, 5 August 1981.

Chapter 1

1. Nikki Finke, "Guys Beat Gal," *Deadline.com*, 14 August 2010, <http://www.deadline.com/2010/08/first-box-office-the-expendables-13m34m-eat-pray-love-8m23m-scott-pilgrim-5m12m/> (18 August 2010).

2. Robert Stam, "Introduction," in *Literature and Film: A Guide to the Theory and Practice of Film Adaptation*, eds. Robert Stam and Alessandra Raengo (Malden: Blackwell Publishing, 2005), 8.

3. Robert Stam, "Beyond Fidelity: The Dialogics of Adaptation," in *Film Adaptation*, ed. James Naremore (New Jersey: Rutgers University Press, 2000), 64.

4. Stam, "Introduction," 11.

5. Another potentially productive framework for analyzing the stylistic relationship between American film and comics may also be found in the work of scholars focusing on intermediality and multimodality (specifically, the works of scholars like Marina Grishakova, Irina O. Rajewsky, and Marie-Laure Ryan). Unfortunately, despite being a substantial field of study across Europe—Rajewsky's work dates back to 2002—much of the scholarship has yet to either be translated into English or made available to North American readers. For instance, an essay by Jeff Thoss on *Scott Pilgrim* in the 2014 anthology *Storyworlds Across Media* largely relies on the author's translation of Rajewsky's scholarship. In a footnote in the same article, Thoss notes how Rajewsky differentiates between the terms: remediation is a "category that describes the relations between media in general from intermediality as a narrower category denoting aesthetic phenomena involving more than one medium in specific texts, films, and so forth" (227). However, despite this gap caused by translation and accessibility, the distinction between the concepts may ultimately turn out to be rather thin. For instance, Thoss uses remediation as a synonym for intermediality ("the relationship

between remediation or intermediality and media rivalry," page 211) and concludes that "both terms are frequently used in both senses" (page 227). Nevertheless, I would cite this avenue as a potent site for additional research by my fellow scholars (on both sides of the pond!). See Jeff Thoss, "Tell It Like a Game: Scott Pilgrim and Performative Media Rivalry," in *Storyworlds Across Media: Toward a Media-Conscious Narratology*, eds. Marie-Laure Ryan and Jan Noël Thon (Lincoln: University of Nebraska Press, 2014), 211–229.

6. Jay David Bolter and Richard Grusin, *Remediation: Understanding New Media* (Cambridge, MA: MIT Press, 1999), 44.

7. Ibid., 86, 15.

8. Pascal Lefèvre, "Incompatible Visual Ontologies?: The Problematic Adaptation of Drawn Images," in *Film and Comic Books*, eds. Ian Gordon, Mark Jancovich, and Matthew P. McAllister (Jackson: University Press of Mississippi, 2007).

9. Edgar Wright, interview with author, 27 July 2010.

10. For simplicity's sake, I am ignoring the three-dimensional quality of McCloud's pyramid by simply dealing with the Retinal and Representational Edges.

11. McCloud, 51.

12. Ibid., 50–51.

13. Scott McCloud, *Understanding Comics*, 114.

14. Thanks to my good friends William Bibbiani and Jennifer Wang for sharing their knowledge of manga with me.

15. Scott McCloud, in his seminal study *Understanding Comics: The Invisible Art* describes six transitions between individual panels: moment to moment, action to action, subject to subject, scene to scene, aspect to aspect, and non-sequitur.

16. McCloud, 94–97.

17. Eisner, 40–41.

18. Notably, David Lynch does not allow DVD and Blu-Ray releases of his films to have chapters because it defaces the theatrical experience.

19. McCloud, 9.

20. Thierry Groensteen, *The System of Comics*, trans. Bart Beaty and Nick Nguyen (Jackson: University of Mississippi Press, 2007), 19.

21. See also Chris Sims, "The Best Video Game Moments in *Scott Pilgrim*," *Comics Alliance*, 28 July 2009, <http://www.comicsalliance.com/2009/07/28/the-best-video-game -moments-in-scott-pilgrim/> (2 August 2010).

22. Edgar Wright, interview with author.

23. Bryan Lee O'Malley, interview with author, 27 July 2010.

24. Bill Gibron, "Game(r) Over," *Popmatters.com*, 16 August 2010, <http://www.popmat ters.com/pm/post/129700-gamer-over/> (18 August 2010).

25. Ibid.

26. Finke, "Guys Beat Gal."

27. Gibron, "Game(r) Over."

28. Drew Morton, "Adam McKay Signs on to Direct R-Rated Superhero Satire *The Boys*," *The Playlist*, 24 July 2010, <http://theplaylist.blogspot.com/2010/07/adam-mckay-signs-on -to-direct-r-rated.html> (18 August 2010).

29. Hollywood budgets are normally defined in vague and slippery terms by the industry. A fair assumption for determining marketing costs is approximately 50 percent the negative cost. Thus, if a film costs $100 million to produce, the studio will probably spend around $50 million to market it.

Chapter 2

1. Bob Rehak, "*Watchmen*'s Frames of Reference: Digital Production Tools and the High-Fidelity Comic Book Adaptation," presentation at the Society for Cinema and Media Studies Conference, 18 March 2010.

2. Bradford W. Wright, *Comic Book Nation: The Transformation of Youth Culture in America* (Baltimore: Johns Hopkins University Press, 2003), 3–4.

3. Ibid., 4.

4. Duncan and Smith, 32.

5. Wright, 13.

6. Duncan and Smith, 33.

7. Jean-Paul Gabilliet, *Of Comics and Men: A Cultural History of American Comic Books*, trans. Bart Beaty and Nick Nguyen (Jackson: University Press of Mississippi, 2010), 22.

8. Ibid.

9. Sabin, 35.

10. Paul Lopes, *Demanding Respect: The Evolution of the American Comic Book* (Philadelphia: Temple University Press, 2009), 32.

11. Ibid., 43.

12. Gabilliet, 39.

13. For more information on the "comic book scare," see David Hajdu, *The Ten-Cent Plague: The Great Comic-Book Scare and How it Changed America* (New York: Farrar, Straus and Giroux, 2008).

14. Wright, 172.

15. Duncan and Smith, 40.

16. Sabin, 68.

17. Ibid., 36–37.

18. Benton, 42.

19. Gabilliet, 202–203.

20. Thomas Doherty, *Teenagers and Teenpics: The Juvenilization of American Movies in the 1950s* (Philadelphia: Temple University Press, 2002), 2.

21. Jake Rossen, *Superman vs. Hollywood: How Fiendish Producers, Devious Directors, and Warring Writers Grounded an American Icon* (Chicago: Chicago Review Press, 2008), 24.

22. The film was edited and aired on television as two episodes of the series in 1953.

23. Lynn Spigel and Henry Jenkins, "Same Bat Channel, Different Bat Times: Mass Culture and Popular Memory," in *The Many Lives of the Batman: Critical Approaches to a Superhero and his Media*, eds. Roberta Pearson and William Uricchio (New York: Routledge, 1991), 123–124.

24. Ibid., 124.

25. Sabin, 61.

26. Les Daniels, *Batman: The Complete History* (San Francisco: Chronicle Books, 1999), 113.

27. See Will Brooker, *Batman Unmasked: Analyzing a Cultural Icon* (New York: Continuum Publishing, 2000), 171–248.

28. Rossen, 52.

29. Frank Miller, "Introduction," *Batman: Year One* (New York: DC Comics, 1988), Page Number Not Listed.

30. Quoted in Rossen, 60.

31. Addison Verrill, "*Superman* Headed Over Budget but Sitting Pretty," *Daily Variety*, 22 July 1977.

32. Army Archerd. Title Unknown, *Daily Variety*, 8 July 1975.

33. Mary Murphy, "Movie Call Sheet: *Superman* Film."

34. See the documentaries *Taking Flight: The Development of Superman* and *Filming the Legend: Making Superman*, both on the *Superman: The Movie* Special Edition DVD (2001).

35. See the commentary by Salkind and Spengler on the 1978 theatrical version, included in the Special Edition DVD.

36. See the documentary *The Magic Behind the Cape* on the Special Edition DVD for a rather simplistic overview of the technologies used in specific sequences.

37. Todd McCarthy, "Salkinds' Lucrative *Superman* Films Also Costly and Litigious," *Variety*, 8 July 1987.

38. Lacey Rose, "Hollywood's Most Expensive Movies," *Forbes*, 18 December 2006.

39. Rossen, 94.

40. Carol Blue and Al Delugach, "*Superman*: Rare Look at Film Finances," *Los Angeles Times*, 3 April 1980.

41. James Harwood, "*Superman* Movie Review," *Variety*, 13 December 1978.

42. See McCarthy, "Salkinds' Lucrative *Superman* Films Also Costly and Litigious" and Rossen, 105–107.

43. Roger Ebert, "*Superman II* Movie Review," *RogerEbert.com*, 1 January 1981, <http://rogerebert.suntimes.com/apps/pbcs.dll/article?AID=/19810101/REVIEWS/101010303/1023> (4 May 2010).

44. Rossen, 135.

45. Ibid.

46. Ibid., 141.

47. See the Starz Channel documentary *Comic Books Unbound*.

48. Catherine Shapcott, "*Superman* Lands in Calgary," *Variety*, 1 September 1982.

49. Roger Ebert, "*Superman III* Movie Review."

50. "An Expensive Duck," *New York Times*, 22 August 1986.

51. Unless otherwise noted, I've taken the production budgets listed at *Box Office Mojo*, <http://www.boxofficemojo.com>.

52. Lawrence Cohn, "*Batman* a 10-Year Journal for Uslan and Melniker; Execs' Next Game: *Monopoly*," *Weekly Variety*, 7 June 1989.

53. See the documentary *Shadows of the Bat: The Cinematic Saga of the Dark Knight* on the *Batman* Special Edition DVD.

54. Duncan and Smith, 46.

55. Ibid., 172.

56. Wright, 234.

57. Duncan and Smith, 59.

58. Wright, 239.

59. Sabin, 127–128.

60. Mark Rogers, "Beyond Bang! Pow! Zap!: Genre and the Evolution of the American Comic Book Industry," PhD dissertation, University of Michigan, 1997, 87–88.

61. See the documentary *Shadows of the Bat: The Cinematic Saga of the Dark Knight* on the *Batman* Special Edition DVD.

62. Jane Lieberman, "Short Brings 'Simple' Approach to Complex Special-Effects Work," *Variety*, 29 April 1988.

63. Allan B. Rothstein, "Mr. Mom as Batman?" *Los Angeles Times*, 3 July 1988.

64. Kathleen A. Hughes, "Batman Fans Fear the Joke's On Them in Hollywood Epic," *Wall Street Journal*, 29 November 1988.

65. Ibid.

66. Nancy Griffin and Kim Masters, *Hit and Run: How Jon Peters and Peter Guber took Sony for a Ride in Hollywood* (New York: Simon and Schuster, 1997), 170–171.

67. Thomas Schatz, "The New Hollywood," in *Film Theory Goes to the Movies*, eds. Jim Collins, Hilary Radner, and Ava Preacher Collins (London: Routledge, 1993), 10.

68. Justin Wyatt, *High Concept: Movies and Marketing in Hollywood* (Austin: University of Texas Press, 1994), 7.

69. David Bordwell, *The Way Hollywood Tells It: Story and Style in Modern Movies* (Berkeley: University of California Press, 2006), 7, 13. Note that Bordwell is working off of a passage written by André Bazin in the second-half of the quote.

70. Geoff King, *New Hollywood: An Introduction* (New York: Columbia University Press, 2002), 5.

71. David Bordwell, Janet Staiger, and Kristin Thompson, *The Classical Hollywood Cinema: Film Style & Mode of Production to 1960* (New York: Columbia University Press, 1985), 70–84.

72. Roger Ebert and Gene Siskel, "*Batman* Review."

73. Anne Thompson and Pat H. Broeske, "Hawking *Batman*," *Entertainment Weekly*, 10 July 1992.

74. See the documentary *Shadows of the Bat: The Cinematic Saga of the Dark Knight* on the *Batman Returns* Special Edition DVD.

75. See the documentary *Shadows of the Bat: The Cinematic Saga of the Dark Knight* on the *Batman Forever* Special Edition DVD. The special edition DVDs are notable for mixing depreciating commentary based on the franchise with small doses of justification.

76. Janet Maslin, "New Challenges for the Caped Crusader," *New York Times*, 16 June 1995.

77. Brooker, 300–301.

78. Ibid.

79. Claudia Eller, "*Tracy* Cost Put at $101 Mil.," *Variety*, 22 October 1990.

80. Charles Fleming, "Naked Hollywood: Bat Out of Hell," *LA Weekly*, 8 August 1997.

81. Ibid.

82. Derek Johnson, "Will the Real Wolverine Please Stand Up?: Marvel's Mutation from Monthlies to Movies," in *Film and Comic Books*, eds.Ian Gordon, Mark Jancovich, and Matthew P. McAllister (Jackson: University Press of Mississippi, 2007), 72.

83. Ibid.

84. See the Starz documentary *Comic Books Unbound*.

85. Bob Rehak, "*Watchmen*'s Frames of Reference: Digital Production Tools and the High-Fidelity Comic Book Adaptation," presentation at the Society for Cinema and Media Studies Conference, 18 March 2010.

Chapter 3

1. Richard Marschall, *America's Great Comic-Strip Artists* (New York: Abbeville Press, 1989), 227.

2. Ibid., 229.

3. Ibid.

4. Gregg Kilday, "Film Clips: *Dick Tracy* to Make Film Debut," *Los Angeles Times*, 26 November 1977.

5. "Film Clips," *Los Angeles Times*, 29 June 1983.

6. Marilyn Beck, "Paramount Drops *Dick Tracy* Project," *Daily News*, 15 January 1986.

7. "Insider," *Los Angeles Magazine*, October 1986.

8. David Ansen, "Tracymania," *Newsweek*, 25 June 1990.

9. Dick Tracy Press Kit, 14.

10. André Bazin, "The Ontology of the Photographic Image," in *What Is Cinema? Volume I*, trans. Hugh Gray (Berkeley: University of California Press, 1967), 13.

11. Ibid.

12. Pascal Lefèvre, "Incompatible Visual Ontologies?: The Problematic Adaptation of Drawn Images," in *Film and Comic Books*, eds. Ian Gordon, Mark Jancovich, and Matthew P. McAllister (Jackson: University Press of Mississippi, 2007), 8.

13. See also Scott McCloud's "The Vocabulary of Comics" in *Understanding Comics*.

14. For simplicity's sake, I am ignoring the second axis, "The Retinal Edge," and the three-dimensional quality of McCloud's pyramid by simply dealing with the Representational Edges, *Understanding Comics: The Invisible Art* (New York: Harper Perennial, 1994), 50–51.

15. Cohen, 13.

16. McCloud, 186–188.

17. Glenn Campbell, "Crimestoppers Textbook," *Cinefex* 44 (November 1990), 32.

18. Cohen, 20.

19. Ray Bennett, "Showing Off: The Unique Look of *Dick Tracy*," *The Hollywood Reporter*, 28 January 1991.

20. Claudia Eller, "*Tracy* Cost Put at $101 Mil.," *Variety*, 22 October 1990.

21. Larry Rohter, "Hollywood Abuzz Over Cost Memo," *New York Times*, 2 February 1991.

22. Tom Spain, "'Dick Tracy': Scaling the Wall," *Washington Post*, 20 December 1990.

23. Letter from Warren Beatty to Ms. Broeske, dated October 11, 1988, found in the *Dick Tracy* clipping file at the Academy of Motion Picture Arts and Sciences' Margaret Herrick Library.

24. Roger Ebert, "*Dick Tracy* Movie Review," *RogerEbert.com*, 15 June 1990, <http://rogerebert.suntimes.com/apps/pbcs.dll/article?AID=/19900615/REVIEWS/6150301/1023> (21 June 2010).

25. Richard Corliss, "Extra! *Tracy* is Tops," *Time*, 18 June 1990, 75.

26. Keith Phipps, "Remember *Dick Tracy*?" *Slate.com*, 21 June 2010 <http://www.slate.com/id/2255746/pagenum/all/#p2> (29 June 2010).

27. Roger Sabin, *Comics, Comix, & Graphic Novels: A History of Comic Art* (New York: Phaidon, 1996), 69.

28. Bradford Wright, *Comic Book Nation: The Transformation of Youth Culture in America* (Baltimore: Johns Hopkins University Press, 2001), 207.

29. Sabin, 74.

30. Wright, 223.

31. Army Archerd, "Just for Variety," *Variety*, 3 April 1996.

32. "From *Hulk* to *Rocket*," *Variety*, 8 July 1997.

33. Chris Petrikin, "U Has *Hulk* Take a Seat," *Variety*, 2 March 1998.

34. See the Starz documentary *Comic Books Unbound*.

35. Zorianna Kit, "Lee Crouching with Uni *Hulk*," *The Hollywood Reporter*, 12–14 January 2001.

36. M. Keith Booker, *May Contain Graphic Material: Comic Books, Graphic Novels, and Film* (Westport: Praeger, 2007), xxxi.

37. Groensteen, 28.

38. Ibid.

39. See the Starz documentary *Comic Books Unbound*.

40. Kerry Lengel, "Graphic Novelist Art Spiegelman Keeps the Faith," *The Arizona Republic*, 29 Janruary 2006.

41. David Bordwell, Janet Staiger, and Kristin Thompson, *The Classical Hollywood Cinema: Film Style & Mode of Production to 1960* (New York: Columbia University Press, 1985), 3.

42. Will Eisner, *Comics & Sequential Art* (Tamarac: Poorhouse Press, 1985), 40.

43. McCloud, 67.

44. Brent Simon, "The Monster Within," *Entertainment Today*, 20–26 June 2003, 6.

45. In the majority of the cases explored in this volume, the scenes and formal attributes under analysis are not a-typical for the film as a whole. To draw on an elementary analogy, they are not the formal equivalents of oases in a vast, classically defined, desert.

46. David Bordwell, *The Way Hollywood Tells It: Story and Style in Modern Movies* (Berkeley: University of California Press, 2006), 173–174.

47. Simon, "The Monster Within."

48. "*Hulk*," *The Art of the Title Sequence*, 11 May 2009, <http://www.artofthetitle.com/2009/05/11/hulk/> (23 August 2010).

49. See *The Unique Style of Editing Hulk* documentary on the special edition DVD.

50. David Bloom, "*Hulk* Edit Nails Feel of Comics," *Variety*, 23 June 2003

51. Lev Manovich, *The Language of New Media* (Cambridge, MA: MIT Press, 2001), 302.

52. Ibid., 324.

53. Ibid., 325–326. Note that the financial disappointment of the film could also be attributed to a bootleg of the film that made its way onto the internet two weeks before the film's release.

54. Hollywood budgets are normally defined in vague and slippery terms by the industry. A fair assumption for determining marketing costs is approximately 50 percent the negative cost. Thus, if a film costs $100 million to produce, the studio will probably spend around $50 million to market it.

55. Ang Lee, director commentary on *Hulk* DVD.

56. Unless otherwise noted, I have taken the production budgets listed at *Box Office Mojo*, <http://www.boxofficemojo.com>.

57. Peter Bart, "Is 'Brainy' a Box Office Turn Off?" *Variety*, 23 June 2003.

58. Roger Ebert and Richard Roeper, "Transcript of *Hulk* Review," *Ebert and Roeper*, 11 June 2003.

59. Andrew Sarris, "Ang Lee's Angst-Ridden *Hulk*: The Not-So-Jolly Green Giant," *New York Observer*, 6 July 2003.

60. Bart, "Is 'Brainy' a Box Office Turn Off?"

Chapter 4

1. Charles Brownstein, *Eisner/Miller* (Milwaukie: Dark Horse Books, 2005), 12–13.

2. Ibid.

3. "May 1998 Comic Book Sales Figures," *The Comics Chronicles*, no date, <http://www.comichron.com/monthlycomicssales/1998/1998-05.html> (27 May 2011).

4. Ibid.

5. Kevin Melrose, "Sales Skyrocket for Miller's *300* Graphic Novel," *Newsarama*, 16 November 2006, <http://blog.newsarama.com/2006/11/16/sales-for-skyrocket-for-millers-300-graphic-novel/> (27 May 2011).

6. Susan Wloszczyna, "An Epic Tale, Told *300* Strong," *USA Today*, 7 March 2007.

7. Ibid.

8. Pamela McClintock, "Warners Bets a Bundle on Swords-and-CGI *300*," *Variety*, 10 October 2005.

9. Pascal Lefèvre, "The Construction of Space in Comics," in *A Comics Studies Reader*, eds. Jeet Heer and Kent Worcester (Jackson: University Press of Mississippi, 2009), 158.

10. Stax, "Attila Leads the *300*," *IGN.com*, 15 August 2005, <http://movies.ign.com/articles/641/641893p1.html> (2 September 2010).

11. "*300* Matches Miller's Style," *Sci Fi Wire*, 27 July 2006, <http://web.archive.org/web/20080610062645/http://www.scifi.com/scifiwire/index.php?category=0&id=37328> (30 August 2010).

12. Charles Brownstein, *Eisner/Miller*, 38–39.

13. *300* Press Kit.

14. Tara DiLullo, *300: The Art of the Film* (Milwaukie: Dark Horse Books, 2007), 14.

15. Ibid.

16. Ibid., 23.

17. Mark Olsen, "An Epic Battle is Pumped Up," *Los Angeles Times*, 14 January 2007.

18. Ibid.

19. "Imax in Day-Date Plan for Warners' *300*," *The Hollywood Reporter*, 26 January 2007.

20. Pamela McClintock, "An Unusual WB Deal," *Variety*, 30 January 2007.

21. Lefèvre, "Incompatible Visual Ontologies?: The Problematic Adaptation of Drawn Images," in *Film and Comic Books*, eds. Ian Gordon, Mark Jancovich, and Matthew P. McAllister (Jackson: University Press of Mississippi, 2007), 1.

22. Ali Jaafar, "Iran President Disses *300*," *Variety*, 22 March 2007.

23. Ian Mohr, "B.O. Hits Greek Peak: $70 Mil," *Variety*, 12 March 2007

24. Richard Roeper, "*300* Movie Review," *RichardRoeper.com*, 9 March 2007, <http://www.richardroeper.com/reviews/300.aspx> (31 August 2010).

25. "*300* (Two-Disc Special Edition) Consumer Reviews," *Amazon.com*, <http://www.amazon.com/Two-Disc-Special-Edition-Gerard-Butler/product-reviews/B00005JPLW/ref=cm_cr_pr_viewopt_kywd?ie=UTF8&showViewpoints=1&sortBy=helpful&reviewerTyp e=all_reviews&formatType=all_formats&filterByStar=all_stars&pageNumber=1&filterByKe yword=look> (27 May 2015).

26. Borys Kit, "*Watchmen* Feeding Off *300* Spoils," *The Hollywood Reporter*, 13 March 2007.

27. Sabin, 162.

28. John Jackson Miller, "*Watchmen* Sales Rankings in its Initial Release," *The Comics Chronicles*, no date, <http://www.comichron.com/special/watchmensales.html> (1 June 2011).

29. Ibid.

30. Peter Aperlo, *Watchmen: The Film Companion* (London: Titan Books, 2009), 119

31. Geoff Boucher, "Now All Eyes Are On that *Watchmen* Guy," *Los Angeles Times*, 1 March 2009.

32. More fan servicing came when Snyder realized he couldn't fit the entire narrative of Moore and Gibbons's 416 page novel into the space of a three hour film. Seemingly prompted by fears that the treatment would be deemed "unfaithful," Snyder and Warner Brothers produced the animated film *Watchmen: Tales of the Black Freighter* (2008) that portrayed the comic within the comic narrative of Moore and Gibbons's book. The short film, clocking in at just under thirty minutes, was later edited into *Watchmen: The Ultimate Cut* (2009), a DVD and Blu-Ray only release that followed the initial home video release of the "Director's Cut" by a few months.

33. Jeff Jensen, "*Watchmen*: An Oral History," *Entertainment Weekly*, 21 October 2005.

34. Note that I'm attributing the comic's visual style to both the writer and the artist, as Moore's original scripts are so meticulous with regard to the composition of space that it seems unjust to simply describe the visual style as being Gibbons's.

35. McCloud, 100.

36. Groensteen, 45.

37. Ibid., 46.

38. Julie Bloom, "Arts, Briefly: Film Trailer Aids Sales of *Watchmen* Novel," *New York Times*, 14 August 2008.

39. The one self-acknowledged problem this volume's financial analysis has is the absence of concrete economic data for ancillary (DVD, Blu-Ray, digital download) media forms. Precise figures for this revenue stream, which can contribute greatly to a film's gross is, like most economic data in Hollywood, difficult if not impossible to attain.

40. Dave McNary and Michael Fleming, "WB, Fox Make Deal for *Watchmen*," *Variety*, 15 January 2009.

41. Nikki Finke, "Deadline Hollywood: *Watchmen* Postmortem," *LA Weekly*, 13 March 2009.

42. Ibid.

43. "New Potter Book Topples U.S. Sales Records," *MSNBC.com*, 18 July 2005, <http://www.msnbc.msn.com/id/8608578/> (31 August 2010).

44. Chris Schillig, "Comic Book Chronicler Harvey Pekar Speaks at Mount Union," *The Alliance Review*, 22 February 2008, <http://www.the-review.com/news/article/3343481> (1 June 2011).

45. See *The Comics Chronicles* sales figure search for *American Splendor*, <http://www.comichron.com/monthlycomicssales.html> (1 June 2011).

46. *American Splendor* Production Notes, 15.

47. David Kunzle, *The Early Comic Strip: Narrative Strips and Picture Stories in the European Broadsheet from c. 1450 to 1825* (Berkeley: University of California Press, 1973), 2.

48. Bill Blackbeard, "Mislabeled Books," *Funny World* 16 (1974), 41.

49. David Carrier, *The Aesthetics of Comics* (University Park: Pennsylvania State University Press, 2000), 4.

50. Groensteen, 18.

51. Ibid., 9.

52. Hight, 180.

53. Ibid., 188.

54. Harvey Pekar and Robert Crumb, "Standing Behind Old Jewish Ladies in Supermarket Lines," *American Splendor: The Life and Times of Harvey Pekar* (New York: Ballantine Books, 2003), page number not given.

55. There is a slight change in the significance of the encounter however. In the comic, Harvey goes back to the market a second time and has a pleasant run in with an older Jewish woman and the cashier is inconsiderate. In the film, the unpleasant encounter ends with animated Harvey encouraging himself to do something with his anger, which inspires him to write a comic book.

56. Carrier, 28.

57. Groensteen, 128.

58. Gregg Kilday, "HBO Finds *Splendor* in Sundance Selections," *The Hollywood Reporter*, 24 January 2003.

59. Jenelle Riley, "There's Always Hope," *Back Stage West Drama-Logue*, 21 August 2003.

60. Daniel Schweiger, "An American Family: The Pekars Talk about Their Splendor," *Venice*, August 2003, 57.

61. "Glossary of Movie Business Terms," *The Numbers*, no date, <http://www.the-numbers .com/glossary.php#production_budget> (29 September 2010).

62. "Based on Comic Book Titles," *The Internet Movie Database*, no date, <http://www .imdb .com/keyword/based-on-comic-book/?sort=release_date> (29 September 2010).

63. Douglas Gomery, *The Hollywood Studio System: A History* (London: BFI Publishing, 2005), 247.

64. Neil Rae and Jonathan Gray, "When Gen-X Meets X-Men: Retextualizing Comic Book Film Reception," in *Film and Comic Books*, eds. Ian Gordon, Mark Jancovich, and Matthew P. McAllister (Jackson: University Press of Mississippi, 2007), 86.

Chapter 5

1. David Gerrold, "Introduction," in *Taking the Red Pill: Science, Philosophy, and Religion in The Matrix*, ed. Glenn Yeffeth (Chichester: Summersdale Publishers Ltd., 2003), 6.

2. Bob Rehak, "The Migration of Forms: Bullet Time as Microgenre," *Film Criticism* 32, No. 1 (2007): 27–28.

3. Joshua Clover, *BFI Modern Classics: The Matrix* (London: British Film Institute, 2004), 25.

4. Gaeta is quoted in Rehak, 33–34.

5. I am referring to Larry and Andy Wachowski, who since the time of this interview have both come out as transgender, by their preferred names of Lana and Lilly.

6. See the featurettes on Darrow and Skroce included on *The Burly Man Chronicles* DVD of the The Ultimate *Matrix* Collection box set.

7. Scott McCloud, *Understanding Comics: The Invisible Art* (New York: Kitchen Sink Press, 1993), 110.

8. Ibid., 112.

9. Robert C. Harvey, *The Art of the Comic Book: An Aesthetic History* (Jackson: University Press of Mississippi, 1996), 187.

10. André Bazin, "The Evolution of the Language of Cinema," in *What Is Cinema? Volume 1*, trans. Hugh Gray (Berkeley: University of California Press, 1967), 24.

11. Ibid., 40.

12. Garrett Stewart, *Framed Time: Towards a Postfilmic Cinema* (Chicago: University of Chicago Press, 2007), 3.

13. Ibid., 2.

14. Ibid., 87–121.

15. Henry Jenkins, *Convergence Culture: Where Old and New Media Collide* (New York: New York University Press, 2006), 293.

16. Ibid., 94.

17. Ibid., 104.

18. Unless otherwise noted, I've taken the production budgets listed at *Box Office Mojo*, <http://www.boxofficemojo.com>.

19. Ibid., 126–127.

20. From the 2010 SCMS panel "Transmedia Studies: The Hollywood Geek Elite Debates the Future of Television," co-chaired by Denise Mann and Henry Jenkins.

21. The term "mothership" is used to describe the source of driving the narrative by industrial practitioners, most notably Damon Lindelof and Carlton Cuse, the showrunners of ABC's transmedia franchise *Lost* (2004–2010).

22. Henry Jenkins, "The Pleasure of *Pirates* and What It Tells Us about World Building in Branded Entertainment," *Confessions of an Aca-Fan*, 13 June 2007, <http://henryjenkins.org/2007/06/forced_simplicity_and_the_crit.html> (24 April 2012).

23. Jenkins, 95.

24. "*300* Comic to Screen Comparison," *Solace in Cinema*, 4 October 2006, <http://www.solaceincinema.com/2006/10/04/300-comic-to-screen-comparison/> (4 October 2010).

25. Chris Carle, "*Enter the Matrix* Video Game Review," *IGN.com*, 20 May 2003, <http://ps2.ign.com/articles/403/403749p1.html> (4 October 2010).

26. Ibid.

27. Frayling, *Spaghetti Westerns: Cowboys and Europeans from Karl May to Sergio Leone*, vii.

28. Adrian Martin, *Once Upon a Time in America* (London: BFI Press, 2008), 4.

29. Simone Castaldi, *Drawn and Dangerous: Italian Comics of the 1970s and 1980s* (Jackson: University Press of Mississippi, 2010), 12.

30. Ibid., 12–13.

31. Christopher Frayling, *Sergio Leone: Something to Do with Death* (London: Faber and Faber, 2000), 7.

32. Ibid., 6.

33. Thierry Groensteen, *The System of Comics*, trans. Bart Beaty and Nick Nguyen (Jackson: University of Mississippi Press, 2007), 40.

34. Roger Ebert, "*The Good, the Bad, and the Ugly* Movie Review," *RogerEbert.com*, 3 August 2003, <http://rogerebert.suntimes.com/apps/pbcs.dll/article?AID=/20030803/REVIEWS08/308030301/1023> (1 November 2010).

35. Frayling, 175, 180.

36. David Colton, "Q&A with Stephen King," *USA Today*, 18 December 2006, <http://www.usatoday.com/life/books/news/2006-12-18-king-qa_x.htm> (12 October 2010).

37. Ibid.

38. "February 2007 Comic Book Sales Figures," *The Comics Chronicles*, no date, <http://www.comichron.com/monthlycomicssales/2007/2007-02.html> (1 June 2011).

39. "Top Comic Books of the 2000s," *The Comics Chronicles*, <http://www.comichron.com/vitalstatistics/topcomics2000s.html> (1 June 2011).

40. Stephen King, *The Gunslinger: Revised and Expanded Edition* (Toronto: Signet Fiction, 2003), xxvii.

41. Patrick McGee, *From Shane to Kill Bill: Rethinking the Western* (Malden: Blackwell Publishing, 2007), 175.

42. Frayling, 160.

43. Peter David, Robin Furth, Jae Lee, and Richard Isanove, *The Dark Tower: The Gunslinger Born* 2 (New York: Marvel Comics, 2007), 5–7.

44. E. H. Gombrich, "The Principles of Caricature," *The Gombrich Archive*, 25 May 1937, <http://www.gombrich.co.uk/showdoc.php?id=85> (1 November 2010).

45. Ibid.

46. Howard Hughes, *Once Upon a Time in the Italian West: The Filmgoer's Guide to Spaghetti Westerns* (London: I.B. Tauris, 2004), 118.

47. McCloud, 24–59.

Chapter 6

1. Michael Chabon, *The Amazing Adventures of Kavalier & Clay* (New York: Picador, 2000), 361.

2. Ibid.

3. Ibid., 362.

4. Chabon later edited a series of *Escapist* comics that are portrayed as being reprints of Kavalier and Clay's work but are the creations of contemporary comic book writers and artists.

5. Orson Welles and Peter Bogdanovich, *This Is Orson Welles* (Boston: Da Capo Press, 1998), 190.

6. Denny O'Neil, phone interview with author, 19 May 2011.

7. Eileen R. Meehan, "'Holy Commodity Fetish Batman!': The Political Economy of the Commercial Intertext," in *The Many Lives of Batman: Critical Approaches to a Superhero and his Media*, eds. Roberta Pearson and William Uricchio (London: Routledge, 1991), 54.

8. Ibid.

9. Les Daniels, *Batman: The Complete History* (San Francisco: Chronicle Books, 1999), 20.

10. Ibid., 21.

11. Ibid., 40.

12. Ibid.

13. Daniel Robert Epstein, "The Joker, the Jewish Museum, and Jerry: Talking to Jerry Robinson," *Newsarama.com*, 18 October 2006,
<http://forum.newsarama.com/showthread.php?t=88092> (7 January 2011).

14. Christopher Sharrett, "Batman and the Twilight of the Idols: An Interview with Frank Miller," in *The Many Lives of Batman: Critical Approaches to a Superhero and His Media*, eds. Roberta Pearson and William Uricchio (London: Routledge, 1991), 37.

15. Brian Bolland, "On Batman: Brian Bolland Recalls The Killing Joke," in *DC Universe: The Stories of Alan Moore* (New York: DC Comics, 2006), 256.

16. *Burton on Burton*, ed. Mark Salisbury (London: Faber and Faber, 2000), 71.

17. Leonard Pierce, "*Batman: The Animated Series*: On Leather Wings," *AVClub.com*, 29 November 2010, <http://www.avclub.com/articles/on-leather-wings,48295/> (15 January 2010).

18. See DVD commentary track for *Batman: The Animated Series*, "On Leather Wings."

19. Denny O'Neil, phone interview with author, 19 May 2011.

20. Ibid.

21. Ibid., 186.

22. Jean-Paul Gabilliet, *Of Comics and Men: A Cultural History of American Comic Books*, trans. Bart Beaty and Nick Nguyen (Jackson: University Press of Mississippi, 2010), 105.

23. "February 2007 Comic Book Sales Figures," *The Comics Chronicles*, <http://www.comichron.com/monthlycomicssales/2007/2007–02.html> (22 June 2011).

24. Grant Morrison and John Van Fleet, *Batman* 663 (New York: DC Comics, 2007), 8.

25. See the reader comments on ReflectingHierophant, "Why So Serious?" *Comic Book Movie.com*, no date, <http://www.comicbookmovie.com/fansites/MyCBMOpinion/news/?a=28648&t=Reflections_of_a_Hierophant_Why_So_Serious> (24 January 2011).

26. Peter Sciretta, "Brian Azzarello's *Joker* Graphic Novel," */Film*, 19 October 2008, <http://www.slashfilm.com/brian-azzarellos-joker-graphic-novel/> (24 January 2011).

27. "2008 Comic Book Sales Figures," *The Comics Chronicles*, <http://www.comichron.com/monthlycomicssales/2008.html> (22 June 2011).

28. Dan Phillips, "The Joker's Wild Ride," *IGN.com*, 23 October 2008, <http://comics.ign.com/articles/923/923283p1.html> (24 January 2011).

29. Bill Ramey, "Lee Bermejo, Part 2," *Batman on Film*, 23 May 2007, <http://www.batman-on-film.com/lee-bermejo_interview-2.html> (24 January 2011).

30. Phillips, "The Joker's Wild Ride."

31. Ramey, "Lee Bermejo, Part 2."

32. Rebecca Murray, "Writer/Director Christopher Nolan Talks about *The Dark Knight*," *About.com*, date unknown, <http://movies.about.com/od/thedarkknight/a/darkknight70408_2.htm> (24 January 2011).

33. Jennifer Vineyard, "*Arkham Asylum* Scribe Grant Morrison Opens Up Heath Ledger's Joker Diary," *MTV.com*, 4 August 2008, <*http://m.mtv.com/blogs/splashpage_post.rbml?id=2008/08/04/arkham-asylum-scribe-grant-morrison-opens-up-heath-ledgers-joker-diary/&weburl=http%3A%2F%2Fsplashpage.mtv.com%2F2008%2F08%2F04%2Farkham-asylum-scribe-grant-morrison-opens-up-heath-ledgers-joker-diary%2F&alt=http%3A%2F%2Fm.mtv.com%2Fblogs%2Fsplashpage.rbml&cid=300*> (16 July 2013).

34. Ibid.

35. Justin Wyatt, *High Concept: Movies and Marketing in Hollywood* (Austin: University of Texas Press, 1994), 7.

36. Ibid., 23.

37. Ibid.

38. Bradford Wright, *Comic Book Nation: The Transformation of Youth Culture in America* (Baltimore: Johns Hopkins University Press, 2001), 266.

39. Ibid., 267.

40. Mike Benton, *The Comic Book in America: An Illustrated History* (Dallas: Taylor Publishing Company, 1989), 84.

41. Roger Sabin, *Comics, Comix, & Graphic Novels: A History of Comic Art* (New York: Phaidon, 1996), 168.

42. Randy Duncan and Matthew J. Smith, *The Power of Comics: History, Form & Culture* (New York: Continuum, 2009), 120.

43. Ibid., 122.

44. Ibid., 89.

45. Charles Brownstein, *Eisner/Miller* (Milwaukie: Dark Horse Books, 2005), 151.

46. Ibid., 26, 153.

47. Claudia Eller, "Orion Reveals Plan for *Robocop II*," *Hollywood Reporter*, 6 August 1987.

48. "Cinefile," *Los Angeles Times*, 19 March 1989.

49. Steve Grant, "Frank Opinions," *Time Out*, 10–17 October 1990, 15.

50. Ibid.

51. Ibid.

52. "Rambling Reporter," *The Hollywood Reporter*, 17 October 1990.

53. "Rambling Reporter," *The Hollywood Reporter*, 19 October 1990.

54. "August 2003 Comic Book Sales Figures," *The Comics Chronicles*, <http://www.comichron.com/monthlycomicssales/2003/2003–08.html> (22 June 2011).

55. Dana Harris, "WB Sends Pi Guy into the Bat Cave," *Variety*, 21 September 2000, 1.

56. Kevin O'Donnell, "Q&A: Frank Miller," *Rolling Stone*, 25 August 2005.

57. Stephen Garrett, "Q&A: Frank Miller," *Esquire*, April 2007.

58. See the feature film commentary on the theatrical release of *Sin City* with Miller and Rodriguez on the Recut, Extended, Unrated DVD or Blu-Ray release (2005).

59. Ibid.

60. See the featurette on the Recut, Extended, Unrated DVD or Blu-Ray entitled *How It Went Down: Convincing Frank Miller to Make the Film* (2005).

61. There are a handful of graphical differences between the comics and the film to acknowledge, most notably the addition of colored mise-en-scène in certain scenes (Miller was very sparse with the use of color, whereas Rodriguez encouraged him to open up the palate a bit more at times). Yet it is telling that one of the most discussed visual differences between the comic and the film is that Nancy (Jessica Alba) is nude in the book and scantily clad in the film. That is how similar these two texts are from a visual standpoint.

62. Art Spiegelman, "Reading Pictures," in *Lynd Ward: Prelude to a Million Years, Song Without Words, Vertigo*, ed. Art Spiegelman (New York: Literary Classics of the United States, 2010), x.

63. Jean-Paul Gabilliet, *Of Comics and Men: A Cultural History of American Comic Books*, trans. Bart Beaty and Nick Nguyen (Jackson: University Press of Mississippi, 2010), 90.

64. I acknowledge that these essays—while foundational texts in studies on film noir— have been complicated and elaborated upon recently, specifically in James Naremore's seminal volume *More Than Night: Film Noir and Its Contexts* (Berkeley: University of California Press, 1998). However, in order to reign in the discussion and to keep a tangent from becoming a digression, I have simplified and generalized my analysis of noir style. The subject of

Frank Miller and the noir style deserves further research and I hope this modest analysis can serve as a stepping stone to a deeper study.

65. Paul Schrader, "Notes on Film Noir," in *Film Noir Reader*, eds. Alain Silver and James Ursini (New York: Limelight Editions, 1996), 57.

66. Ibid.

67. Frank Miller, *Sin City: The Hard Goodbye* (Milwaukie: Dark Horse Comics, 2005), 127.

68. Ibid., 138.

69. Janey Place and Lowell Peterson, "Some Visual Motifs of Film Noir," in *Film Noir Reader*, eds. Alain Silver and James Ursini (New York: Limelight Editions, 1996), 67–69.

70. Frank Miller, *Sin City: That Yellow Bastard* (Milwaukie: Dark Horse Comics, 2005), 93.

71. Schrader, 54.

72. Brownstein, 87–88.

73. "May 2005 Comic Book Sales Figures," *The Comics Chronicle*, <http://www.comichron.com/monthlycomicssales/2005/2005–05.html> (22 June 2011).

74. Jeff Goldsmith, "*Spirit* Moves Him," *Variety*, 26 July 2007, A2.

75. Ibid.

76. Geoff Boucher, "Revenge of the Dark Knight," *Los Angeles Times*, 29 April 2007, E5.

77. See the *Green World* featurette on *The Spirit* Special Edition DVD or Blu-Ray.

78. Geoff Boucher, "*The Spirit* Moved Him," *Los Angeles Times*, 2 November 2008.

79. Ibid.

80. Ibid.

81. Frank Miller, "Introduction," in *Eisner/Miller*, by Charles Brownstein (Milwaukie: Dark Horse Books, 2005), 3.

82. Brownstein, 87.

83. Ibid., 88.

84. Duncan and Smith, 142.

85. Michael Barrier, "About *The Spirit* and Will Eisner," in *A Smithsonian Book of Comic Books*, eds. Michael Barrier and Martin Williams (New York: Smithsonian Institution Press and Harry N. Abrams, 1981), 270.

86. Brownstein, 96–97.

87. Ibid., 17.

88. Schrader, 61.

89. Jondough, "Jondough Deems Frank Miller's *The Spirit* the Worst Movie He's Ever Seen!!" *Ain't It Cool News*, 15 December 2008, <http://www.aintitcool.com/node/39450> (14 March 2011).

90. Ranylt Richildis, "*The Spirit* Movie Review," *Pajiba*, 30 December 2008, <http://www.pajiba.com/film_reviews/spirit-the-review.php> (7 February 2011).

91. Nathan Rabin, "*The Spirit* Movie Review," *The AV Club*, 24 December 2008, <http://www.avclub.com/articles/the-spirit,17083/> (7 February 2011).

92. *Green World* featurette.

93. See the filmmaker commentary track on *The Spirit* DVD or Blu-Ray.

94. Iann Robinson, "The Redemption of Frank Miller," *Crave Online*, 12 January 2009, <http://www.craveonline.com/entertainment/comics/article/the-redemption-of-frank-miller-72867> 7 February 2011.

95. Rabin, "*The Spirit* Movie Review."

96. Jean-Paul Gabilliet, *Of Comics and Men: A Cultural History of American Comic Books*, trans. Bart Beaty and Nick Nguyen (Jackson: University Press of Mississippi, 2010), 21.

97. Alex Segure, "What's Next for Frank Miller and Jim Lee?" *The Source*, 2 April 2010, <http://dcu.blog.dccomics.com/2010/04/02/whats-next-for-frank-miller-and-jim-lee/> (7 February 2011).

Conclusion

1. Jean-Paul Gabilliet, *Of Comics and Men: A Cultural History of American Comic Books*, trans. Bart Beaty and Nick Nguyen (Jackson: University Press of Mississippi, 2010), 73.

2. Denny O'Neil, phone interview with author, 19 May 2011.

3. Ibid.

4. Ibid.

5. Mark C. Rogers, "License Farming and the American Comic Book Industry," *International Journal of Comic Art* 1, no. 2 (1999), 134.

6. Denny O'Neil, phone interview with author, 19 May 2011.

7. Ibid. When I asked former DC president and editor Paul Levitz if he was available for a similar interview, he said he was interested but needed clearance approval from Time Warner publicity due to confidentiality agreements he was still being held to. It goes without saying that these clearances are difficult, if not impossible, to receive.

8. Brooks Barnes and Michael Cieply, "Movie Studios Reassess Comic-Con," *New York Times*, 12 June 2011.

9. Mike Fleming, "Universal Nixes Stephen King's *Dark Tower*—No Ambitious Film Trilogy or TV Series," *line.com*, 18 July 2011, <http://www.line.com/2011/07/universal-wont-scale-stephen-kings-the-dark-tower-studio-declines-to-make-ambitious-trilogy-and-tv-series/> (20 July 2011).

10. Gabilliet, 207.

11. Ibid., 208.

12. Ibid., 210.

13. Julia Round, "'Is This a Book?' DC Vertigo and the Redefinition of Comics in the 1990s," in *The Rise of the American Comics Artist: Creators and Contexts*, eds. Paul Williams and James Lyons (Jackson: University Press of Mississippi, 2010), 25.

14. Jochen Ecke, "Spatializing the Movie Screen: How Mainstream Cinema Is Catching Up on the Formal Potentialities of the Comic Book Page," in *Comics as a Nexus of Cultures: Essays on the Interplay of Media, Disciplines and International Perspectives*, eds. Mark Berninger, Jochen Ecke, and Gideon Haberkorn (Jefferson: McFarland and Company, 2010), 19.

15. It should be noted that formal influence is not the central thesis of Round's essay and that it is largely a tangential observation that works in dialogue with her central thesis: the ways in which DC imprint Vertigo have redefined the form. She does include industrial analysis, but its chief focus is the comic book industry, not the overlap between the comic book and film industries.

16. Lev Manovich, *The Language of New Media* (Cambridge, MA: MIT Press, 2001), 322.

17. Ibid., 324.

18. Ibid., 326.

19. David Bordwell, *The Way Hollywood Tells It: Story and Style in Modern Movies* (Berkeley: University of California Press, 2006).

20. Sean Cubitt, *The Cinema Effect* (Cambridge, MA: MIT Press, 2005), 5.

21. David Bordwell, Janet Staiger, and Kristin Thompson, *The Classical Hollywood Cinema: Film Style & Mode of Production to 1960* (New York: Columbia University Press, 1985), 70.

22. Ibid.

23. Bordwell, Staiger, and Thompson's *The Classical Hollywood Cinema* does not mention transtexual motivation. Bordwell later elaborates on his taxonomy of motivations in *Narration in the Fiction Film,* which informs Kristin Thompson's usage of the term in her monograph *Breaking the Glass Armor.*

24. Ibid., 77.

25. Ibid.

26. Ibid.

27. Kristin Thompson, *Breaking the Glass Armor: Neoformalist Film Analysis* (Princeton: Princeton University Press, 1988), 18.

28. Ibid., 19.

BIBLIOGRAPHY

Allen, Michael. "The Impact of Digital Technologies on Film Aesthetics." In *The New Media Book*. Edited by Dan Harries. London: BFI Publishing, 2002.

Allen, Robert C. "The Movies in Vaudeville: Historical Context of the Movies as Popular Entertainment." In *The American Film Industry*. Edited by Tino Balio. Revised edition. Madison: University of Wisconsin Press, 1985.

Amdler, Meredith, and Dade Hames. "Not So Jolly Green Giant." *Variety*, 24 June 2003.

American Splendor Production Notes.

Andrew, Dudley. *Concepts in Film Theory*. Oxford: Oxford University Press, 1984.

"An Expensive Duck." *New York Times*, 22 August 1986.

Ansen, David. "Tracymania." *Newsweek*, 25 June 1990.

Aperlo, Peter. *Watchmen: The Film Companion*. London: Titan Books, 2009.

Archerd, Army. Title Unknown. *Daily Variety*, 8 July 1975.

Archerd, Army. "Just for Variety." *Variety*, 3 April 1996.

"August 2003 Comic Book Sales Figures." *The Comics Chronicles*. No date. <http://www.comichron.com/monthlycomicssales/2003/2003-08.html> (22 June 2011).

"August 2007 Comic Book Sales Figures." *The Comics Chronicles*. No date. <http://www.comichron.com/monthlycomicssales/2007/2007-08.html> (1 June 2011).

Azzarello, Brian, and Lee Bermejo. *The Joker*. New York: DC Comics, 2008.

Barnes, Brooks, and Michael Cieply. "Movie Studios Reassess Comic-Con." *New York Times*, 12 June 2011.

Barol, Bill. "Batmania." *Newsweek*, 26 June 1989, 70.

Barrier, Michael. "About *The Spirit* and Will Eisner." In *A Smithsonian Book of Comic Books*. Edited by Michael Barrier and Martin Williams. New York: Smithsonian Institution Press and Harry N. Abrams, 1981.

Bart, Peter. "Is 'Brainy' a Box Office Turn Off?" *Variety*, 23 June 2003.

"Based on Comic Book Titles." *The Internet Movie Database*. No date. <http://www.imdb.com/keyword/based-on-comic-book/?sort=release_date> (29 September 2010).

Bazin, André. "The Ontology of the Photographic Image." In *What Is Cinema? Volume I*. Translated by Hugh Gray. Berkeley: University of California Press, 1967.

———. "The Evolution of the Language of Cinema." In *What Is Cinema? Volume I*. Translated by Hugh Gray. Berkeley: University of California Press, 1967.

205

————. "Adaptation, or the Cinema as Digest." In *Film Adaptation*. Edited by James Naremore. New Jersey: Rutgers University Press, 2000.

Beaty, Bart. "Introduction to In Focus: Comics Studies, Fifty Years After Film Studies." *Cinema Journal* 50, no. 3 (2011): 106–110.

Beck, Marilyn. "Paramount Drops *Dick Tracy* Project." *Daily News*, 15 January 1986.

Bendazzi, Giannalberto. *Cartoons: One Hundred Years of Cinema Animation*. Bloomington: Indiana University Press, 1994.

Bennett, Ray. "Showing Off: The Unique Look of *Dick Tracy*." *The Hollywood Reporter*, 28 January 1991.

Benton, Mike. *The Comic Book in America: An Illustrated History*. Dallas: Taylor Publishing Company, 1989.

Blackbeard, Bill. "Mislabeled Books." *Funny World* 16 (1974).

Blackbeard, Bill, and Martin Williams, eds. *The Smithsonian Collection of Newspaper Comics*. Washington, DC: Smithsonian Institution Press and Harry N. Abrams, 1977.

Blackton, J. Stuart. "Lecture Given at the University of Southern California, February 29, 1929." In *Hollywood Directors: 1914–1940*. Edited by Richard Koszarski. New York: Oxford University Press, 1976.

Blair, Preston. *Cartoon Animation*. Laguna Hills: Walter Foster Publishing, 1994.

Bloom, David. "*Hulk* Edit Nails Feel of Comics." *Variety*, 23 June 2003.

Bloom, Julie. "Arts, Briefly: Film Trailer Aids Sales of *Watchmen* Novel." *New York Times*, 14 August 2008.

Blue, Carol and Al Delugach. "*Superman*: Rare Look at Film Finances." *Los Angeles Times*, 3 April 1980.

Bluestone, George. *Novels into Film*. Baltimore: Johns Hopkins University Press, 2003.

Bolland, Brian. "On Batman: Brian Bolland Recalls *The Killing Joke*." In *DC Universe: The Stories of Alan Moore*. New York: DC Comics, 2006.

Bolter, Jay David, and Richard Grusin. *Remediation: Understanding New Media*. Cambridge, MA: MIT Press, 1999.

Booker, M. Keith. *May Contain Graphic Material: Comic Books, Graphic Novels, and Film*. Westport: Praeger, 2007.

Bordwell, David, Janet Staiger, and Kristin Thompson. *The Classical Hollywood Cinema: Film Style & Mode of Production to 1960*. New York: Columbia University Press, 1985.

Bordwell, David. *Narration in the Fiction Film*. Madison: University of Wisconsin Press, 1985.

Bordwell, David. *On the History of Film Style*. Cambridge, MA: Harvard University Press, 1997.

————. *The Way Hollywood Tells It: Story and Style in Modern Movies*. Berkeley: University of California Press, 2006.

Boucher, Geoff. "Joker Creator Jerry Robinson Reflects on Gotham and the Golden Age." *Los Angeles Times*, 6 May 2009.

————. "Now All Eyes Are on That *Watchmen* Guy." *Los Angeles Times*, 1 March 2009.

————. "Revenge of the Dark Knight." *Los Angeles Times*, 29 April 2007, E5.

————. "*The Spirit* Moved Him." *Los Angeles Times*, 2 November 2008.

Boyer, Peter J. "Film Clips: As Batman, West is Out of Movie Lineup." *Los Angeles Times*, 5 August 1981.

Brennan, Steve. "Universal is Hulking Up." *The Hollywood Reporter*, 10 May 1999.

Brewster, Ben, and Lea Jacobs. *Theatre to Cinema: Stage Pictorialism and the Early Feature Film*. Oxford: Oxford University Press, 1997.

Brooker, Will. *Batman Unmasked: Analyzing a Cultural Icon*. New York: Continuum Publishing, 2000.

Brownstein, Charles. *Eisner/Miller*. Milwaukie: Dark Horse Books, 2005.

Brubaker, Ed, Doug Mahnke, and David Baron. *Batman: The Man Who Laughs*. New York: DC Comics, 2005.

Bukatman, Scott. "Comics and the Critique of Chronophotography, or 'He Never Knew When It Was Coming!'" *Animation: An Interdisciplinary Journal* 1, no. 1 (2006): 83–103.

———. "Online Comics and the Reframing of the Moving Image." In *The New Media Book*. Edited by Dan Harries. London: BFI Publishing, 2002.

The Burly Man Chronicles. Directed by Josh Oreck. 95 min. Warner Bros., 2004. DVD.

Campbell, Glenn. "Crimestoppers Textbook." *Cinefex* 44 (November 1990).

Canby, Vincent. "A Cartoon Square Comes to Life in *Dick Tracy*." *New York Times*, 15 June 1990.

Canemaker, John. *Winsor McCay: His Life and Work*. Revised edition. New York: Harry Abrams Publishers, 2005.

Carle, Chris. "*Enter the Matrix* Video Game Review." *IGN.com*. 20 May 2003. <http://ps2.ign.com/articles/403/403749p1.html> (4 October 2010).

Carlin, John, Paul Karasik, and Brian Walker, eds. *Masters of American Comics*. New Haven: Yale University Press, 2005.

Carlson, Johanna and KC. "What's the Point of a Motion Comic?" *DVDs Worth Watching*. 23 August 2009. <http://comicsworthreading.com/2009/08/23/whats-the-point-of-a-motion-comic/> (21 March 2011).

Carrier, David. *The Aesthetics of Comics*. University Park: Pennsylvania State University Press, 2000.

Castaldi, Simone. *Drawn and Dangerous: Italian Comics of the 1970s and 1980s*. Jackson: University Press of Mississippi, 2010.

Chabon, Michael. *The Amazing Adventures of Kavalier & Clay*. New York: Picador, 2000.

Chisholm, Brad. "Colonizing the Comic Book Industry." Presentation at the Society for Cinema and Media Studies Conference, 10 March 2007.

"Cinefile." *Los Angeles Times*, 19 March 1989.

Clover, Joshua. *BFI Modern Classics: The Matrix*. London: British Film Institute, 2004.

Cohen, Michael. "*Dick Tracy*: In Pursuit of a Comic Book Aesthetic." In *Film and Comic Books*. Edited by Ian Gordon, Mark Jancovich, and Matthew P. McAllister. Jackson: University Press of Mississippi, 2007.

Cohn, Lawrence. "*Batman* a 10-Year Journal for Uslan and Melniker; Execs' Next Game: *Monopoly*." *Weekly Variety*, 7 June 1989.

Colton, David. "Q&A with Stephen King." *USA Today*. 18 December 2006. <http://www.usatoday.com/life/books/news/2006-12-18-king-qa_x.htm> (12 October 2010).

Comic Books Unbound. Director unknown. 59 min. Starz, 2008. DVD.

Corless, Richard. "Extra! *Tracy* is Tops." *Time*, 18 June 1990.

Crafton, Donald. *Emile Cohl, Caricature, and Film*. Princeton: Princeton University Press, 1990.

Crafton, Donald. *Before Mickey: The Animated Film 1898–1928*. 2nd ed. Chicago: University of Chicago Press, 1993.

Craven, Thomas, ed. *Cartoon Cavalcade*. Chicago: Consolidated Book Publishers, 1945.

Crook, Marshall, and Peter Sanders. "Will Marketing Change After Star's Death?" *Wall Street Journal*. 24 January 2008. <http://online.wsj.com/article/SB120113527501911813.html> (24 January 2011).

Cubitt, Sean. *The Cinema Effect*. Cambridge, MA: MIT Press, 2005.

Daniels, Les. *Batman: The Complete History*. San Francisco: Chronicle Books, 1999.

David, Peter, Stephen King, Robin Furth, and Jae Lee. *The Dark Tower: The Gunslinger Born*. New York: Marvel Comics, 2007.

"DC Universe November 2009 Release Calendar." *DCComics.com*. No date. <http://www .dccomics.com/dcu/comics/> (01 November 2009).

Dick Tracy Press Kit.

DiLullo, Tara. *300: The Art of the Film* (Milwaukie: Dark Horse Books, 2007).

Doherty, Thomas. *Teenagers and Teenpics: The Juvenilization of American Movies in the 1950s*. Philadelphia: Temple University Press, 2002.

D'Orazio, Valeria. "What Makes a Comic Book A Success Nowadays?" *Comic Book Junction*. 9 March 2009. <http://www.comicbookjunction.com/2009/03/09/what-makes-a -comic-book-a-success-nowadays/> (9 April 2010).

Duncan, Randy, and Matthew J. Smith. *The Power of Comics: History, Form, & Culture*. New York: Continuum, 2009.

Ebert, Roger. "*Superman* Movie Review." *RogerEbert.com*. 15 December 1978. <http://rog erebert.suntimes.com/apps/pbcs.dll/article?AID=/19781215/REVIEWS/41011001/1023> (4 May 2010).

———. "*Superman II* Movie Review." *RogerEbert.com*. 1 January 1981. <http://rogerebert. suntimes.com/apps/pbcs.dll/article?AID=/19810101/REVIEWS/101010303/1023> (4 May 2010).

———. "*Superman III* Movie Review." *RogerEbert.com*. 17 June 1983. <http://rogerebert.sun times.com/apps/pbcs.dll/article?AID=/19830617/REVIEWS/306170302/1023> (9 April 2010).

———. "*Dick Tracy* Movie Review." *RogerEbert.com*. 15 June 1990. <http://rogerebert.sun times.com/apps/pbcs.dll/article?AID=/19900615/REVIEWS/6150301/1023> (13 July 2010).

———. "*Batman Forever* Movie Review." *RogerEbert.com*. 16 June 1995. <http://rogerebert .suntimes.com/apps/pbcs.dll/article?AID=/19950616/REVIEWS/506160301/1023> (15 May 2010).

———. "*The Good, the Bad, and the Ugly* Movie Review." *RogerEbert.com*. 3 August 2003. <http://rogerebert.suntimes.com/apps/pbcs.dll/article?AID=/20030803/ REVIEWS08/308030301/1023> (1 November 2010).

———. "*Sin City* Movie Review." *RogerEbert.com*. 31 March 2005. <http://rogerebert.sun times.com/apps/pbcs.dll/article?AID=/20050331/REVIEWS/50322001/1023> (24 January 2011).

———. "*The Spirit* Movie Review." *RogerEbert.com*. 23 December 2008. <http://rogerebert .suntimes.com/apps/pbcs.dll/article?AID=/20081223/REVIEWS/812239987> (24 January 2011).

———. "*Year One* Movie Review," *RogerEbert.com*, 17 June 2009, <http://rogerebert.sun
times.com/apps/pbcs.dll/article?AID=/20090617/REVIEWS/906179997> (27 July 2010).

Ebert, Roger and Richard Roeper. "Transcript of *Hulk* Review." *Ebert & Roeper*, 11 June 2003.

Ebert, Roger, and Gene Siskel. "*Batman* Movie Review." *At the Movies*. Unknown Date.
<http://bventertainment.go.com/tv/buenavista/atm/reviews.html?sec=1&subsec=170>
(15 May 2010).

Ecke, Jochen. "Spatializing the Movie Screen: How Mainstream Cinema Is Catching Up on
the Formal Potentialities of the Comic Book Page." In *Comics as a Nexus of Cultures:
Essays on the Interplay of Media, Disciplines and International Perspectives*. Edited by
Mark Berninger, Jochen Ecke, and Gideon Haberkorn. Jefferson: McFarland and Company, 2010.

Eisner, Will. *The Best of the Spirit*. New York: DC Comics, 2005.

———. *Comics and Sequential Art*. Tamarac: Poorhouse Press, 1985.

Eller, Claudia. "Orion Reveals Plan for *Robocop II*." *The Hollywood Reporter*, 6 August 1987.

———. "*Tracy* Cost Put at $101 Mil." *Variety*, 22 October 1990.

Epstein, Daniel Robert. "The Joker, the Jewish Museum, and Jerry: Talking to Jerry Robinson." *Newsarama.com*. 18 October 2006. <http://forum.newsarama.com/showthread
.php?t=88092> (7 January 2011).

"February 2007 Comic Book Sales Figures." *The Comics Chronicles*. No date. <http://www
.comichron.com/monthlycomicssales/2007/2007-02.html> (1 June 2011).

Feininger, Lyonel. *The Kin-der-Kids*. New York: Dover Publications, 1980.

Fell, John L. *Film and the Narrative Tradition*. Berkeley: University of California Press, 1974.

"Film Clips." *Los Angeles Times*, 29 June 1983.

Filming the Legend: Making Superman. Directed by Michael Thau. 31 min. Warner Bros.,
2001. DVD.

Fineberg, Jonathan. *Art Since 1940: Strategies of Being*. 2nd ed. Upper Saddle River: Prentice
Hall, 2000.

Finke, Nikki. "Deadline Hollywood: *Watchmen* Postmortem." *LA Weekly*, 13 March 2009.

———. "Guys Beat Gal." *Deadline.com*. 14 August 2010. <http://www.deadline.com/2010/08/
first-box-office-the-expendables-13m34m-eat-pray-love-8m23m-scott-pilgrim-5m12m/>
(18 August 2010).

Fisher, Bud. *A. Mutt: A Complete Compilation: 1907–1908*. Edited by Bill Blackbeard. Westport: Hyperion Press, 1977.

Fleming, Charles. "Naked Hollywood: Bat Out of Hell." *L.A. Weekly*, 8 August 1997.

"Forget the Stars; Studios Pay Most for FX." *The Internet Movie Database*. 15 May 2006.
<http://www.imdb.com/news/sb/2006-05-15#film1> (07 April 2010).

Fleming, Mike. "Universal Nixes Stephen King's *Dark Tower*—No Ambitious Film Trilogy or
TV Series." *Deadline.com*. 18 July 2011. <http://www.deadline.com/2011/07/universal
-wont-scale-stephen-kings-the-dark-tower-studio-declines-to-make-ambitious-trilogy
-and-tv-series/> (20 July 2011).

Frayling, Christopher. *Spaghetti Westerns: Cowboys and Europeans from Karl May to Sergio
Leone*. London: I.B. Tauris, 1998.

———. *Sergio Leone: Something to Do With Death*. London: Faber and Faber, 2000.

"From *Hulk* to *Rocket*." *Variety*, 8 July 1997.

Gabilliet, Jean-Paul. *Of Comics and Men: A Cultural History of American Comic Books.* Translated by Bart Beaty and Nick Nguyen. Jackson: University Press of Mississippi, 2010.

Garrett, Stephen. "Q&A: Frank Miller." *Esquire*, April 2007.

George, Richard. "*300* in Film." *IGN.com.* 8 March 2007. <http://comics.ign.com/articles/771 /771698p1.html> (07 April 2010).

Gerrold, David. "Introduction." In *Taking the Red Pill: Science, Philosophy, and Religion in The Matrix.* Edited by Glenn Yeffeth. Chichester: Summersdale Publishers Ltd., 2003.

Gibron, Bill. "Game° Over." *Popmatters.com.* 16 August 2010. <http://www.popmatters.com/ pm/post/129700-gamer-over/> (18 August 2010).

Giroux, Jack. "Kevin Smith talks *Scott Pilgrim vs. the World.*" *The Film Stage.* 3 March 2010. <http://thefilmstage.com/2010/03/03/exclusive-kevin-smith-talks-scott-pilgrim-vs-the -world/> (3 August 2010).

Glanzer, David, and Gary Sassaman. *Comic-Con 40 Souvenir Book.* San Diego: San Diego Comic-Con International, 2009.

"Glossary of Movie Business Terms." *The Numbers.* No date. <http://www.the-numbers .com/glossary.php#production_budget> (29 September 2010).

Goldberg, Jordan, Long Vo, Joe Ng, and Crystal Reid. *Inception: The Cobol Job.* No date. <http://movies.yahoo.com/feature/inception-comic.html> (18 March 2011).

Goldsmith, Jeff. "*Spirit* Moves Him." *Variety*, 26 July 2007, A2.

Gombrich, E. H. "The Principles of Caricature." *The Gombrich Archive.* 25 May 1937. <http:// www.gombrich.co.uk/showdoc.php?id=85> (1 November 2010).

Gomery, Douglas. *The Hollywood Studio System: A History.* London: BFI Publishing, 2005.

Gopalan, Nisha. "Stephen King Reveals Long-Awaited *Tower* Scoop at Comic-Con." *Entertainment Weekly.* 26 February 2007. <http://popwatch.ew.com/2007/02/26/with_tooth pick_/> (12 October 2010).

Gordon, Ian, Mark Jancovich, and Matthew P. McAllister, eds. *Film and Comic Books.* Jackson: University Press of Mississippi, 2007.

Gordon, Ian. "Making Comics Respectable: How *Maus* Helped Redefine a Medium." In *The Rise of the American Comics Artist*, editors Paul Williams and James Lyons. Jackson: University Press of Mississippi, 2010.

Grant, Steve. "Frank Opinions." *Time Out*, 10–17 October 1990, 15.

Greenfield, Daniel. "Gunslinger #3-*Stephen King's The Dark Tower-The Gunslinger Born* Three." *Hubpages.* No date. <http://hubpages.com/hub/Gunslinger_3_-_Stephen_Kings _The_Dark_Tower_-_The_Gunslinger_Born_Three> (07 April 2010).

Green World. Director unknown. 12 mins. Lionsgate, 2009. DVD.

Griffin, Nancy, and Kim Masters. *Hit and Run: How Jon Peters and Peter Guber Took Sony for a Ride in Hollywood.* New York: Simon and Schuster, 1997.

Groensteen, Thierry. *The System of Comics.* Translated by Bart Beaty and Nick Nguyen. Jackson: University of Mississippi Press, 2007.

Gronsky, Daniel Gaines Edward. "Frame to Frame: A Historical Analysis of the Evolution and Propagation of the Comic Book Film." PhD dissertation, University of Connecticut, 2008.

Gunning, Tom. *D. W. Griffith and the Origins of American Narrative Film: The Early Years at Biograph.* Urbana: University of Illinois Press, 1991.

———. "'Primitive' Cinema-A Frame-up? or The Trick's on Us." *Cinema Journal* 28, no. 2 (1989): 3–12.

Gustines, George Gene. "A Comic Book Superhero is Headed to Small Screens." *New York Times*, 14 July 2008.

Hajdu, David. *The Ten-Cent Plague: The Great Comic-Book Scare and How It Changed America*. New York: Farrar, Straus and Giroux, 2008.

Harris, Dana. "WB Sends *Pi* Guy into the Bat Cave." *Variety*, 21 September 2000, 1.

Harvey, Robert C. *The Art of the Comic Book: An Aesthetic History*. Jackson: University Press of Mississippi, 1996.

Hight, Craig. "*American Splendor*: Translating Comic Autobiography into Drama-Documentary." In *Film and Comic Books*. Edited by Ian Gordon, Mark Jancovich, and Matthew P. McAllister. Jackson: University Press of Mississippi, 2007.

Hughes, Howard. *Once Upon a Time in the Italian West: The Filmgoers' Guide to Spaghetti Westerns*. London: I.B. Tauris, 2004.

How It Went Down: Convincing Frank Miller to Make the Film. Director unknown. 6 mins. Miramax, 2009. DVD.

Hughes, Kathleen. "Batman Fans Fear the Joke's on Them in Hollywood Epic." *Wall Street Journal*, 29 November 1988.

"*Hulk*." *The Art of the Title Sequence*. 11 May 2009. <http://www.artofthetitle.com/2009/05/11/hulk/> (23 August 2010).

"Imax in Day-Date Plan for Warners' *300*." *The Hollywood Reporter*, 26 January 2007.

"Insider." *Los Angeles Magazine*, October 1986.

Jaafar, Ali. "Iran President Disses *300*." *Variety*, 22 March 2007.

Jenkins, Henry. *Convergence Culture: Where Old and New Media Collide*. New York: New York University Press, 2006.

———. "The Pleasure of *Pirates* and What It Tells Us about World Building in Branded Entertainment." *Confessions of an Aca-Fan*. 13 June 2007. <http://henryjenkins.org/2007/06/forced_simplicity_and_the_crit.html> (24 April 2012).

———. *What Made Pistachio Nuts?: Early Sound Comedy and the Vaudeville Aesthetic*. New York: Columbia University Press, 1992.

Jensen, Jeff. "*Watchmen*: An Oral History." *Entertainment Weekly*, 21 October 2005.

Johnson, Derek. "Will the Real Wolverine Please Stand Up?: Marvel's Mutation from Monthlies to Movies." In *Film and Comic Books*. Edited by Ian Gordon, Mark Jancovich, and Matthew P. McAllister. Jackson: University Press of Mississippi, 2007.

Jondough. "Jondough Deems Frank Miller's *The Spirit* the Worst Movie He's Ever Seen!!" *Ain't It Cool News*. 15 December 2008. <http://www.aintitcool.com/node/39450> (14 March 2011).

Jones, Matthew T. *Found in Translation: Structural and Cognitive Aspects of the Adaptation of Comic Art to Film*. Saarbrücken: VDM Verlag, 2009.

Kilday, Gregg. "Film Clips: *Dick Tracy* to Make Film Debut." *Los Angeles Times*, 26 November 1977.

———. "HBO Finds *Splendor* in Sundance Selections." *The Hollywood Reporter*, 24 January 2003.

King, Geoff. *New Hollywood Cinema: An Introduction*. New York: Columbia University Press, 2002.

King, Stephen. *The Gunslinger: Revised and Expanded Edition*. Toronto: Signet Fiction, 2003.

Kit, Borys. "*Watchmen* Feeding Off *300* Spoils." *The Hollywood Reporter*, 13 March 2007.

Kit, Zorianna. "Lee Crouching with Uni *Hulk*." *The Hollywood Reporter*, 12–14 January 2001.

Klenotic, Jeffrey F. "The Place of Rhetoric in 'New' Film Historiography: The Discourse of Corrective Revisionism." *Film History* 6, no. 1 (1994): 45–58.

Kunzle, David. *The Early Comic Strip: Narrative Strips and Picture Stories in the European Broadsheet from c. 1450 to 1825*. Berkeley: University of California Press, 1973.

———. *The History of the Comic Strip: The Nineteenth Century*. Berkeley: University of California Press, 1990.

———. "Some Supplementary Notes by David Kunzle." *Film Quarterly* 26, no. 1 (1972): 19–23.

Lacassin, Francis. "The Comic Strip and Film Language." *Film Quarterly* 26, no. 1 (1972): 11–19.

Lane, Anthony. "*City of God* Movie Review." *New Yorker* 20 (2003).

Lee, Stan and Jack Kirby. *The Essential Incredible Hulk, Vol. 1*. New York: Marvel Comics, 2006.

Lefèvre, Pascal. "The Construction of Space in Comics." In *A Comics Studies Reader*. Edited by Jeet Heer and Kent Worcester. Jackson: University Press of Mississippi, 2009.

———. "Incompatible Visual Ontologies?: The Problematic Adaptation of Drawn Images." In *Film and Comic Books*. Edited by Ian Gordon, Mark Jancovich, and Matthew P. McAllister. Jackson: University Press of Mississippi, 2007.

Lengel, Kerry. "Graphic Novelist Art Spiegelman Keeps the Faith." *Arizona Republic*, 29 January 2006.

Lopes, Paul. *Demanding Respect: The Evolution of the American Comic Book*. Philadelphia: Temple University Press, 2009.

The Magic Behind the Cape. Directed by Michael Thau. 24 min. Warner Bros., 2001. DVD.

Manovich, Lev. *The Language of New Media*. Cambridge, MA: MIT Press, 2001.

Marschall, Richard. *America's Great Comic-Strip Artists*. New York: Abbeville Press, 1989.

Martin, Adrian. *Once Upon a Time in America*. London: BFI Press, 2008.

"May 1998 Comic Book Sales Figures." *The Comics Chronicles*. No date. <http://www.comichron.com/monthlycomicssales/1998/1998-05.html> (27 May 2011).

"May 2005 Comic Book Sales Figures." *The Comics Chronicle*. <http://www.comichron.com/monthlycomicssales/2005/2005-05.html> (22 June 2011).

McAllister, Matthew P., Ian Gordon, and Mark Jancovich, "Blockbuster Meets Superhero Comic, or Art House Meets Graphic Novel?: The Contradictory Relationship Between Film and Comic Art." *Journal of Popular Film and Television* 34 (Fall 2006).

Mcbride, Sarah. "Web Draws on Comics." *Wall Street Journal*, 18 July 2008.

McCarthy, Todd. "Salkinds' Lucrative *Superman* Films Also Costly and Litigious." *Variety*, 8 July 1987.

McCay, Winsor. *Little Nemo in Slumberland: Many More Splendid Sundays!* Edited by Peter Maresca. Palo Alto: Sunday Press Books, 2009.

———. "Little Sammy Sneeze." *New York Herald*, 24 September 1905.

———. *Little Sammy Sneeze: So Many Splendid Sundays!* Edited by Peter Maresca. Palo Alto: Sunday Press Books, 2006.

McClintock, Pamela. "An Unusual WB Deal." *Variety*, 30 January 2007.

———. "Warners Bets a Bundle on Swords-and-CGI *300*." *Variety*, 10 October 2005.

McCloud, Scott. *Understanding Comics: The Invisible Art.* New York: Kitchen Sink Press, 1993.

———. *Reinventing Comics: How Imagination and Technology Are Revolutionizing an Art Form.* New York: HarperCollins, 2000.

McDonnell, Patrick, Karen O'Connell, and Georgia Riley de Havenson. *Krazy Kat: The Comic Art of George Herriman.* New York: Harry N. Abrams, 1986.

McFarlane, Brian. *Novel to Film: An Introduction to the Theory of Adaptation.* Oxford: Oxford University Press, 1996.

McGee, Patrick. *From Shane to Kill Bill: Rethinking the Western.* Malden: Blackwell Publishing, 2007.

McGovern, Adam, Arlen Schumer, Steve Lawrence, and Robert Lawrence. "Animatters: Marvel Man." *Jack Kirby Collector* 42 (2004).

McLuhan, Marshall. *Understanding Media: The Extensions of Man.* Cambridge, MA: MIT Press, 1994.

McManus, George. *Bringing Up Father.* Edited by Herb Galewitz. New York: Charles Scribner's Sons, 1973.

McNary, Dave, and Michael Fleming. "WB, Fox Make Deal for *Watchmen.*" *Variety*, 15 January 2009.

McNary, Dave, and Michael Schneider. "Towering Challenge." *Variety*, 9 September 2010.

Meehan, Eileen R. "'Holy Commodity Fetish Batman!': The Political Economy of the Commercial Intertext." In *The Many Lives of Batman: Critical Approaches to a Superhero and His Media.* Edited by Roberta Pearson and William Uricchio. London: Routledge, 1991.

Melrose, Kevin. "Sales Skyrocket for Miller's *300* Graphic Novel." *Newsarama.* 16 November 2006. <http://blog.newsarama.com/2006/11/16/sales-for-skyrocket-for-millers-300-graphic-novel/> (27 May 2011).

Miller, Frank, David Mazzucchelli, and Richmond Lewis. *Batman: Year One.* New York: DC Comics, 1988.

Miller, Frank, Klaus Janson, and Lynn Varley. *Batman: The Dark Knight Returns.* New York: DC Comics, 1997.

Miller, Frank, and Lynn Varley. *300.* Milwaukie: Dark Horse Publishing, 1999.

Miller, Frank. "Introduction." In *Batman: Year One.* New York: DC Comics, 1988.

———. "Introduction." In *Eisner/Miller.* Edited by Charles Brownstein. Milwaukie: Dark Horse Books, 2005.

———. *Sin City: The Big Fat Kill.* Milwaukie: Dark Horse Publishing, 2005.

———. *Sin City: Booze, Broads, & Bullets.* Milwaukie: Dark Horse Publishing, 2010.

———. *Sin City: A Dame to Kill For.* Milwaukie: Dark Horse Publishing, 2005.

———. *Sin City: Family Values.* Milwaukie: Dark Horse Publishing, 2005.

———. *Sin City: Hell and Back.* Milwaukie: Dark Horse Publishing, 2005.

———. *Sin City: That Yellow Bastard.* Milwaukie: Dark Horse Comics, 2005.

———. *Sin City: The Hard Goodbye*. Milwaukie: Dark Horse Comics, 2005.

Miller, John Jackson. "*Watchmen* Sales Rankings in its Initial Release." *The Comics Chronicles*. No date. <http://www.comichron.com/special/watchmensales.html> (1 June 2011).

Mitchell, Elvis. "A Comics Guy, Outside the Box." *New York Times*, 15 August 2003.

———. "Ang Lee on Comic Books and *Hulk* as Hidden Dragon." *New York Times*, 22 June 2003.

Mohr, Ian. "B.O. Hits Greek Peak: $70 Mil." *Variety*, 12 March 2007.

Moore, Alan, and David Gibbons. *Watchmen*. New York: DC Comics, 1995.

Moore, Alan, and David Lloyd. *V for Vendetta*. New York: Vertigo Comics, 2008.

Morrison, Grant, and John Van Fleet. *Batman* 663. New York: DC Comics, 2007.

Morton, Drew. "Adam McKay Signs on to Direct R-Rated Superhero Satire *The Boys*." *The Playlist*. 24 July 2010. <http://theplaylist.blogspot.com/2010/07/adam-mckay-signs-on-to-direct-r-rated.html> (18 August 2010).

———. "Comics Jump to the Big Screen." *Milwaukee Journal Sentinel*. 26 August 2002.

———. "Comics to Film (and Halfway Back Again): A DVD Essay." *Flow TV* 5, no. 11 (2007).

———. "Godard's Comic-Strip Mise-en-Scène." *Senses of Cinema* 53 (2009).

———. "Sketching Under the Influence? Winsor McCay and the Question of Aesthetic Convergence Between Comic Strips and Film." *Animation: An Interdisciplinary Journal* 5, no. 3 (2010): 295–312.

Murphy, Mary. "Movie Call Sheet: *Superman* Film." *Los Angeles Times*. 9 August 1975.

Murray, Rebecca. "Writer/Director Christopher Nolan Talks about *The Dark Knight*." *About.com*. No date. <http://movies.about.com/od/thedarkknight/a/darkknight70408_2.htm> (24 January 2011).

Naremore, James. "Introduction." In *Film Adaptation*. Edited by James Naremore. New Jersey: Rutgers University Press, 2000.

———. *More than Night: Film Noir in Its Contexts*. Berkeley: University of California Press, 1998.

Newell, Kathleen Ellen. "What We Talk about When We Talk about Adaptation." PhD dissertation, University of Delaware, 2005.

"New Potter Book Topples U.S. Sales Records." *MSNBC.com*. 18 July 2005. <http://www.msnbc.msn.com/id/8608578/> (31 August 2010).

North, Dan. "Virtual Actors, Spectacle and Special Effects: Kung Fu Meets 'All That CGI Bullshit.'" In *The Matrix Trilogy: Cyberpunk Reloaded*. Edited by Stacy Gillis. New York: Wallflower Press, 2005.

Nystrom, Elsa A. "A Rejection of Order, the Development of the Newspaper Comic Strip in America." PhD dissertation, Loyola University of Chicago, 1989.

O'Donnell, Kevin. "Q&A: Frank Miller." *Rolling Stone*, 25 August 2005.

Oliff, Steve. "The Image Era Changes Comic Color." *Olyoptics.com*. No date. <http://www.olyoptics.com/test/Timeline1992Page1.htm> (19 May 2011).

Olsen, Mark. "An Epic Battle is Pumped Up." *Los Angeles Times*, 14 January 2007.

O'Neil, Dennis, Jerry Ordway, and Steve Oliff. *Batman: A DC Movie Special*. New York: DC Comics, 1989.

O'Sullivan, Judith. *The Great American Comic Strip: One Hundred Years of Cartoon Art*. Boston: Bulfinch Press, 1990.

Peary, Danny, and Gerald Peary, eds. *The American Animated Cartoon: A Critical Anthology*. New York: E. P. Dutton, 1980.

Pekar, Harvey, and Robert Crumb. "Standing Behind Old Jewish Ladies in Supermarket Lines." In *American Splendor: The Life and Times of Harvey Pekar*. New York: Ballantine Books, 2003.

Pekar, Harvey. *American Splendor: The Life and Times of Harvey Pekar*. New York: Ballantine Books, 2003.

Petrikin, Chris. "U Has *Hulk* Take a Seat." *Variety*, 2 March 1998.

Phillips, Dan. "The Joker's Wild Ride." *IGN.com*. 23 October 2008. <http://comics.ign.com/articles/923/923283p1.html> (24 January 2011).

Phillips, Michael, and A. O. Scott. "*Scott Pilgrim vs. the World*." *At the Movies*, 14 August 2010.

Phipps, Keith. "Remember *Dick Tracy*?" *Slate.com*. 21 June 2010. <http://www.slate.com/id/2255746/pagenum/all/#p2> (29 June 2010).

Pierce, Leonard. "*Batman: The Animated Series*: On Leather Wings." *AVClub.com*. 29 November 2010. <http://www.avclub.com/articles/on-leather-wings,48295/> (15 January 2010).

Place, Janey, and Lowell Peterson, "Some Visual Motifs of Film Noir." In *Film Noir Reader*. Edited by Alain Silver and James Ursini. New York: Limelight Editions, 1996.

Puckett, Kelley, Martin Pasko, and Ty Templeton. *The Batman Adventures*. New York: DC Comics, 1992.

Quigley, Adam. "Matthew Vaughn Agreed to Direct *X-Men: First Class* Because He Believes Superhero Movies Will Be Dead Soon." *Slashfilm.com*. 7 August 2010. <http://www.slashfilm.com/2010/08/07/matthew-vaughn-agreed-to-direct-x-men-first-class-because-he-believes-superhero-movies-will-be-dead-soon/> (18 August 2010).

Rabin, Nathan. "*The Spirit* Movie Review." *The AV Club*. 24 December 2008. <http://www.avclub.com/articles/the-spirit,17083/> (7 February 2011).

Rae, Neil, and Jonathan Gray, "When Gen-X Meets X-Men: Retextualizing Comic Book Film Reception." In *Film and Comic Books*. Edited by Ian Gordon, Mark Jancovich, and Matthew P. McAllister. Jackson: University Press of Mississippi, 2007.

"Rambling Reporter." *The Hollywood Reporter*, 17 October 1990.

"Rambling Reporter." *The Hollywood Reporter*, 19 October 1990.

Ramey, Bill. "Lee Bermejo, Part 2." *Batman on Film*. 23 May 2007. <http://www.batman-on-film.com/lee-bermejo_interview-2.html> (24 January 2011).

ReflectingHierophant, "Why So Serious?" *Comic Book Movie.com*. No date. <http://www.comicbookmovie.com/fansites/MyCBMOpinion/news/?a=28648&t=Reflections_of_a_Hierophant_Why_So_Serious> (24 January 2011).

Rehak, Bob. "The Migration of Forms: Bullet Time as Microgenre." *Film Criticism* 32, No. 1 (2007).

———. "*Watchmen*'s Frames of Reference: Digital Production Tools and the High-Fidelity Comic Book Adaptation." Presentation at the Society for Cinema and Media Studies Conference, 18 March 2010.

Rhode, Michael, and Manfred Vogel. *Film & TV Adaptations of Comics: 2007 Edition*. Location Unknown: Lulu.com Press, 2007.

Richildis, Ranylt. "*The Spirit* Movie Review." *Pajiba*. 30 December 2008. <http://www.pajiba.com/film_reviews/spirit-the-review.php> (7 February 2011).

Richards, Dave. "Cassaday on the *Astonishing X-Men* Motion Comic." *Comic Book Resources*. 23 October 2009. <http://www.comicbookresources.com/?page=article&id=23421> (14 March 2011).

Riley, Jenelle. "There's Always Hope." *Back Stage West Drama-Logue*, 21 August 2003.

Robinson, Iann. "The Redemption of Frank Miller." *Crave Online*. 12 January 2009. <http://www.craveonline.com/entertainment/comics/article/the-redemption-of-frank-miller-72867> (7 February 2011).

Roeper, Richard. "*300* Movie Review." *RichardRoeper.com*. 9 March 2007. <http://www.richardroeper.com/reviews/300.aspx> (31 August 2010).

Rogers, Mark. "Beyond Bang! Pow! Zap!: Genre and the Evolution of the American Comic Book Industry." PhD dissertation, University of Michigan, 1997.

———. "License Farming and the American Comic Book Industry." *International Journal of Comic Art* 1, no. 2 (1999).

Rohter, Larry. "Hollywood Abuzz Over Cost Memo." *New York Times*, 2 February 1991.

Rose, Lacey. "Hollywood's Most Expensive Movies." *Forbes*, 18 December 2006.

Rossen, Jake. *Superman vs. Hollywood: How Fiendish Producers, Devious Directors, and Warring Writers Grounded an American Icon*. Chicago: Chicago Review Press, 2008.

Rothstein, Allan B. "Mr. Mom as Batman?" *Los Angeles Times*, 3 July 1988.

Round, Julia. "'Is This a Book?' DC Vertigo and the Redefinition of Comics in the 1990s." In *The Rise of the American Comics Artist: Creators and Contexts*. Edited by Paul Williams and James Lyons. Jackson: University Press of Mississippi, 2010.

Sabin, Roger. *Comics, Comix, & Graphic Novels: A History of Comic Art*. New York: Phaidon Press, 1996.

Salisbury, Mark, ed. *Burton on Burton*. London: Faber and Faber, 2000.

Sanders, Noah B. "The Importance of Being Clad in Spandex: The Comic Book Film in Contemporary America." Honors thesis, Whitman College, 2003.

Sarris, Andrew. "Ang Lee's Angst-Ridden *Hulk*: The Not-So-Jolly Green Giant." *The New York Observer*, 6 July 2003.

Schatz, Thomas. "The New Hollywood." In *Film Theory Goes to the Movies*. Edited by Jim Collins, Hilary Radner, and Ava Preacher Collins. London: Routledge, 1993.

Schedeen, Jesse. "Why *The Dark Tower* Matters." *IGN.com*. 17 September 2010. <http://movies.ign.com/articles/112/1121704p1.html> (12 October 2010).

Schillig, Chris. "Comic Book Chronicler Harvey Pekar Speaks at Mount Union." *Alliance Review*. 22 February 2008. <http://www.the-review.com/news/article/3343481> (1 June 2011).

Schrader, Paul. "Notes on Film Noir." In *Film Noir Reader*. Edited by Alain Silver and James Ursini. New York: Limelight Editions, 1996.

Schweiger, David. "An American Family: The Pekars Talk about Their Splendor." *Venice*, August 2003.

Sciretta, Peter. "Brian Azzarello's *Joker* Graphic Novel." /*Film*. 19 October 2008. <http://www
.slashfilm.com/brian-azzarellos-joker-graphic-novel/> (24 January 2011).

Seidman, Robert. "Cable Top 25." *TV by the Numbers*. 15 March 2011. <http://tvbythenum
bers.zap2it.com/2011/03/15/cable-top-25-jersey-shore-wwe-raw-the-best-player-sponge
bob-lakersheat-top-weekly-cable-viewing/85817> (21 March 2011).

Segure, Alex. "What's Next for Frank Miller and Jim Lee?" *The Source*. 2 April 2010. <http://
dcu.blog.dccomics.com/2010/04/02/whats-next-for-frank-miller-and-jim-lee/> (7 February 2011).

Shadows of the Bat: The Cinematic Saga of the Dark Knight. 30 min. Warner Bros., 2005. DVD.

Sharrett, Christopher. "Batman and the Twilight of the Idols: An Interview with Frank
Miller." In *The Many Lives of Batman: Critical Approaches to a Superhero and His Media*.
Edited by Roberta Pearson and William Uricchio. London: Routledge, 1991.

Simon, Brent. "The Monster Within." *Entertainment Today*, 20–26 June 2003, 6.

Sims, Chris. "The Best Video Game Moments in *Scott Pilgrim*." *Comics Alliance*. 28 July 2009.
<http://www.comicsalliance.com/2009/07/28/the-best-video-game-moments-in
-scott-pilgrim/> (2 August 2010).

Siuntres, John. "Word Balloon: *Watchmen Motion Comics*' Jake Hughes." *Newsarama.com*. 28
January 2009. <http://www.newsarama.com/comics/010928-WB-Watchmen-Motion
.html> (15 March 2011).

Sneddon, Laura. "Full and Uncut Interview with Grant Morrison." 29 September 2011.
<http://www.comicbookgrrrl.com/2011/09/29/full-and-uncut-interview-with-grant
-morrison/> (16 January 2012).

Spain, Tom. "'Dick Tracy': Scaling the Wall." *Washington Post*, 20 December 1990.

Spiegelman, Art. "Reading Pictures." In *Lynd Ward: Prelude to a Million Years, Song Without
Words, Vertigo*. Edited by Art Spiegelman. New York: Literary Classics of the United
States, 2010.

Spigel, Lynn, and Henry Jenkins, "Same Bat Channel, Different Bat Times: Mass Culture and
Popular Memory." In *The Many Lives of the Batman: Critical Approaches to a Superhero
and His Media*. Edited by Roberta Pearson and William Uricchio. New York: Routledge,
1991.

Stam, Robert. "Beyond Fidelity: The Dialogics of Adaptation." In *Film Adaptation*. Edited by
James Naremore. New Jersey: Rutgers University Press, 2000.

———. "Introduction." In *Literature and Film: A Guide to the Theory and Practice of Film
Adaptation*. Edited by Robert Stam and Alessandra Raengo. Malden: Blackwell Publishing, 2005.

Stax. "Attila Leads the *300*." *IGN.com*. 15 August 2005. <http://movies.ign.com/articles/641
/641893p1.html> (2 September 2010).

Steiling, David. "Icon, Representation and Virtuality in Reading the Graphic Narrative." PhD
dissertation, University of South Florida, 2006.

Stewart, Garrett. *Framed Time: Towards a Postfilmic Cinema*. Chicago: University of Chicago
Press, 2007.

Taking Flight: The Development of Superman. Directed by Michael Thau. 30 min. Warner
Bros., 2001. DVD.

Thompson, Anne, and Pat H. Broeske. "Hawking *Batman*." *Entertainment Weekly*, 10 July 1992.

Thompson, Kristin. *Breaking the Glass Armor: Neoformalist Film Analysis*. Princeton: Princeton University Press, 1988.

"*300* Comic to Screen Comparison." *Solace in Cinema*. 4 October 2006. <http://www.solaceincinema.com/2006/10/04/300-comic-to-screen-comparison/> (4 October 2010).

"*300* Matches Miller's Style." *Sci Fi Wire*. 27 July 2006. <http://web.archive.org/web/20080610062645/http://www.scifi.com/scifiwire/index.php?category=0&id=37328> (30 August 2010).

300 Press Kit.

300 (Two-Disc Special Edition) Consumer Reviews," *Amazon.com*. No date. <http://www.amazon.com/Two-Disc-Special-Edition-Gerard-Butler/product-reviews/B00005JPLW/ref=cm_cr_pr_viewopt_kywd?ie=UTF8&showViewpoints=1&sortBy=helpful&reviewerType=all_reviews&formatType=all_formats&filterByStar=all_stars&pageNumber=1&filterByKeyword=look> (27 May 2015).

Thoss, Jeff. "Tell It Like a Game: Scott Pilgrim and Performative Media Rivalry." In *Storyworlds Across Media: Toward a Media-Conscious Narratology*. Edited by Marie-Laure Ryan and Jan Noël Thon. Lincoln: University of Nebraska Press, 2014.

"Top Comic Books of the 2000s." *The Comics Chronicles*. <http://www.comichron.com/vitalstatistics/topcomics2000s.html> (1 June 2011).

Toro, Gabe. "New *Sucker Punch* Trailer Confirms Zack Snyder Needs to Back Away from His Anime Collection Slooowly." *The Playlist*. 27 July 2010. <http://theplaylist.blogspot.com/2010/07/new-sucker-punch-trailer-confirms-zack.html> (24 August 2010).

Trimble, Marian Blackton. *J. Stuart Blackton: A Personal Biography by His Daughter*. Metuchen, NJ: Scarecrow Press, 1985.

"2008 Comic Book Sales Figures." *The Comics Chronicle*. No date. <http://www.comichron.com/monthlycomicssales/2008.html> (22 June 2011).

The Unique Editing Style of Hulk. 5 min. Universal, 2003. DVD.

Varnum, Robin, and Christina T. Gibbons, eds. *The Language of Comics: Word and Image*. Jackson: University Press of Mississippi, 2001.

Verrill, Addison. "*Superman* Headed Over Budget but Sitting Pretty." *Daily Variety*, 22 July 1977.

Vineyard, Jennifer. "*Arkham Asylum* Scribe Grant Morrison Opens Up Heath Ledger's Joker Diary." *MTV.com*. 4 August 2008. <http://m.mtv.com/blogs/splashpage_post.rbml?id=2008/08/04/arkham-asylum-scribe-grant-morrison-opens-up-heath-ledgers-joker-diary/&weburl=http%3A%2F%2Fsplashpage.mtv.com%2F2008%2F08%2F04%2Farkham-asylum-scribe-grant-morrison-opens-up-heath-ledgers-joker-diary%2F&alt=http%3A%2F%2Fm.mtv.com%2Fblogs%2Fsplashpage.rbml&cid=300> (16 July 2013).

"*Watchmen: The Complete Motion Comic*—DVD Sales." *The Numbers*. No date. <http://www.the-numbers.com/movies/2009/0WCMC-DVD.php> (21 March 2011).

Weiner, Stephen. "How the Graphic Novel Changed American Comics." In *The Rise of the American Comics Artist: Creators and Contexts*. Edited by Paul Williams and James Lyons. Jackson: University Press of Mississippi, 2010.

Welles, Orson, and Peter Bogdanovich. *This is Orson Welles*. Boston: Da Capo Press, 1998.

Wells, Paul. *Animation: Genre and Authorship*. London: Wallflower Press, 2002.

Wershler, Darren. "Digital Comics, Circulation, and the Importance of Being Eric Sluis." *Cinema Journal* 50, no. 3 (2011): 127–134.

Wilkerson, David B. "Disney to Acquire Marvel Entertainment for $4B." *MarketWatch*. 31 August 2009. <http://www.marketwatch.com/story/disney-to-acquire-marvel-entertainment-for-4b-2009-08-31> (07 April 2010).

Williams, Paul, and David Lyons. "Introduction." In *The Rise of the American Comics Artist: Creators and Contexts*. Edited by Paul Williams and David Lyons. Jackson: University Press of Mississippi, 2010.

Winchester, Mark. "Cartoon Theatricals from 1896 to 1927: Gus Hill's Cartoon Shows for the American Road Theatre." PhD dissertation, Ohio State University, 1995.

Wloszczyna, Susan. "An Epic Tale, Told 300 Strong." *USA Today*, 7 March 2007.

Wood, Mary. "The Yellow Kid on the Paper Stage." *University of Virginia*. No date. <http://xroads.virginia.edu/~MA04/wood/ykid/yellowkid.htm> (09 June 2009).

Wright, Bradford W. *Comic Book Nation: The Transformation of Youth Culture in America*. Baltimore: Johns Hopkins University Press, 2003.

Wright, Edgar. "Liner Notes." *Scott Pilgrim vs. the World: Original Motion Picture Soundtrack*. New York: ABKCO Records, 2010.

Wyatt, Justin. *High Concept: Movies and Marketing in Hollywood*. Austin: University of Texas Press, 1994.

INDEX

Academy of Motion Picture Arts and Sciences, 47, 76, 85, 185n2, 193n23

Action Comics, 3, 42, 48

Action lines. *See* Motion lines

Adaptation: defined, 6–8, 22–25; high-fidelity, 40, 60–62, 90; as industrial practice, 3, 5, 11, 15–18, 37–39, 41, 46, 49, 167–73; and remediation, 6–8, 22–23, 28, 65–70, 85–86, 93, 115, 136–37

American Splendor (comic), 87, 101–4

American Splendor (2003 film), 37, 87, 101–9, 196n55

Andrew, Dudley, 3, 6

Artifice: and camp, 54; in comics, 17, 90; in *Dick Tracy*, 67–72, 75; in film, 79, 92–93, 121–22; and the Joker, 152

Avengers, The, 17

Avengers, The (2012 film), 5, 38, 178

Azzarello, Brian, 150, 152–54, 173

Balloons. *See* Word and thought balloons

Batman: in comics, 3, 9, 23, 42–43, 46, 53, 61, 131, 142–54, 172; and fans, 46, 54–55; hero, 9, 17, 61, 95; on television, 14–15

Batman (1940s serials), 45

Batman (1966 film), 3

Batman (1966 television series), 10, 15–16, 24, 40–41, 45–46, 51, 54, 59

Batman (1989 film): and conglomeration, 8, 109–10; and cultural prestige, 11–12, 15–16, 40–41; and influence of, 12, 141;

production of, 51, 53–58, 66, 175–77; success of, 5, 74–75

Batman: A DC Movie Special (comic), 23, 139–41, 143

Batman: The Animated Series, 15, 41, 53, 147–48, 173

Batman: The Dark Knight Returns (comic), 10–11, 24, 53–54, 94, 145–47, 155–56, 173

Batman: The Killing Joke (comic), 143, 145–46

Batman: The Long Halloween (comic), 41, 61

Batman: Year One (comic), 46, 55, 61, 156, 158

Batman Adventures, The (comic), 148–49

Batman and Robin, 59–60, 76, 170

Batman Begins, 7, 41, 61, 68, 70, 150, 152, 159

Batman Forever, 58–59

Batman Returns, 57–59, 146

Bazin, André, 67, 70, 121–22, 191n69

Beatty, Warren, 7, 16, 59, 62, 65–75, 85–86, 153

Bermejo, Lee, 152–53

Blockbusters: and advertising, 116, 152; and budgets, 49, 87, 101; and reception, 59; and superhero films, 3, 5, 13, 40–41, 110

Bolland, Brian, 143, 145, 148

Bolter, Jay David, and Richard Grusin, 6–7, 23–24

Booker, M. Keith, 3, 12, 77

Borde, Raymond, and Étienne Chaumeton, 164, 167

221

Bordwell, David: on blockbusters, 3; on film style, 56–57, 77, 79, 127, 181–82, 204n23; on *Hulk*, 82–83, 127

Box office grosses: and *American Splendor*, 108; and *Batman* franchise, 54–55, 57–60, 74, 146, 152, 159, 177; and *Dick Tracy*, 74; and Hollywood, 10, 60, 84, 88, 110, 196n39; and *Hulk*, 84–85; and *The Matrix* franchise, 123; and Michael Cera, 37–38; and *Robocop* franchise, 156–57; and *Scott Pilgrim*, 22; and *Sin City*, 165; and *The Spirit*, 170; and *Superman* franchise, 49–51; and *300*, 93; and *Watchmen*, 99–100

Brando, Marlon, 9, 15, 47, 50

Brooker, Will, 46, 59, 123

Budget: and *American Splendor*, 101, 108; and *Batman* franchise, 54, 57–58, 60, 124, 152, 159, 176; and *Dick Tracy*, 59, 66–67, 74–75; and Hollywood, 6, 9–10, 12, 51, 85–88, 109–10, 177–80, 189n29, 194n54, 198n18; and *Hulk*, 76–77, 83–84; and *Kick-Ass*, 37; and *The Matrix* franchise, 123; and Michael Cera, 38; and *Robocop* franchise, 156; and *Scott Pilgrim*, 22, 39; and *Sin City*, 39, 158–59; and *The Spirit*, 165; and *Superman* franchise, 40, 46–49, 175; and *300*, 89, 93; and *Watchmen*, 94, 99–100

Bullet time, 17, 22, 115–22, 125, 136, 172, 177

Burton, Tim: and Batman, 5, 8, 16, 54–61, 141, 150, 153–54; and style, 41, 68, 146–48, 176

Camp: and *Batman*, 10–11, 15–16, 40, 45–46, 51–59; and *The Spirit*, 170; and *Superman*, 9–11, 16, 47

Caricature: in comics, 17, 93; in *Dick Tracy*, 7, 62, 67, 72–74, 86; in film, 7; in *The Good, the Bad, and the Ugly* and *The Dark Tower*, 130, 132–34; in *Sin City*, 161

Carrier, David, 105, 107

Cera, Michael, 28, 35, 37–38

CGI. *See* Computer-generated imagery

Chabon, Michael, 138–39, 199n4

Cinematography, 62, 65, 76, 86, 161, 167

Classical Hollywood system: defined, 77–80, 127, 180–82, 204n23; and high-concept and post-classical films, 56–57, 101, 154; and *Hulk*, 111; and Sergio Leone, 127–30; and *Sin City*, 164

Closure, 6, 31, 79–82, 117–19, 127

Cohen, Michael, 67–68, 71–72

Color: in comics, 13, 25, 31, 35, 96, 131–32, 147; and comic publishing, 28; in *Dick Tracy*, 71–72, 74; in film, 7, 48, 59, 68; and film noir, 161, 167, 170–72, 201n61; in *300*, 88, 91–93

Comic books: and audience, 43–45, 52–53, 100, 110; and cultural prestige, 9–12, 37–41, 52–55, 95; defined, 5–7, 24–25, 30, 164, 166–67; and film adaptations, 3, 5–6, 13, 15, 60–62, 83–85; history as industry, 41–62, 101, 155–56, 176–79; and iconography, 24–25, 66–76, 91–93, 132, 136, 142–54, 159; international differences, 13–14, 27–28, 126–27; printing, 71, 88; and reading, 28, 77–80; and sound, 15, 24, 28, 82; and space, 6, 24, 30, 77–80, 88, 90, 130, 134; and television, 15; and temporality, 6, 14, 28–29, 96, 117, 119–21; and text, 24–25, 103–7

Comics Code, 9–10, 16, 40, 44, 52–53, 76, 176

Computer-generated imagery (CGI): cost of, 76–77, 86, 100, 109, 180; evolution of, 12–13, 15, 111; use of, 35, 65, 67, 83, 100, 109, 122, 158, 177

Conglomeration: and stylistic remediation, 6, 8–9, 12, 22, 83, 109; and Warner Bros., 16, 41, 101, 141, 153, 175–78

Continuity and discontinuity editing. *See* Classical Hollywood system

Crumb, Robert, 52, 101, 104, 106

Cubitt, Sean, 181, 183

Dark Horse Comics, 88, 101, 156, 186n23

Dark Knight, The, 38, 76, 123–24, 150–54

Dark Knight Rises, The, 5, 178

Dark Tower, The (comic), 17, 115, 128, 130–37

Dark Tower, The (2017 film), 178–79

David, Peter, 131–32, 134–36

DC Comics: and Batman, 139–56, 172–73; history of, 42–43, 52, 76, 179; industrial structure, 8–9, 40, 176–77, 203n7; publishing, 10, 39, 101, 138, 186n23; and Superman, 45–47, 175; and *Watchmen*, 94, 110

Del Toro, Guillermo, 11, 61

Detective Comics, 3, 42, 142–45

Diamond Comic Distributors, 9, 88, 101, 164

Dick Tracy (comic), 65–66, 74, 132, 139, 167

Dick Tracy (1990 film): and box office, 87, 109–10, 177, 180; production of, 5, 39, 59, 61–62, 153; and remediation, 7, 16, 65–76, 86

Digital cinema, 6, 62, 83, 93, 111, 122, 165, 179–83

Donner, Richard, 3, 10, 47–50

Duncan, Randy, 10, 14, 52, 155–56, 167

Ebert, Roger, 50, 57, 75, 85, 108, 129

Eisner, Will: as artist and writer, 13, 17, 88, 121, 155, 165–73; as theorist, 28, 79

Eisner Awards, 88, 164–65

Fans: and Batman, 11, 16, 41, 54–57, 59, 75–76, 146–54, 173, 176; engagement, 12, 15, 52–53, 60–62, 103, 110, 136, 177–80; 195n32; growth of, 8–9, 16, 38–39, 62; and *The Spirit*, 165–67, 170, 172; and Superman, 50; and transmedia, 123–24; and *Watchmen*, 86, 94–95, 99–100

Fantastic Four, The (comic), 76

Film: defined against television, 15; history as industry, 41–62; as medium, 5–6, 25, 182; and space, 17, 82; and temporality, 6, 18, 28–29; and viewer, 29; and visual representation, 25, 28, 67–75, 127

Film noir: in *Batman*, 16, 55, 58, 147, 152; in comics, 5; as genre, 159–61, 164, 182, 201n64; in *Sin City*, 17, 23, 142, 155, 159–66; in *The Spirit*, 166–73

Finger, Bill, 3, 42, 142–43, 148

Fox Broadcasting Company, 147

Frayling, Christopher, 126, 128–30, 132, 134–37

Furst, Anton, 55–56

Gabilliet, Jean-Paul, 43, 148, 159, 172, 176, 178–79

Gaiman, Neil, 14, 150, 158

German Expressionism, 41, 55, 138, 159

Gibbons, Dave, 10, 14–15, 53, 61–62, 94–95, 98, 110, 195n32

Good, the Bad, and the Ugly, The, 17, 115, 128–32, 135, 137

Gould, Chester, 62, 65–67, 70–76, 86, 132, 134, 167

Graphical remediation, 28, 33, 35, 65–75, 87, 106–7, 139–73

Groensteen, Thierry, 30, 77, 96, 98, 105, 108, 127–30

Guber, Peter, 51, 55

Harvey, Robert C., 121–22

High-concept films, 56–57, 154–55, 177

Horizontal integration, 6, 8, 12, 75, 109, 175

Hulk, 52, 76

Hulk (2003 film), 4–7, 37, 41, 61–62, 65, 76–87, 100, 109–11, 177–83

Intermediality, 187n5

Isanove, Richard, 131–36, 158

Janson, Klaus, 10, 53, 155, 173

Jaws (1975 film), 3, 40, 49

Jenkins, Henry, 35, 45, 122–24

Joker (2008 comic), 152–54, 173

Joker, the, 54–55; design of, 17, 139–55, 172–73; and Jack Nicholson, 11, 139

Kane, Bob, 3, 42, 54–55, 61, 142–43, 145, 148, 176

Keaton, Michael, 11, 54–55, 57–58, 139, 176

Kick-Ass (2010 film), 17, 22, 37–38, 179

King, Stephen, 130–31, 134, 136, 178

Kirby, Jack, 76, 78–80

Ledger, Heath, 150–54

Lee, Ang, 5, 7, 15, 62, 65, 76–86, 109, 181

Lee, Jae, 131–36

Lee, Stan, 52, 76, 78–80, 155

Lefèvre, Pascal, 24, 89, 93

Leone, Sergio, 17, 126–37

Lester, Richard, 10, 49–50

Licensing, 9, 41, 44, 58, 60, 75, 109, 146, 175–77

Lucas, George, 10, 51, 83, 116

Manga, 13–14, 25, 28, 31, 116, 148

Man of Steel, 13, 18, 178

Manovich, Lev, 83–84, 111, 122, 179–83

Man Who Laughs, The (1928 film), 143, 146

Marketing: and *Batman* franchise, 55, 153–56, 173; and fans, 11–12, 39, 45, 178–79, 189n29, 194n54; and high concept, 57; and *The Matrix*, 116, 123; and remediation, 17, 87, 91, 94, 100, 110; and *Scott Pilgrim*, 22; and *Speed Racer*, 8–9; and *The Spirit*, 170–72

Martin, Adrian, 126, 130, 137

Marvel Comics, 14, 52, 60, 156, 176; and licensing, 51, 60; and published titles, 17, 39, 130–31, 155

Matrix, The (1999 film), 8, 17, 22, 86, 115–26, 136, 156, 177–78

Maus: A Survivor's Tale, 10, 53, 77

McCloud, Scott: defining comics, 30, 77, 79, 82, 105; on Japanese comics, 14, 27; on movement, 117–19; on representation, 25, 67–68, 71–73, 135, 145, 192n14; on temporality, 28–29, 89, 96, 188n15

Media specificity, 6–7, 23–31, 39, 108, 166, 179–80, 187n5

Meehan, Eileen, 8, 141–42, 154

Miller, Frank: as auteur, 17, 41, 55, 155–58, 165–73, 180; and *Batman: The Dark Knight Returns*, 10–11, 53–54, 145–48; and *Batman: Year One*, 46; and *Sin City*, 5, 23, 61–62, 142, 158–65; and *300*, 13, 15, 17, 88–94

Moore, Alan: and Batman, 41, 143–46, 173; career of, 14; and *From Hell*, 105; and *Watchmen*, 10, 53, 93–95, 98, 100, 195n32

Morrison, Grant, 14, 150–54, 173

Motion lines, and action lines, 17, 89, 115–21

Multiframe: in *American Splendor*, 108; in *Batman*, 140, 145, 150; in *The Dark Tower: The Gunslinger Born*, 134; in *Hulk*, 4–6, 62, 65–66, 76–87, 111, 181, 183; in *Scott Pilgrim*, 31; in *300*, 89–90; in *Watchmen*, 96, 98

Multimodality, 187n5

Muybridge, Eadweard, 117, 119, 136

New Batman Adventures, The (television series), 41, 147

Nicholson, Jack, 11, 15, 139

Nolan, Christopher: and Batman, 5, 7, 41, 68, 70, 110, 147, 150, 152–54, 158, 174; as director, 15, 61, 164; as producer, 18

O'Malley, Bryan Lee, 15, 21, 24–37

180-degree rule, 71, 79–82

O'Neil, Dennis, 139–41, 147, 176–77

Oscars. *See* Academy of Motion Picture Arts and Sciences

Paramount Pictures, 43, 45, 60, 66, 94

Pekar, Harvey, 87, 101–9

Photography, 25, 67, 70, 117, 121, 159

Place, Janey, and Lowell Peterson, 159, 161, 163–64

Post-classical Hollywood, 56–57, 101

Pulcini, Robert, and Shari Springer Berman, 87, 101, 105–8

Puzo, Mario, 9, 47, 49

Rabin, Nathan, 170, 172

Radomski, Eric, 147–48

Raimi, Sam, 61, 110

Realism: and *Batman*, 16–18, 41, 46; and cinema, 122, 182; and *Dick Tracy*, 75; and Frank Miller, 91; and remediation, 86; and *Scott Pilgrim*, 28; and *Superman*, 10, 40, 47–50

Rehak, Bob, 40, 61–62, 116, 125

Remediation: compared to adaptation, 7–8, 16–17, 22–23, 137, 139–42; defined, 5–8, 22–24; and multimodality and intermediality, 186n5; and transmedia, 31–39

Robertson, Paul, 35–37

Robinson, Jerry, 139, 143, 148

Robocop franchise, 139, 156–58

Rodriguez, Robert, 13, 23, 61–62, 93, 155, 158, 165

Rogers, Mark, 53, 88, 101, 177

Rossen, Jake, 46, 49–50, 176

Round, Julia, 179, 186n24

Sabin, Roger, 14, 43, 52, 76, 94, 155

Salkind, Alexander and Ilya, 9, 46–51, 175–76

San Diego Comic-Con International (SDCC), 11–12, 21–22, 37, 62, 95, 110, 166, 178–79

Schrader, Paul, 159, 161, 164, 167

Schumacher, Joel, 16, 41, 58–60, 152

Scott Pilgrim (comic), 13, 15, 22, 25–29, 31–37

Scott Pilgrim vs. the World (2010 film): and box office, 16–17, 39, 110; and remediation, 13, 15, 21–39, 177–79, 187n5; and transmedia, 7, 15; and video games, 7, 22, 31, 33, 35–39

Shuster, Joe, 3, 42, 156

Siegel, Jerry, 3, 42, 156

Sin City (comic), 4–5, 23–24, 155–56, 158–66, 170, 186n23

Sin City (2005 film): and box office, 89; and CGI, 13, 93, 100–101, 158; and fans, 125; and film noir, 17, 159–66, 172–73;

production of, 23–24, 39, 41, 61–62, 125, 142, 158, 201n61

Singer, Bryan, 12, 15, 60–61

Slybert, Richard, 67, 71, 74

Smith, Matthew J., 10, 14, 52, 155–56, 167

Snyder, Zack: as director, 180, 183; and *Man of Steel*, 18; and *300*, 12–13, 17–18, 36, 85–94, 165; and *Watchmen*, 16, 18, 61–62, 94–100, 110, 195n32

Spatial remediation, 28–31, 83–84, 89–98, 122, 127–36, 180–83

Spatiotemporality, 6, 18, 29, 79–85, 89–99, 115, 127

Special effects: and budgets, 109; and bullet time, 117, 120–22, 126, 136; in *Dick Tracy*, 66–67, 72–75; evolution of, 6, 10, 12, 51; in *Hulk*, 80–85; in *Superman*, 48–49; visual norms of, 16. *See also* Computer-generated imagery

Spengler, Pierre, 9, 46–49

Spider-Man (comic), 9, 52; franchise, 60–61; hero, 95, 110; on television, 14

Spider-Man (2002 film), 60–61, 84, 110

Spiegelman, Art, 10, 53, 77, 159

Spirit, The (comic), 17, 121, 155, 165–70, 173

Spirit, The (2008 film), 17, 142, 155, 165–73

Split-screen, 6, 62, 66, 77, 81, 82, 84–86, 181

Star Wars franchise, 35, 48–49, 116, 124, 156

Stewart, Garrett, 122

Storaro, Vittorio, 67, 71

Storyboard, 5, 13, 30, 62, 65, 77, 89, 95, 117

Stylistic remediation: in adaptations, 16; in *American Splendor*, 101–9; and Batman, 140–54, 173; beyond adaptations, 17, 115, 173; and *The Dark Tower*, 130–37; defined, 8, 15–17, 23–24; and economics, 85–87, 109–11; and Frank Miller, 155–73; history of, 40–62, 177–80; in *The Matrix*, 115–26, 136; and remediation, 5–6; in *Scott Pilgrim*, 21–25, 31, 33, 35–39; and Sergio Leone, 126–30, 137; and sound, 24; and style, 180–83; on television, 15; in *300*, 13, 88–94; and transmedia, 22, 31, 35–39; in *Watchmen*, 94–101

Superman (comic), 9, 150; franchise, 50–51, 54, 59–60, 75, 178, 183; hero, 3, 17, 43; on television, 14, 45

Superman (1978 film), 3, 9–10, 13, 16, 46–51, 66, 109, 175–76; and realism, 11, 16, 47–51, 54

Superman Returns (2006 film), 12, 61

Television: and Batman, 40–41, 45–46, 51, 54, 59, 147–48; and film, 109; and Hulk, 76; and marketing, 12, 154, 178; and Michael Cera, 37; and remediation, 7, 14–17, 23–24, 80, 83, 180; and Superman, 45, 48

Temporal remediation: defined, 24, 28–29, 31, 119, 122, 180; and *Hulk*, 6, 80–83; and Sergio Leone, 130, 134–36; and *Watchmen*, 18, 89, 95–99

Thompson, Kristin, 56, 77, 181–83, 204n23

Thought balloons. *See* Word and thought balloons

300 (comic), 17, 88–92, 135, 155–56, 158, 165, 186n23

300 (2006 film), 175; and box office, 37, 85; and critics, 100; and fans, 125; and marketing, 36, 172; and remediation, 41, 87–95, 179; and technology, 12–13, 111; and Zack Snyder, 17–18, 165, 177

Timm, Bruce, 147–48

Transmedia: franchise, 7, 177–79; storytelling, 35–37, 122–25, 136, 141; style, 15, 22, 31, 35–39, 125–26, 136

Transtextual motivation, 182–83

Twentieth Century-Fox, 11, 21, 45–46, 60, 99, 110

Underground comics, 52–53

Universal Studios: and *Batman*, 51; and *The Dark Tower*, 178–79; and *Hulk*, 76, 83–84, 109; and *Scott Pilgrim*, 22, 36–37, 177

Uslan, Michael, 51, 53, 165

Varley, Lynn, 10, 13, 53, 88–92

Wachowski, Lilly and Lana, 8, 115–17, 121, 197n5

Walt Disney Studios, 44, 59, 61, 66, 74–75, 178

Warner Bros.: and Batman, 5, 11, 41, 53–55, 57, 60, 110, 146, 152–54, 173, 177–78; and comic book titles, 44, 142, 203n7; and *The Matrix*, 116, 123–24; structure of, 8, 40, 47, 109; and Superman, 3, 9, 47, 49–51, 175–76; and *300*, 89, 93–94; and *Watchmen*, 62, 99–100, 110, 195n32

Watchmen (comic), 9–10, 53, 61, 86, 94–100, 110, 134, 195n34

Watchmen (2009 film), 16, 18, 61–62, 86–89, 93–100, 109–10, 175, 195n32

Welles, Orson, 138–39, 163

Wertham, Fredric, 43–44, 59, 176

Word and thought balloons, 24, 79, 96, 102–8

Wright, Bradford, 42, 52, 155

Wright, Edgar, 15, 21–22, 24, 28–29, 31, 33–37

Wyatt, Justin, 56–57, 154–55

X-Men (comic), 88; franchise, 50, 60–61; on television, 14

X-Men (2000 film), 50, 60, 110

CPSIA information can be obtained
at www.ICGtesting.com
Printed in the USA
BVOW06*0324021116

466558BV00003B/3/P